The privatised world

International Library of Sociology

Founded by Karl Mannheim

Editor: John Rex, University of Warwick

Arbor Scientiae
Arbor Vitae

A catalogue of the books available in the **International Library of Sociology** and other series of Social Science books published by Routledge & Kegan Paul will be found at the end of this volume.

The privatised world

Arthur Brittan

Routledge & Kegan Paul
London, Henley and Boston

First published in 1977
by Routledge & Kegan Paul Ltd
39 Store Street,
London WC1E 7DD,
Broadway House,
Newtown Road,
Henley-on-Thames,
Oxon RG9 1EN and
9 Park Street,
Boston, Mass. 02108, USA
Photoset in 10 on 11 Times
by Kelly and Wright, Bradford on Avon, Wiltshire
and printed in Great Britain by
Lowe & Brydone Ltd

British Library Cataloguing in Publication Data

Brittan, Arthur

The privatised world.__(International
library of sociology).
1. Privatization
I. Title II. Series
301.11'3   HM136   77–30276

ISBN 0 7100 8769 1
ISBN 0 7100 8768 3 Pbk

For Eileen, Jessica and Daniel

Contents

Preface

This book is about the experience of privatisation in capitalist society, and the way in which this experience is reflected in the tensions of humanistic sociology. It is also about the entrapment of sociologists and other social scientists in the enclosed and fragmented world in which the divorce between theory and practice is daily growing more acute. Hence I am concerned with offering *both* a critique of humanism in sociology *and* examining the problem of privatisation as a dominant aspect of everyday life.

My central argument is that the experience of privatisation is mainly responsible for the proliferation of partial theories of social life which promote an obsessive concern with individual autonomy at the expense of political involvement.

Nevertheless, despite the pessimistic self-indulgence of some of these theories I find it difficult simply to dismiss them out of hand. The growing number of viewpoints which demote or deny the significance of such topics as the self or consciousness are just as misconceived as those advocating the autonomy of personal life. Consequently my defence of what I call concrete humanism is a recognition that sociology cannot call itself emancipatory unless it allows some kind of theoretical expression to privatised and fragmented experience.

I would like to express my thanks to Andy Tudor whose advice and help was invaluable in enabling me to avoid a number of logical and stylistic infelicities.

1 Introduction: the negation of the self

The crisis in self confidence that sociology is experiencing is reflected in the spectacular rate at which traditional concepts, theories and arguments are being jettisoned. This process is not some paradigmatic shift from one consensual commitment to another; it is not an intellectual regrouping of the discipline's resources so that sociologists can more easily catch the flux of social reality in a more appropriate theoretical framework. Rather, it is a surrender, an abandonment, of the very idea of sociology as a form of consciousness and critique of the social world. In this context, the self concept, is seen as an irrelevance, a piece of academic garbage to be thrown out along with other sociological monstrosities.

The socialised self has become so much a part of the folklore of sociology that it comes as a surprise when its privileged status is challenged. Although the myth of the solitary and unitary ego has long been relegated to the scrap heap of intellectual history, the self concept assumed central importance in the accounts that sociologists and social psychologists gave of the way in which animal nature was transformed into human nature. Accordingly, it was a cardinal premise of this position that the self has no existence independent of the set of social relationships which it presupposes. What seemed revolutionary when Cooley and Mead first articulated the notion that the self is a social process, a sequence of interactions between society and organism, is now established orthodoxy. The challenge to this orthodoxy is not simply a question of academic reassessment, but derives from the tensions and ambiguities of the sociological enterprise itself.

The negation of the self is a feature of the attack on sociology, both from some of its own practitioners, and its enemies. Friend and foe alike have questioned the usefulness of a concept which they believe belongs to a more primitive age of explanation. However, it is not the adequacy or inadequacy of concepts that concerns me here. What I am concerned with are the consequences of the flight from self consciousness which is a dominant characteristic of contemporary social thought. The sources of this negation are various, but three themes are paramount.

1 Historical irrelevance

For so many sociologists the hostility they encounter from other academics and professional humanists is an unavoidable aspect of their professional personas. Moreover, there are some sociologists who positively revel in their pariah status, in their marginality and in their sheer academic non-respectability. For those amongst us who are lapsed Marxists, or consider ourselves radical sociologists, the attractions of bourgeois sociology were overwhelming. We argued that sociology could be changed from within, that it could be made to act as an agency of social change in spite of the institutional constraints which tended to inhibit any attempt to translate our theoretical understanding into practice. The sheer romanticism and self indulgence of this attitude seems unbelievable in terms of the realities of the academic scene and the historical situation in which we find ourselves.

Indeed, the earlier euphoria has been replaced by guilt. How can sociology justify itself in the context of a social and political crisis which seems to be outside the control and competence of rational men? It is obvious that there can be no justification for a discipline which claims legitimacy on the basis of its marginality. More specifically, how can we continue to employ the concepts and theories that we do, especially concepts relating to the self and private troubles? If there is a justification for sociology, then presumably this can only derive from its ability to respond to the world as it is, and not from concentrating on individual consciousness.

Sociology must do without the self. It cannot afford to spend countless hours in the search for the structure of consciousness when consciousness itself is in danger of being swamped by events. Hence, the accusation of mysticism, romanticism and subjectivism levelled against social phenomenologists, symbolic interactionists and even those practitioners who define themselves as Humanistic Marxists, must be seen in the light of the cold facts and imperatives that are apparently self evident to the dispassionate gaze of the hard political and social analyst. What relevance can the self concept have when one is faced with the increasing pauperisation of the so-called underdeveloped world? What use can the analysis of consciousness have for the confrontation between Black and White in South Africa, or Jew and Arab in the Middle East?

If we are to banish the self and consciousness from serious sociological discussion, then what kind of sociology does this presuppose? Are we to believe that we can demystify sociology by simply turning to the central structural concerns of Marx, Durkheim and Weber? John Rex, for one, has no doubts that this is the way out of our present discontents:

> What we are proposing is a double task and a double revolution in sociology. First we have to eliminate the unnecessary difficulties which the arcane languages of the most recent sociologies have placed in the way of anyone seeking to achieve a real understanding of the world. Second, we have to recall sociology to an interest in the central structural problems which face us in the social world we inhabit. This book should be, above all, a testament of faith that this is possible and that sociology is available as an instrument of social and self understanding, as well as of emancipation to anyone who wishes to use it.[1]

Certainly this is not a proposal to construct a macro-sociology without taking consciousness into account, but it is a proposal to return to a sociology which is morally committed to 'public issues'. It follows that obsessive interest in the romantic consciousness of the disenchanted intellectual has no real significance for sociology. Those concepts we employ to describe the private encapsulation of the individual in the network of social relationships are interesting to the novelist or the poet; they are not of relevance to a sociology of 'public issues'. To put it another way, the illlusions of individual middle-class sociologists about the 'self' and 'consciousness' are illustrative of the 'idealist' mess that so much social thought finds itself in, a mess in which the suffering of the individual is not located in a given historical situation, but is dependent on existential choices that may, or may not be, available at a given moment in time.

Barrington-Moore[2] has argued that the prime task of the social and political theorist is to articulate the objective reasons for human misery. These are found in institutional factors, in certain constancies in the relationships between exploiters and exploited, in the persistence of war and in the increasing polarisation of the world into rich and impoverished societies. Human suffering and misery, are, by this token, not only available in the testimony of individual human beings, but are objectively 'there' as aspects of the real world. There is no illusion about the facts of poverty. Misery, in this sense, is indivisible. In the institutional

3

arrangements of western industrial capitalism there can be no doubt that 'objective' reasons for human misery can be studied and described as social and political facts.

Both John Rex and Barrington-Moore, in their different ways, are reacting against trends in the social sciences which subjectivise human suffering. Moreover, the rejection of 'subjectivism' means that certain concepts and modes of argument are ruled out of court because they do not meet the criterion of relevance, a criterion which stresses the urgency and immediacy of social and economic imperatives. Those sociologists who have constructed an elaborate system of concepts to handle the minutiae of self–other interactions are squandering their intellectual resources at a time when sociology should be engaged in an objective critique of the institutional malaise of industrialised societies. Ultimately, the sociology of the small-scale, the micro-world of interpersonal encounters, can only be justified if it illuminates structural forces. The 'reification' of the 'definition of the situation' into an over-arching explanatory principle has distorted the historical task of sociology; it has detracted sociologists from real understanding of power and social change when such an understanding is perhaps the only justification for sociology as an academic subject.

2 Anthropologisation

Those sociologists who define themselves as symbolic interaction-ists have for a long time monopolised the sociological discussion of the self and socialisation. There have, of course, been significant contributions from Parsons and others, but on the whole Mead's image of the self as process has been dominant. This is to say, that a particular version of the Median self has been accepted as the cornerstone of socialisation theory in sociology. In general, this version emphasises the subjection of human spontaneity to the 'generalised other'. Subjective certainty is replaced by the importation of the objective world of social relationships into the psychic structure of the individual – a process which it is presumed resolves the apparent conflict between the individual and society. The autonomous individual's illusion of subjective being is a fiction, directly attributable to the powerful influence of socialisation pressures. In a sense Descartes is inverted here. Instead of 'I' think, therefore 'I' am, we have in this Meadian version, 'They think, therefore I am'.

The trouble with this reading of Mead is that there are other possible interpretations available. Like Marx and Freud, Mead's interpreters tend to contradict themselves. Nevertheless, there does seem to be a paradox in Mead's discussion of the 'self', namely, his advocacy of social determinism on the one hand, and his commitment to impulsive voluntary action on the other. This paradox is very clear in his treatment of the relationship between the 'I' and the 'Me'.

Mead claims that the origin of self consciousness is in the original 'act' or impulse, but at the same time he tends to confuse the issue by implying that the 'Me' is the source of the 'I'. He presupposes the original act towards the other. Gibson Winter puts it this way:

> The actor's gesture . . . is presupposed. however, the 'I' through whom the gesture originates cannot be presupposed in the account without reducing the 'I' to the 'Me', and this is precisely what has happened among the social scientists, with some notable exceptions, who have gained most from Mead's breakthrough. The initiation of the gesture presupposes the 'I' and the relatedness of the 'I' to that toward which it moves; moreover, the understanding of the meaning of the gesture for the other presupposes 'meaning' and grasp of meaning. In general, sociality and meaning are presupposed as the milieu in which the 'me' emerges, and the initiating gesture of the 'I' is the element in which those presuppositions come to focus. The 'I' who gestures and the 'I' who interprets the gesture in his response are both presupposed in the account of the emergence of mind, self, and society.[3]

If the 'I' is reduced to the 'Me', then it follows that the self is redundant because it becomes impossible to differentiate between self and 'other'. This, I believe, was not intended by Mead, yet it has become so much a part of role and socialisation theory that it is difficult to envisage a viable alternative without abandoning entrenched assumptions about the nature of social nature. It has been suggested by Maurice Natanson[4] that the socialisation 'reading' of Mead is an unavoidable consequence of the neglect of phenomenological themes in his work. However, a phenomenological reading does not mean that we can talk about a self which is grounded in 'taken for granted' inter-subjectivity. The truth of the matter is, I suppose, that symbolic interactionists read into Mead whatever they want to read into Mead. What emerges from this multiplicity of 'readings' is the peculiar ambivalent status that the self concept has in social theory.

Mead attempted to bridge the divide between the 'isolated consciousness' and the objective world of social relationships. The very depths of subjective being were not, in his view, divorced from social influence. There is no dichotomy between 'private troubles' and 'public issues' – no dualism of subject and object in his formulation of social genesis of the self. Self and society are in dynamic relationship to each other. There can be no society without self consciousness, and no self consciousness without society. But, self consciousness does not emerge like some phoenix from the heat of social relationships. Its emergence is fundamentally dependent on communication, on language, on symbolic interaction.[5] Language, for Mead, is the crucial dimension in his description of social processes – it constitutes the prime stuff of mind and society. The dualism of mind and matter, self and society, which had so plagued European philosophy and social thought since Descartes, was, in Mead's eyes, a result of the inadequate understanding of the nature of symbolic communication. Both society and the self are inconceivable outside a symbolic context – their existence depends on symbolic mutuality, not on the duality of meaning and matter.

In a crude sense, we could say that the self that Mead posits is a symbolic self, reflexively engaging other selves to constitute society. Although Mead firmly located his social philosophy in an evolutionary organistic framework, it is not this element in his thought which has generally been absorbed into symbolic interactionism. Looked at from the outside, symbolic interactionism presents two contrasting pictures. The *first* has strong affinities with linguistic relativism, the *second* with what could be called symbolic romanticism. Linguistic relativism asserts the reality of symbolic forms in the shaping of self and society – language becomes *the* 'paramount reality'. Symbolic romanticism stresses the indeterminacy of self other interactions; language becomes a means for the negotiation and renegotiation of identity. In the first case, critics have pointed to the submergence of structure in culture, a tendency in which there seems to be no room for the action of economic and political forces, and in which the internalisation of norms and values ensures the cohesion of society. Language is poured into man – the self being nothing more than a repository of symbols. In the second case, criticism is directed against the haphazard way in which language becomes a set of labels to categorise internal states. Individuals name themselves, devise social strategies and construct identities at will. Such a perspective, it is argued, fits in nicely with bourgeois romantic individualism.

If symbolic interactionism is castigated for its subjective idealism as in the second case discussed above, then it is not surprising that the whole gamut of interpretative and humanistic approaches in the social sciences are under similar attack. The relative eclipse of existentialism in France, and its replacement by 'structuralism' is not simply an exercise in academic trendiness; it is rather an expression of the impatience that various practitioners feel about the scientific limitations of the social sciences. In their different ways Lévi-Strauss, Althusser and Foucault have rejected the 'subject' and 'consciousness', and in so doing have deliberately set their face against humanism, whether of the Marxist, or academic, kind. The subject disappears and is replaced by a stringent concern with linguistic structures. Foucault[6] dissolves the subject by an act of exclusion from language, language being the only pure objective reality or structure. Althusser's disgust with Marxist humanism sums up the movement away from the romantic excesses deriving from the discovery of the '1844 Manuscripts' and their interpretation as a charter for the ideology of freedom. Freedom is bourgeois luxury:

> Thus, in a very exact sense, the bourgeoisie *lives* in the ideology of *freedom*, the relation between it and its conditions of existence: that is, its real relation (the law of a liberal capitalist economy) *but invested in an imaginary relation* (all men are free, including the free labourers). Its ideology consists of this play on the word *freedom*, which betrays the bourgeois wish to mystify those ('free men'!) it exploits, blackmailing them with freedom so as to keep them in harness, as much as the bourgeoisie's need to *live* its own class rule as the freedom of those it is exploiting. Just as a people that exploits another cannot be free, so a class that uses an ideology is its captive too. So when we speak of the class function of an ideology it must be understood that the ruling ideology is indeed the ideology of the ruling class and that the former serves the latter not only in its rule over the exploited class, *but in its own constitution of itself as the ruling class*, by making it accept the lived relation between itself and the world as real and justified.[7]

In this respect not only does the bourgeoisie 'live in the ideology of "freedom"', but this includes the countless practitioners who earn a living in academic establishments, particularly those concerned with the human and social sciences. Traditionally, the Marxist attack on academic social science has always been in terms of its ideological taint, but in Althusser's reading of Marx, ideology is not an aspect of 'consciousness' — it is profoundly unconscious. Hence the rhetoric of self consciousness that informs the theoretical work of academic sociologists and the like reflects an outmoded non-scientific mode of ideological discourse which is incapable of recognising its own 'lived relation' with the world. Not only is 'subjective humanism' ideological in character, it is also rooted in idealism. While Althusser is primarily concerned with the refutation of Marxist humanism, he is at one with Lévi-Strauss and Foucault in their savage onslaught on the idea of man in the social sciences. Lévi-Strauss's[8] debate with Sartre on the nature of human freedom, if nothing else, has crystallised the arguments on both sides in such a way that we are impelled to accept their terms of reference. In denying Sartre's image of history, in denying the conception of the historical production of human nature, Lévi-Strauss is simply reaffirming the unity of culture and nature. Culture is not an excrescence on the surface of society, nor is it the antithesis of society. Society, culture, nature and consciousness are constituted by analogous coding mechanisms – it is the code which demonstrates the naturalness of culture, and it is language which provides us with evidence of universal structures of mind and society. Individual consciousness and personal identity cannot provide the starting point for a scientific understanding of human nature and culture. Such an understanding can only be found in the permanent and logical structures of the mind. Hence, Lévi-Strauss is advancing a strong determinist thesis in which there can be no room for conscious intentionality, or to put it another way, consciousness can only be an object of study if it is seen in the context of unconscious structure. This is, of course, completely antithetical to existential phenomenology and interpretative sociology.

The structuralist attempt to expel consciousness from the human and social sciences is not a reductionist strategy, at least not in the conventional sense. Structuralism, in the broadest view, is concerned with isomorphies. Both Foucault and Lévi-Strauss see an isomorphism between linguistic structures and social structures – the problem being adequately to describe the operation of the transformation rules between one structure and another. *Superficially*, this project could be seen as giving pride of place to linguistic rules which shape and influence other structures, but this is too simple an interpretation of the structuralist project, more or less implying that once language is externalized in speech and text, it somehow subverts reality. Nevertheless, structuralism is determinist – it makes no allowances for self definition or self determination.

If, as Foucault has argued, the idea of man and the individual are epistemological disasters, then the social and human sciences must indeed be in a precarious position:

'Anthropologisation' is the great internal threat to knowledge in our day. We are inclined to believe that man has emancipated himself from himself since his discovery that he is not at the centre of creation, nor in the middle of space, nor even perhaps the summit and culmination of life; but though man is no longer sovereign in the kingdom of the world, though he no longer reigns at the centre of being, the human sciences are *dangerous intermediaries* in the space of knowledge. The truth of the matter is, however, that this very posture dooms them to an essential instability. What explains the difficulty of the 'human sciences', their precariousness, their uncertainty as sciences, their dangerous familiarity with philosophy, their ill-defined reliance upon other domains of knowledge, their perpetually secondary and derived character, and also their claims to universality, is not, as is often stated, the extreme density of their object; it is not the metaphysical status or the inerasable transcendence of this *man* they speak of, but rather the complexity of the epistemological configuration in which they find themselves placed.[9]

We are confronted in the theorising of Althusser, Foucault and Lévi-Strauss, not merely with a revision of established epistemological procedures in the social sciences, but with a direct challenge to their very existence as modes of discourse. There have been other dismissals of the 'subject' and 'consciousness' from sociology, psychology and politics – behaviourism and mechanism for example, except that their denial of subjectivity did not involve the denial of their object of study. Behavioural psychology does not dissolve man, it reduces him to a stimulus-response mechanism, and, surprisingly, it is claimed by such an elegant apologist for behaviourism as Homans, that the behaviourist project in sociology reintroduces man back into sociology. Be that as it may, psychologism, sociologism, or as Foucault puts it 'anthropologism' are recent 'inventions' in discourse, inventions which have outlived their welcome and usefulness. It is true that the implications of this retreat from 'man' are not common intellectual currency. Structuralism is fashionable, but it is not fashionable for its hostility to humanism. Neither Foucault nor Althusser lend themselves to popularisation; they are not easily assimilated into 'recipe' games. Nevertheless, the social sciences, humanities and literary criticism have been infiltrated. Whether it is acknowledged or not, 'structuralism' and its modes have so permeated academic consciousness that it is now almost impossible to engage in discourse without assuming that, behind the surface, there is some vital and unconscious linguistic 'structure'. The current vogue for textual exegesis, coupled with the practice of 'code-breaking' provides an obvious example of this tendency.

Of course, such phrases as the 'dissolution of man' tend to assume a superficial glibness when taken out of context. They are meaningless if they are used as catch-phrases in recipe games where the object is to demonstrate intellectual modernity. However, structuralism is not a game played for the benefit of disillusioned existentialists. It represents a serious endeavour to delimit and demythologise the human and social sciences, not only as an exercise in academic debunking, but also as a contribution to the analysis of social and economic formations. In rejecting the concept of human nature, structuralists argue that the social sciences have too easily adapted facile assumptions from humanism, which situates man in the centre of things, as the 'subject' of history. In other words, human nature is a construction, an invention. Hence, whatever meaning we assign to the concept 'human nature', we do so in terms of categories which are specific to the 'invention' of the human sciences – the idea of man is *not* a datum of inquiry, nor is the sociological model of the self.

It is an open question whether or not the abandonment of human nature and the elimination of subjectivity from the social sciences is feasible, or even desirable. Certainly, for those of us brought up on conventional liberal or even Marxist humanism, such a project would seem to be a disaster. Nevertheless, the possibility remains that the price of any further advance in the social sciences might well be the discarding of liberal illusions about the freedom of the individual and human spontaneity. However, this would be to admit that the last hundred years of the social sciences have been a tragic failure, a monumental waste of time, and this is not an admission that most of us are likely to make. Moreover, although subjective humanism is under great pressure, the alternatives stemming from such sources as the 'Frankfurt School', social phenomenology and mainstream sociology have not been swept aside by the structuralist tide – on the contrary, they often proceed as if structuralism is irrelevant, or does not even exist. In the final analysis, it is not structuralism that poses the greatest danger to the social sciences' continued existence – the danger comes from an excessive commitment to consciousness as the focus of inquiry – a disembodied consciousness in which symbolic systems, culture and ideology are treated as if they were independent of and different from economic and structural forces. A sociology which gives allegiance to the slogan 'meaning without structure' is just as misconceived as a sociology which advocates 'structure without meaning'. It is not a question of the epistemological status of such concepts as the 'self' and the 'individual' which are at stake in the critique of subjective humanism, rather, it is the belief that all such concepts entail explication which is different in kind from that employed in a sociology or politics of public issues. The structuralist negation of consciousness, whatever its deficiencies, points to the *natural* base of human conduct, and in this respect it

10

rejects the dualism of consciousness and nature which permeates social thought. But, even if dualism is rejected, it would seem to me that this does not necessarily destroy humanism in the social sciences. This is a theme to which I will return later in this book.

3 Rhetorical artifice

The recent discovery of Wittgenstein as a sociological resource has opened up all sorts of possibilities for internal criticism. For those practitioners who have made this discovery, most of main-stream sociology is a linguistic maze, in which confused concepts and motives are given misleading theoretical respectability. Also, the verbal opaqueness of so much sociology tends to support their view, that as a discipline, it is a special kind of rhetoric, which at best generates a sense of passionate commitment, and at worst declines into triviality. This suggests that the very notion of rhetoric entails a spurious intellectual facade behind which dubious arguments are constructed in order to bolster up shaky theoretical foundations. Hence, the language of sociology and the other social sciences is dissected, concepts are analysed and found to be inadequate and, in general, analysis becomes the tool for the exposure of rhetorical artifice.

Nothing can stand up to the ferocity of this analytical attack. The traditional stock of sociological concepts and theories is subjected to the most ardent examination and found to be meaningless; terms like 'structure', 'culture', 'role', 'system', 'class', and a whole host of associated concepts, disappear under the analytic axe. The absorption of the later Wittgenstein into ethnomethodology, and into other types of sociological analysis, does not simply mean that sociologists are becoming linguistic philosophers; this would be a too arrogant and inaccurate description of their theoretical work, but it does mean that for some practitioners the analysis of linguistic practices is the real ground for sociological inquiry. The sloughing off of two centuries of sociological and political theory, and the substitution of a sociology which is a compendium of language games, may seem to some practitioners to be a strange fate for a discipline which defined itself in terms of structural concerns like 'class' and 'power'.

If we take this position to its logical ending point, then not only does the study of sociology become the study of language in use, but the problem of the self becomes a problem of word play. In other words, the naming of parts, the reflexive recognition of self, the negotiation of meanings and motives, and the construction of theories of social structure, are merely different aspects of the way

11

in which men use language, or perhaps, of the way in which language uses men. If there is a 'ghost in the machine', then it is a language ghost. Selves dissolve into occasions – into episodes for the language ghost to play its little games. Taking their cues from linguistic philosophers, ethnomethodologists criticise Mead's 'lodged' self and Goffman's artful 'performer'. From their point of view, sociology, especially symbolic interactionism, ignores the *instability* of language games and the volatile nature of meanings. The symbolic self is not derived from a common set of meanings which all men acknowledge; there is no core symbolic universe in which meaning can be found, and consequently the 'self' can never be 'built up', or 'constructed'. The only thing to be said about the self is that under certain circumstances a rule can be invoked that allows us to use self referring concepts. What such a rule looks like, of course, will vary according to context, or its 'indexicality'. Very simply, this means that the self can never be lodged in an individual, nor can it be the end product of a period of socialisation. Such a hypostatisation of a process cannot be taken seriously – it belongs to an earlier period of discourse.

Yet, even though the sociological 'self' disappears from ethnomethodology, the notion of reflexivity does not, although what is meant by reflexivity is open to debate

> Most ethnomethodologists agree that reflexivity is fundamental to ethnomethodology. Nonetheless, there is deep disagreement concerning its meaning. Some treat reflexivity as a phenomenon, some as a theory. Still others, claim that reflexivity is a method, or call it a theology.[10]

Both symbolic interactionists and ethnomethodologists are concerned with reflexivity as a central dimension of human interaction, but this duality of interest is rooted in opposed assumptions about 'meaning' and 'everyday reality'. The 'self' that symbolic interactionism projects is grounded in symbolic reciprocity; that is, in the belief that reflexivity is an *unavoidable phenomenon* of language – ethnomethodology makes no such assumptions about the unavoidability of phenomena; it does not posit a 'self' or 'I' which reflexively engages other selves in a symbolic dialogue. For ethnomethodologists, all such assumptions are problematic, needing investigation and analysis. At best, all that can be hoped for is the description of rules which allow us to employ reflexive strategies in various situations. However, rules are not found in a dictionary of ready-made definitions of what is appropriate or inappropriate in this or that context. In 'everyday life' rules for self reference are not generally available as objects of discourse; 'everyday life' is not constituted by rules discovered by social scientists. Philosophers and sociologists might talk about reflexivity and the self, psychologists may try to operationalise the self as an intervening variable etc., but all such attempts are illegitimate if they get away from concrete instances of human interaction.

Now, while the main thrust of the 'linguistic turn' in sociology has been humanistic (in the sense documented by Maurice Roche[11]), there is an associated aspect of the analytic critique which is not interested in 'going beyond sociology', but in completely analysing it out of existence. For many analytic philosophers, sociology is a meaningless farago of half-baked empirical generalisations and conceptual muddles. In general, the analytical attack on sociology is reminiscent of the deep suspicion of metaphysics so typical of British empiricism, a suspicion which manifests itself in the way in which continental philosophy is defined as being obscurantist and rhetorical. Sociologists are accused of being victims of their own verbal excesses; they are accused of constructing an encapsulated world of meaning which is completely cut off from human reality, and from the ordinary practices of ordinary people. Hence, what remains of sociology after being exposed to *analytical surgery*, is a discipline without any rationale at all, except as an appendage to history or psychology. These are perennial criticisms of sociology, but today sociologists themselves are becoming proficient practitioners of *analytical surgery*. Sociology has no need for external analysis; it is too busy dismantling and dissecting its own structure and history with the tools provided by analytical philosophers. Self criticism has been replaced by self surgery. Certainly the language of sociology needs to be constantly examined for rhetorical artifice, but this is not the same as the complete dismantling of its theoretical structure.

I have suggested that the humanistic commitment in sociology is under severe pressure from three sources. This pressure must be seen in the context of a historical situation which threatens daily to undermine the explanatory relevance of all the social sciences. The accusation of historical irrelevance levelled at sociology by John Rex and others is an echo of similar accusations which are Marxist in origin. The denial of subjective humanism emanating from French 'structuralist' sources is premised on the belief that the human sciences are anachronistic or ideological; they are epistemologically bankrupt because they have anthropologised the study of social structures. Structuralism is utterly opposed to the reification of the process of self creation so essential to Sartre's version of Marxism. From a completely different perspective, a number of sociologists have turned to linguistic analysis for their concepts or 'anti-concepts'. Their critique of sociology is primarily

13

directed at the postulate of an 'independently existing social order'. If there is any order, then this derives from the way in which individuals try to make sense of each other's talk and behaviour – hence, talking and listening are critical elements in the constitution of the belief in order and rule-following. It follows that both the 'self' and 'social structure' are problematic; they cannot be taken for granted except as convenient fictions to facilitate a practitioner's understanding of the 'talk' he is endeavouring to describe.

I started this chapter by referring to the 'crisis in self confidence that sociology is experiencing'. The whittling away of this self confidence is not necessarily evident in the everyday talk of sociologists, or for that matter in their academic talk in lectures and seminars. For years, I suppose, some of us have played around with such themes as the 'ivory tower' alienation of social scientists, their political ineffectiveness, their inability to demystify their own concepts, let alone the myths and ideologies of the world around them – yet this self disgust was somehow accompanied by a rather naïve hope that time was on our side, that if we were patient there was bound to be some epoch-making theoretical breakthrough which would immediately transform sociology from its woolly eclecticism into a force to be reckoned with on the intellectual and academic scene. In the United States, Parsons had seemed to fulfil this requirement in the 1950s, but certainly this is not the case today, while in Europe and Britain the classic tradition was continuously rediscovered and reinterpreted. Sociology was incorporated into standard social science courses – it became 'respectable' as a university subject, that is, until it came to be associated with student revolt in the 1960s. From the 1960s onwards, it has had the dubious distinction of being denigrated by the rest of the academic community as being subversive and non-scholarly, and, simultaneously, attacked by the 'old' and 'new' left as a form of bourgeois self indulgence which hampers any genuine attempt to understand and change society.

A vote of no confidence of such an extent did not provide the climate for theoretical advance. If there have been new theoretical 'breakthroughs', these have not been sociological in origin, but are located in the emergence of the 'new linguistics' as a dominant intellectual preoccupation. Indeed, it has become very fashionable to be able to spell out the intricacies of Chomsky's 'transformational grammar' as a substitute for sociological argument – linguistics is in the process of being elevated to the 'master social science'. Everybody is now concerned with language, communication, grammars, deep and surface structures – and from a different set of premises, structuralists place language at the heart

14

of their account of the naturalness of human conduct. Lévi-Strauss's programatic slogan 'Whoever says "Man" says "Language", and whoever says "Language" says "Society"' sums up the current commitments of hundreds of practitioners in the social and human sciences.

Where does this leave 'the sociology of public issues'? Can there be a sociology of public issues when everybody seems to be preoccupied with language? What happens to radical and humanist commitments when the social sciences seem to be moving in directions which, on the face of it, seem to negate and deny the historical roots of social structures? And is there any point in defending the social origin of 'individual consciousness' as a key component in our understanding of 'human nature'? It would seem to me that these questions must somehow be answered, they cannot be ignored and pushed aside as if they were meaningless. It might well be that a sociology of public issues is not tenable, except as a forlorn hope of social transformation, yet this is not demonstrated by the history of the social sciences. The fact that Marx, Weber and Durkheim saw no real discontinuity between public issues and private troubles cannot be discounted as if it has no consequence for contemporary sociology. If we decide the answers to these are in the negative, then sociologists have good reason for their anxiety about their discipline's viability. They might as well hand over to other practitioners and begin to write their memoirs.

Part one

2 Everyday life and reality

While it is true that humanism seems to be on the defensive in the social sciences, this is not to say that in the everyday world of social encounters men and women have suddenly discovered a new dispassionate and neutral rhetoric in which to relate to each other and the world. In this everyday reality, emotions are negotiated and confirmed, consciousness is assumed, the self is taken for granted – subjective reality is not questioned – it is accepted as given. Nobody attempts to deny the intractable 'givens' of existence: the body's limitations, its inevitable decay, its capacity for pain and pleasure – the way in which *others* are believed to limit and define the boundaries of each individual's freedom of action, the sheer monumental 'obviousness' of economic and social imperatives; and yet this intractability is often treated by social scientists as if it was problematic, as if it was a chimerical reality which disappears when investigated and analysed. But the routine and boring visceral world does not go away even when it is translated into the turgidity of social theory – it has a habit of subverting the academic 'account' offered by social science.

Certainly, 'everyday life' has become a fashionable concept, often replacing traditional theoretical categories by an almost mystical belief in its liberating qualities. Nevertheless, 'everyday life' is not simply an attempt to construct an alternative sociological universe; in a sense it *is* the paramount reality in which most of us conduct our daily lives, although 'paramount reality' might itself be subverted by illusion, or 'false consciousness'. The point is that in everyday life participants do not question or deny their feelings, their emotions, their motives; they do not question the reality of what others do to them, and what they do to others; nor do social scientists 'live' their *own* lives as if they were subject to a different reality. There are, of course, competing ways of looking at 'everyday life', just as there are competing images of consciousness. When one starts to disentangle the ambiguous nature of both concepts, one is left with a feeling that nothing can be usefully said that does not further obscure an already obscure aspect of contemporary social thought. However, these problems are not simply conceptual, but are rooted in the actuality of everyday life, as well as in the distortions of everyday life that inform social and political theory, especially in the context of the supposed estrangement between 'private troubles' and 'public issues'.

What options are available in any attempt to come to terms with everyday life? And in what way is this concern with the 'mundane' world any different from traditional concerns in Marx, Weber, Durkheim, Simmel, Mead, etc., etc.? Are we saying that everyday life should have priority in our understanding of the social world? These questions are perhaps best answered by examining different strands of thought which supposedly display everyday life. It might well be that all these different strands are alternative ways of looking at 'paramount reality', but this is not demonstrable, except as an ontological commitment, a commitment which often manifests itself in an over-arching and unavoidable reification of the 'obvious'. Everyday life at one level is a tautology because, by definition, it is impossible to conceive of a reality which is not contained in somebody's everyday life. Furthermore, *my* mundane existence might be *your* idea of the extra-mundane. In other words, paramount reality consists of a multiplicity of realities, each of which has a claim to ontological priority. The trouble is that most of us tend to equate our own particular versions of reality with paramount reality. What I want to do now is to look at five versions of everyday life in the extant literature.

1 Everyday life as routine

To a certain extent, everyday life has become a topic of interest in the social sciences because of a growing awareness of the influence of phenomenology in European philosophy and social thought. Until very recently, this influence was not direct; it was mediated through such practitioners as Schutz, Scheler and, latterly, Berger and Luckmann. In general, sociologists did not read Husserl and Heidegger at first hand, but relied on secondary sources, although this is probably not true of French sociologists who had been exposed to phenomenology through its association with the work of Sartre and Merleau-Ponty. What emerged from this kindling of interest in phenomenology was an alternative language to handle social phenomena. The 'common-sensical' everyday world is given the status of such concepts like 'social structure' and 'culture'. If there is a problem of order in sociology, then it is not to be understood in terms of 'value consensus', 'legitimation', 'authority', 'class', 'power', or any of the elaborations to be found in standard sociological texts.

What 'orders' social life is precisely the mundane routines ignored by other sociologists. There is nothing problematic about the accomplishment of a routine activity for traditional sociology – in principle, it can be accounted for by referring to 'role performance', or it can be seen as being a consequence of adherence to a rule, or norm. What is taken for granted by sociology is problematic for phenomenology. The question is, I suppose, is routine problematic to participants? If we observe somebody getting on to a bus every morning at the same time and getting off a bus at the same time every evening, then there seems to be no difficulty in trying to account for the perceived regularity. He catches the bus in the morning in order to get to work in time, while in the evening he goes through the reverse routine. Catching a bus might not be an exciting problem for social investigation, nor is it likely to stimulate much interest amongst participants, except in so far as routines are subject to disturbance or alteration. If there is a breakdown, for example, or if there is a bus strike, then routine may be freshly conceived of as being problematic, as dependent on an acceptance of the taken-for-granted regularity of everyday life. Yet participants do not usually have a theory of routine, they do not articulate the ordinaryness of everyday life. Catching buses, going to the toilet, observing traffic rules, going to a pub, eating with knives and forks, talking to one's friends, mowing the lawn, all the mundane activities informing social existence, are not questioned in a systematic manner. Provided nothing interrupts the flow of mundane happenings, there is no apparent need to theorise about the world. For participants, the routinised world is reality, its appearance is not superficial, there is nothing beyond routine because routine is all there is – at least, they do not question its apparent ubiquity. In so far as participants are not *conscious* of the ordinariness of everyday routine, they have no need to examine the typicality of the world they live in. But, of course, the world does not stand still, routines are interrupted, personal and social crises infringe on the calm of mundane reality. The ebb and flow of everyday life involves more than routine, it involves *consciousness of* differences between the boring present and the threatening future, the possibility of pain and suffering, and, more appositely, *consciousness of* the actuality of personal troubles.

Routines are not monolithic, nor is everyday life experienced as a unity – on the contrary, paramount reality is fragmented into a multiplicity of realities, or what Berger *et al.* call 'pluralisation of life worlds'. Thus the routines of everyday life can be grasped in their concrete particularity, and it is in the confrontation between personal troubles and public issues that this concreteness is most apparent.

> The capacity to move from what Schutz calls the 'paramount reality' of everyday life to other spheres of meaning may be assumed to be anthropologically given. What happens under modern conditions, however, is that this given capacity is vastly intensified. Plurality becomes a basic theme of life. With this pluralisation, the creation of any over-arching symbolic universe becomes increasingly more difficult. Different realities are defined and legitimated in quite discrepant ways, and the construction of an over-arching world view that will embrace all of them becomes highly problematic.[1]

Whether or not it was ever possible to construct over-arching world views, the fact remains that pluralisation is the 'normal' way in which participants live their lives today. Everyday life, from this point of view, is a mish-mash of unrelated and encapsulated routines, each of which is taken-for-granted by participants. The classic inference that is usually drawn from pluralisation is that of the fragmentation of consciousness and the disintegration of the self. These are familiar enough themes – they are based on the assumption that the growth of industrial capitalism, and the increasing elaboration of the division of labour, is accompanied by the splitting of consciousness into private and public dimensions. Hence, the 'givens' of mundane existence are experienced by practitioners, not simply as 'being there' in this or that reality, but as being perfectly normal, as being consistent with their everyday participation in the world. If I spend my entire day in some stuffy office as an invoice clerk, and my evenings playing squash or experimenting with drugs, then all these activities have equal value, they are all routinised and accepted as normal and non-problematic. Fragmentation is not questioned, unless some other disturbing reality overwhelms the particularity of the life-world in which the individual is currently involved. Hence, if we claim that everyday life is the 'paramount reality', then it follows that *all* routines have their being in the taken-for-granted world, and yet we know this to be problematic, especially in the context of economic and political structures. Certainly we can talk about everyday life at these levels, but it has a different significance and connotation. It is precisely these areas of experience that provide the disturbing realities which interrupt the taken-for-granted world.

2 Everyday life as politics

It is very easy to make grandiose statements about the universality of exploitation. Exploitation is not a simple concept which lends itself to logical explication or definition; nevertheless, in everyday life, exploitation is not a mystery, but is experienced and understood without the benefit of a philosophical or theoretical gloss. No doubt, there are countless millions of people who are not able to verbalise their exploited state – very few Blacks in South Africa describe their everyday lives in terms of alienation, or false consciousness. There is no need for them to do so – the evidence of their situation is all round them. Their everyday routines are bounded and shaped by law-enforcement agencies, by Apartheid legislation, by police action, by the crude exploitation in mines and factories, by the constant reminder of their deprived and subjected status. Paramount reality is not subverted by simple access to 'life-worlds' in which everyday life can be forgotten or repressed – in South Africa paramount reality is political reality. Whatever alternative life-worlds are available, are not available as an escape from the routine of everyday life; rather they represent attempts to hide from the terrifying intrusion of the racist state into every aspect of one's life. Certainly we can speak of the pluralisation of life-worlds in the way in which the political and private experiences of the different strata of South Africa society tend to be insulated from each other. The private lives of the white middle class in Johannesburg proceeds as if the world outside was a convenient backdrop to their highly privatised lifestyle, but this is not equivalent to saying they are escaping everyday life – more realistically, they are victims of everyday life, they are deluded by their apparent ability to play middle-class games in which the limits are circumscribed by the definite prescriptions of the law and state. Moreover, their lifestyle is dependent on their location in a society in which 'the rules of the game' are not open to alternative interpretation. They take these rules for granted, they are the way the world works, they represent a degree of permanence which seems to ground the reality of everyday life in brute necessity.

In recognising and resisting the exploitative reality of everyday life in a society like South Africa it is impossible to privatise political action. Acts of defiance are not exercises in fantasy. If a Black deliberately breaks the pass laws, or if he engages in trade-union activity, there is certainly no point in seeing these acts as 'escape attempts' – they represent resistances to South African paramount reality. Millions of Blacks are in the same situation; their paramount reality is precisely determined by the

23

nature of South African society, a society whose structure must be understood historically. Hence, 'everyday life' is economic and political reality from which there is no escape. Those white middle-class swingers in the northern suburbs of Johannesburg who have constructed an elaborate and cosmopolitan lifestyle do not escape from the ugliness of the world around them. On the contrary, their encapsulation in enclaves of apolitical neutralism is a myth, because whether they like it or not, they are located in a pattern of exploitation which mocks their bourgeois sensibility. To feel guilty in such a situation, or to indulge in radical talk as a mode of action, are the classic responses of liberalism. In South Africa, 'liberal' Whites escape into fantasy, having no future, except as actors in a historical drama in which the 'exploiters become victims', and in which the only viable escape is the trip to Europe or Australia. Indeed, one's options are severely limited by the intractability and coercive nature of the racist state. The only way in which everyday political reality can be subverted and negated, is not by a journey into the self, but by committing oneself fully to the collective action of those millions who will bring the whole rotten apparatus down. Such a commitment is not lightly made – it is in this context that we can perhaps understand the 'defeatism' of so many 'liberals' and their subsequent retreat into privatised worlds of interpersonal experience.

I have laboured this point, because everyday life as an academic topic frequently seems to be primarily associated with 'routine', as if routine has no connection with pain, poverty and politics. Everyday life is not a late twentieth-century invention – its current vogue recapitulates earlier themes in social thought and literature – it appears in Marx and Engels as the grounding of their description of the condition of the working class – it appears in the novels of Balzac, Stendhal, Dickens and Dostoevsky, but, more importantly, it continues to appear in the 'lived' experience of classes, and the colonised masses of the world. Everyday life is, therefore, more than a rallying cry for phenomenological and ethnomethodological attacks on traditional social theory – it is the very essence of the social world, a world in which it is difficult to discover any reasonable grounds for the end of human misery, except in the fantasies of optimism which constitute the rationale for the consumer ethic of present-day capitalism. Behind the theories, behind the insipid academic debates there remains a substrate of suffering and struggle – one does not have to be a Marxist to realise that this substrate is 'where the action is', nor does one have to travel to South Africa or Chile to 'find' the political dimension of everyday life.

3 Everyday life as deception

The routines of everyday life are often discussed by various practitioners as though they were a 'staged' set of performances in which all experience is considered to be theatrical. As they go about their daily lives, individuals try to create meaning out of chaos by imbuing the world with dramatic significance. In confronting each other, they lie, cheat and mask motives in order to save face and maintain self esteem. This image of human nature which underpins the 'dramatistic approach' in social theory has its counterpart in the rhetoric of the ad-man and the mass-media. Dramatism may be American in origin, but its language is the lingua franca of the advertising world. The persona of the con-man is now taken to be an appropriate symbol of the quality of everyday life. The con-man image is universalised to cover the entire spectrum of cultural and social life so that we are presented with a terrifying picture of human emptiness conditioned by the rhetoric and ideology of consumer capitalism:

Is not the rhetoric of our society, permeating social language, literature and imagination with its ceaseless intrusions upon our daily experience and our more intimate aspirations? Is it not on the way to becoming the main ideology of our time, and is not this fact confirmed by the importance and efficiency of propaganda modelled on advertising methods? Has not institutionalised advertising replaced former modes of communication, including art, and is it not in fact the sole and vital mediator between producer and consumer, theory and practice, social existence and political power? But what does this ideology disguise and shape, if not that specific level of social reality we call everyday life, with all its 'objects – clothing, food, furnishing?[2]

Everyday life has lost its immediacy, it is distorted by market mechanisms and corrupted by the ideology of affluence (an image common both to radical and conservative critiques of contemporary industrial capitalism) and, consequently, paramount reality is visualised in terms of a game of hypocrisy and deception in which the players communicate with each other by advertising their products. This view of the loss of innocence implies that human nature is so far removed from its original instinctual source, that it is no longer possible to speak of desire, feeling, emotion – what we are left with is the artificial fantasy life induced by the seductive influence of the mass-media. Whether or not this image has any

25

validity, it certainly dominates a great deal of thinking of social critics both on the left and right. It has affinities with the 'Mass Society thesis' as well as with popularised versions of 'Critical Theory', but it also provides the stock-in-trade of various forms of dramatism which have elevated the 'performed self' to the status of a master principle of social existence.

Dramatism advances two strands of argument about the way in which actors perform in everyday life situations.

The *first* strand has its roots in the belief that social life is *naturally* theatrical, and that ultimately the constants of human experience are dramatically realised. Hence, religion, rites of passage, sex, death, war, the passions – all the perplexities of social life, are given universal dramatic significance. In encountering each other in everyday life situations, humans respond in terms of dramatic imperatives. The point is that 'the dramatic mode is seen to be the human mode', and in this context we can trace strong connections with other interpretative humanisms, both in the social sciences, and the humanities. What this entails is a view of the world which is fundamentally optimistic in spite of the tragic constants of everyday life.

The *second* strand of argument in dramatism focuses on the image of contemporary industrial capitalism as the source of the fraudulent performances of human actors in everyday life. It tends to pay particular attention to the tactics of deception. This, of course, is Goffman territory, but equally it is of relevance to the perennial attack on urbanism and industrialism which undergirds so much of the 'loss of community' literature. There is a deep-rooted pessimism at work here – it assumes that men are the victims of manipulative techniques over which they have no control – there is also a despairing sense of moral outrage about the depersonalization of everyday life, a life which seems to be devoid of spontaneity and imagination.

For a great many sociologists, cultural commentators, literary critics and other professional pessimists, despair and pessimism seem endemic in the human situation. Pessimism is the only realistic position to take in respect to everyday life, to the threat of universal bureaucracy and the commercialisation of art and cultural products. In sociology, pessimism has a very respectable pedigree – Durkheim and Weber, in their different ways, were profoundly pessimistic about industrial capitalism, but the mood of despair in sociology reached its climax in the context and aftermath of Fascism and war. Whatever illusions American sociologists had about progress and social engineering were not shared by Europeans – in France, existentialism exercised a pervasive influence, while the Frankfurt School never really recovered from its disillusionment with Stalinism, and its exposure to the first blooming of Nazism in the Weimar Republic. Hence, although one may exaggerate the intensity of European pessimism since the First World War, there can be no doubt that its articulation reflected an almost apocalyptic mood of despair in which the twin spectres of totalitarianism and bureaucracy loomed large as the logical future of industrial society. This mood is still with us today in the depressing picture of ecological and thermonuclear extinction which has become part and parcel of the currency of everyday pessimism, an everyday pessimism which both the mass-media and social sciences have found apposite, and for which they have been partly responsible.

4 Everyday life as a concentration camp?

Everyday pessimism is reflected in mundane consciousness. In a peculiar sense, human beings are conceived of as victims, as passive spectators to their own subjection. Resistance to the state, to authority, to the system, is considered to be useless. The only possible kind of resistance open to 'victims' is in gratuitous action or in fantasies of dissent. Accordingly, individual survival depends on an ability fraudulently to project identities consonant with the requirements of the *status quo*. Moreover, so many people have internalised this notion of the state as the Leviathan remorselessly grinding human life into anonymity and meaninglessness, that it seems unlikely that acts of resistance can be anything more than empty gestures. The totalitarian concentration camp image of society is replicated in mass society literature as well as influencing aspects of dramaturgical theory, although this is not intentional in the latter case. For instance, in Goffman's model of Total Institutions, the prison or asylum seems to have a far wider significance than a 'place' where inmates are isolated from society. 'In Asylums . . . a hidden motif is that society itself is a "total institution", a mental hospital, a concentration camp.'[3]

But, as Geoffrey Pearson points out, Goffman's 'Asylums' can be given an optimistic reading, a reading which has a political flavour:

> If we make the imaginative effort to understand Goffman's Asylums, and all the associated work, as politics . . . then if it is the politics of a one-dimensional world it is also clearly a politics of optimism which puts social structure up for grabs. Goffman's mental patients flap at powerful institutions, and they appear to vanish. Similarly in Garfinkel's work, social structures almost seem to fall down of their own accord.[4]

Nevertheless, if it is true that Goffman is concerned with a politics of optimism 'which puts social structure up for grabs', then it is a politics of gesture, not a politics of direct confrontation. It is a politics of gesture in which inmates and victims can transcend the bounds of everyday life by symbolic voyages of defiance. Society, or the concentration camp, can be subverted and vanquished by individual 'escape attempts', or by journeys into the world of drugs, alcohol and 'hard porn'. These journeys may have a political significance if their end result is really to challenge agencies of social control. In the concentration camp, petty acts of defiance could and did provide the means whereby 'inmates' managed to construct alternative identities, but these acts were not collective – they were basically strategies of *individual* survival. In everyday life, individual acts of resistance against institutions and the state assume political status only if they have roots in the structure of domination. A Black in South Africa who spits at a White is not simply expressing personal dislike – more often than not he is demonstrating his pent-up frustration and his sense of political deprivation. Admittedly, this one act will not bring down 'the racist state' – indeed it is likely to get him to prison, but it is not an expression of the need for *individual* survival – it is a political act. Although, in a manner of speaking, this particular act may be reminiscent of Goffman's patients 'flapping' at institutions, the resemblance is fragile. Can we really accept the hypothesis that inmates in 'mental' hospitals are in the same political situation as Blacks in South Africa? Acts of 'situational self-sabotage', whether they be in mental hospitals or in concentration camps, are political in so far as they directly or indirectly challenge the structure of authority, but surely we are not talking of great pockets of collective resistance – what we are talking about is the way in which some victims manage to find 'space' by dramatising the absurdity of their situation, and, in the case of mental hospitals, by the tacit mocking of the custodians. If there is any optimism to be found in this kind of resistance then it must be grounded in a view of human stoicism which, to say the least, is heroic. Goffman's patients are, therefore, condemned to an unending game of symbolic resistance which can never be translated into decisive political action because there is no way in which they can effectively change the conditions of their imprisonment.

While the concentration camp image of contemporary industrial society has some force, it is obviously a one-sided and distorted reification of social forces and tendencies. Moreover, although we cannot afford to ignore the terrible historical and traumatic lessons of the 'concentration camp' era, we should not be pushed into a position in which we mistakenly identify symptoms with causes. Concentration camps are not independently existing institutions which shape social reality – they are symptomatic of processes which are understandable historically in the context of a general analysis of industrial capitalism.

However, the deep pessimism of so much of the dramaturgical literature, as well as the defeatism of social science in general, cannot be shrugged off as bourgeois self indulgence. 'Everyday life', 'paramount reality' – call it what you like – has become saturated and contaminated by terminal scenarios of the death of civilisation. These scenarios are given daily prominence by the media – the apocalypse has always been news, but never to the extent of today's mass production of appropriate 'endings'. The 'doomster' syndrome – the 'sense of an ending' – is not confined to the mass-media; it has infiltrated 'liberal' social science where 'technology' and 'bureaucracy' have had a long history as enemies of human values.

> The civilization malaise, in a word, reflects the inability of a
> civilization directed to material improvement – higher
> incomes, better diets, miracles of medicine, triumphs of applied
> physics and chemistry – to satisfy the human spirit. To say as
> such is not to denigrate its achievements, which have been
> colossal, but to bring to the forefront of our consciousness a
> fact that I think must be reckoned with in searching the mood
> of our times. It is that the values of an industrial civilization,
> which have for two centuries given us not only material
> advance but also a sense of clan and purpose, now seem to be
> losing their self-evident justification. As yet, the doubts and
> disillusions as to that civilization are only faint breezes that stir
> the leaves of the tree and will certainly not uproot a way of life
> anchored deeply in the earth of our beings. But the breezes
> blow and the stirrings they cause must be added to the sense of
> sometimes indefinable unease that is so much a part of our
> age.[5]

'Civilizational malaise' is a mild way of describing the crescendo of voices raised in horror at the coming of the apocalypse, yet it catches the feeling of anxiety which informs contemporary discussion of urbanism and technology, and the problem of economic overdevelopment. Eschatological metaphors have become popular for the first time since the Middle Ages, and they are not only concerned with the totalitarian concentration camp nightmare but with the diametrically opposed theme of a runaway technological society beyond human control. This 'loss of control' theme has become strident in the last two decades, especially in the

29

context of the supposed 'crisis' of population and resources. Everything has become too complicated, too complex, too remote, too depersonalised. It is argued that governments can no longer make effective decisions, because they are not capable of understanding the intricacies and mechanisms of the 'state' machine. Hence, instead of the uniformity of everyday life which the concentration camp image presupposes, the lack of control theme points to the fragmentation of experience, and to an urban existence literally split into thousands of isolated life-worlds. Loss of control is not only experienced by the 'masses' – it is also experienced by bureaucrats and experts who find it impossible to break out of their functionalised prisons. For Weber, the image of the future was one of increasing rationalisation in which the majority of individuals were divorced from organisations and decision-making processes, but he did not envisage a situation whereby the bureaucrats themselves lost control of the organisations – there was no question of the organisation and the state existing independently of the participation of human actors. Weber's pessimism was centred on the inevitability of the triumph of 'rationalisation', but he was not a prophet of the disintegration of social organisation – on the contrary, he hoped the crust of rationalisation would eventually be broken by some powerful charismatic thrust. Be that as it may, the fragmentation thesis is firmly entrenched in the consciousness of experts and laymen. Both in private and public consciousness it is this pessimistic mood which dominates discourse.

5 Everyday life as spectacle

Perhaps the notion of everyday life as deception lacks conviction because it is too 'individualistic', too rooted in American social experience. For various reasons, European radical social theorists have not taken much interest in the world of small-scale episodic encounters. They tend to devalue practitioners like Goffman – it is a simple exercise to point to the ideological biases in his work. How can one defend a sociology which apparently does not challenge the established order? What justification can one advance for a perspective that seems to wallow in the artificiality of an urban society, where the 'rules of the game' are those of the con-man? Con-men do not make themselves – they do not arrive on the 'scene' as fully operational tricksters – they must have some starting point, some history. In other words, if society is a gigantic con-game, then surely, we are entitled to ask 'why should this be so?' Marxists give one sort of an answer, academic sociologists another, but there is one thing upon which they all tend to agree, namely, that the fragmentation of industrialised societies is intimately related to processes such as the social division of labour and the accumulation of capital. The way men live in society at any moment of historical time must, of necessity, be dependent on structural forces which 'seem' to have a constraining reality – a reality which is not wished away by retreating into fantasy, or explained by treating it as a con-game. Moreover, the 'reality' *or* 'illusion' of the 'self' as an active participant in the construction of the 'game' must also relate to 'moments of historical time'.

We are, of course, venturing into that peculiar and indeterminate discussion of the opposition of self and society (a debate which seemed to be resolved in the 1950s when socialisation was sanctified as *the* master social process). This was particularly true of American sociology where Parsons, Bales and others thought they had ironed out most of the difficulties arising out of the traditional problem of the tension between individual and society. In those halcyon days, American sociology's optimism about the world in general, and American society in particular, seems to belong to the realm of mythology. The belief in a benign pluralism in which conflict was contained by commitment to an ultimate realm of value provided theorists with ammunition to defend western industrial society as a proving ground for individual achievement. We have come a long way since those days – the tensions and disjunctions of late capitalism can no longer be hidden behind the facade of the pluralist consensus. The pendulum has swung the other way.

Optimism has been replaced by an ambivalent pessimism which pictures social reality as the fraudulent product of the media-industry. Hence, we are presented with an image of society which emphasises the episodic, the fleeting moment, the scene, the happening and so forth. Such an image presupposes that participants or actors have no historical consciousness – they can only relate to the 'here' and 'now'. Aspects of contemporary sociological practice have reflected this 'modernist' obsession with movement and the immediacy of experience. Aesthetically, this means that 'everyday life' is seen as though it were in a continuous state of spontaneous combustion – a near-ending 'trip' punctuated by 'highs' and 'lows'.

It is in the United States that the language of the drug culture has been partly absorbed into social science discourse, so that it is perhaps possible to talk of a psychedelic politics and sociology which seriously challenges traditional main-stream assumptions about the historicity of the self and society. This challenge cannot be dismissed too cavalierly. Key figures in the counter-culture, such as Kesey, Tom Wolfe, Leary, Reich, Marcuse and others, have

31

exercised an astoundingly strong influence on the concepts and rhetoric of deviance theory, as well as transforming the lifestyle of hundreds of sociologists. What distinguishes this new sociology of the 1960s was not so much its rediscovery of the early Marx, but its emphasis on the need for a 'total' confrontation with the 'immediacy' of social problems. In confronting the trivia of everyday life – the petty oppressions in the family, the indifference of the educational establishment, in confronting the countless situations in which somebody is being 'got at' – the tactic of this new sociology is not simply to expose and demystify the fraudulent structure of society; rather it is to engage in what could be called a praxis of spontaneity. Each situation becomes the critical focus of social inquiry and action.

However, the praxis of spontaneity found its real home in Europe with the emergence of 'Situationism', particularly in Holland and the France of De Gaulle. It was Henri Lefebvre who gave theoretical coherence to 'Situationism', especially in his attempt to delimit the parameters of everyday life. He argued that 'everyday life' was the contemporary setting for the development of a new and vicious form of alienation which supplemented the alienation of the factory. Everyday life had degenerated into a passive adjunct to consumer capitalism – all human relationships were conceived of as extensions of the market, and accordingly, the individual simply exists as a consumer and as a spectator of the 'show' – a show incorporating the entire world stage. The consumer as a spectator is the typical alienated human being of the twentieth century. As Lefebvre writes:

> It has substituted for the image of active man that of the consumer as the possessor of happiness and of perfect rationality, as the ideal become reality ('me', 'the individual', 'living', 'active subject become objective'). Not the consumer nor even that which is consumed, is important in this image, but the vision of consumer and consuming as art of consumption. In this process of ideological substitutions and displacements man's awareness of his own alienation is repressed, or even suppressed, by the addition of a new alienation to the old.[6]

Consumption, mediated through advertising, becomes the means whereby capitalism manages to maintain its hold upon the masses. The world is dramatised and cinematised – it is presented as a never-ending cascade of 'goodies' supposedly within the reach of all consumers. Spectacles are produced with the object of depoliticising and defusing resistance and spontaneity, but, more than this, 'the spectacle' *becomes* everyday life.

The 'Situationists' as a group are difficult to categorise. They range from Lefebvre's sociological position to the group of activists in the 'Situationist International'. Although ostensibly having a French connection, their international influence has been considerable. They represent a mood, rather than a really worked-out theoretical position – it is not only in the context of May 1968 that we can point to their undoubted significance for 'Leftist' politics, but also in their radical critique of everyday life. The spectacle will be replaced by the festival, by the domain of free play to be established by direct and continuous attack on the social order. Although there are overlaps with Marcuse's analysis of one-dimensionality, the thrust of the Situationist argument is somehow to radicalise the working classes by an aesthetic praxis fusing individual dissent with the poetry of collective revolution. In other words, everyday life must be rediscovered in a world in which the 'spectacle' has overwhelmed art and life. As against, the profound pessimism of Marcuse and other members of the Frankfurt School, the Situationist solution is optimistic, in that they believe in the possibility of a genuine human future.

Problems

The five themes we identified as expressing aspects of the current interest in everyday life as a resource for political and social discourse cannot be formulated into a consistent theoretical scheme – they are far too disparate. What this means, therefore, is that there are a number of problems connected with the 'everyday life' debate which are relevant to our concerns.

I The problem of structure

The interplay between everyday life and structure is replicated in the interminable discussion about the relative primacy of levels of reality – a discussion which attempts to bridge the supposed gap between micro and macro processes, or, alternatively, highlights the tension between the sociology of 'private troubles' and 'public issues'. There are a host of proposed solutions to this problem, ranging from a rigid and distorted reading of Durkheim's advocacy of the autonomy of social facts, to Parsons's notion of the 'inter-penetration of levels'. More usually, the solution is reductionist as in various psychological and behaviourist versions, or it is imperialist, submerging all over levels in the sea of normative determinism.

Of course, many practitioners find it difficult to incorporate the micro and macro levels under one conceptual umbrella – there seem to be two separate universes of discourse, which at best co-exist in an 'uneasy dualism', and at worst are 'split' into competing areas of *reciprocal misunderstanding*. When we try to come to grips with 'everyday life' and oppose it to 'structure', then it seems to me we are on very tricky ground indeed. Are we saying that 'structure' is non-ordinary, or extraordinary, as if it had the same sort of status which the 'sacred' possesses *vis-à-vis* the profane? Obviously, this is nonsense, or if it is not nonsense, then this must imply that structure is something outside the day-to-day experiences of practically all living human beings. The real question is whether mundane reality can be described independently of structure. In the earlier discussion about 'exploitation' it was suggested that 'everyday life' was not a bounded area divorced from economic and political imperatives. If you are starving in the slums of Calcutta, this is everyday life. Moreover, privileged castes, or classes, are embedded in the *same* network of relationships as the starving poor. Everyday life is *structured* for the rich and poor, for capitalist and proletarian, and for Black and White – what is at issue is the nature of structure, not its insulation from the mundane world. We might want to talk of levels of everyday life, or the pluralisation of life-worlds, but we cannot talk of everyday life as if it were a special area of experience reserved for the exploited – exploitation binds both exploiters and exploited in a set of relationships. All this may seem to be tautological and obvious, but its sheer obviousness is overlooked when we become too obsessed with searching for a theoretical rationale for an interest in everyday life.

II The problem of reality

If, as Schutz has maintained, the one paramount reality is the reality of everyday life, then this must mean that any competing claims are not claims about reality, but claims about *aspects* of paramount reality.

In everyday life, we are faced with opposed views of what constitutes reality; there is the reality of the factory floor, the reality of the bus queue, the reality of the kitchen, the reality of visceral discomfort and the seductive reality of fantasy. They all demand allegiance and total commitment. For the woman caught up in the monotonous routine of household chores 'reality' is the kitchen, the bedroom and the interminable sameness of the shopping round, in the constant battle to maintain her self esteem. There are no obvious escape routes, except perhaps through divorce, or an affair, and until the advent of the women's movement, there was no viable political alternative. It is *one* reality in a male-dominated society in which housewives frequently internalise the metaphors and mechanisms of their own subjection – it is a reality which assumes the aspect of an overpowering reification, because it allows for no alternatives to the taken-for-granted obviousness of the housewife's world. However, this reality is *not* sacrosanct – it is constructed and can be taken apart – it does not exist as an eternal verity, although various males, academic and otherwise, act and talk as if this is the case. The reality which confronts the housewife is obviously one which intersects with the reality of the family – the family itself constitutes a battleground of opposed realities, and, to take it a step further, the family is located in a nexus of institutional forces which function as arbiters of reality.

Reality is where you find it – for the housewife it is found in the prison-house of the family, for the worker it is in the factory, and for the artist it is in the acuity of the imagination, for the sociologist in the magic of his constructs and for the Fascist it is in the personification of the 'enemy'. In a sense, all realities have equal status, all are paramount, all have claims to ontological priority. There is no way in which the reality of the kitchen sink is any more significant than the reality of the sociological imagination:

> It is my contention that every reality is equally real. No single reality contains more of the truth than any other. From the perspective of Western everyday life, Western everyday life will appear paramount, just as Schutz maintains. But from the perspective of scientific theorising or dreaming, or mediating, each of these realities will appear just as paramount.[7]

The question of whether or not it makes sense to talk about paramount reality is a philosophical problem, just as the question of whether reality is 'one' or 'manifold' is philosophical, but in spite of this, social scientists have not been remiss in making claims about the ontological priority of their pet realities. This perhaps explains the 'reaction' of the 'new' wave of phenomenological viewpoints in social theory, especially in the context of their attack on reification as an unwarranted abstraction from 'everyday life'. In this exercise they have demonstrated quite successfully, I think, that a great deal of theorising in sociology is flawed by premature closure and an excessive addition to tautology, but whether the solutions they offer can remedy this must depend on their capacity to come to terms with tension points which traditionally have been the concern of practitioners in 'main-stream sociology'.

Presumably, the object of dereification is to lay bare the processes whereby· practitioners accomplish, or construct, a theoretical account of reality. For instance, what is involved when the practitioner tries to explain and understand the phenomenon known as class? From one perspective, class can be defined as a marriage between two realms, two sets of language games, those of participants and practitioners. Traditionally, it could be argued, practitioners have tended to lose sight of the 'grounding' of their language game in the everyday language and practice of participants. Inevitably, this leads to reification, and the sociological concept 'class' is treated as if it had an independent existence or reality. What is irretrievably lost is the reality of the language game of the participants themselves. The only way in which this reality can be retrieved for the purposes of social inquiry is somehow to let the phenomena speak for themselves, and this involves the practitioner in the most stringent act of self denial – he must literally abandon the distorting mirror of his own convoluted language game, a task which, by definition, is beyond the competence of most ordinary mortals. And even if this is possible, after the use of the entire battery of techniques and methods which the 'tape-recorder' has to offer, there is no guarantee the 'reality' caught by these techniques is pristine or uncontaminated.

Andy Tudor has suggested that the quest for the 'integrity of the phenomenon' is not confined to 'everyday lifers':

> It is likely that most sociologists, of whatever persuasion, would claim that they were trying to *approximate* the true state of affairs in the phenomena they study. The everyday lifers differ in taking this claim very literally.[8]

'To the phenomena themselves' might sound like a revolutionary programme for sociology, but I suspect that this is equally true for those practitioners who have found their data and phenomena in language and in the discovery of the symbol as the fount of sociological illumination.

III The problem of meaning

The fact that language has become such a central element in social analysis has entailed an almost obsessive concentration on meaning and on the semantics of everyday life. At one level, we have symbolic interactionists focusing on language as the negotiating medium of identity and motive attribution, and, at another level, we have structuralists telling us that language is the code underpinning the fabric of social and cultural life. For symbolic interactionists 'the definition of the situation' comes to serve as paramount reality, and as the source of our sense of social structure.

One implication of picturing everyday life as a web of symbolic negotiation is that it becomes difficult to root experience in other domains. Typically, the so-called regularities of everyday living are described in terms of interpretative procedures highly suffused with symbolic content. The trivia of existence are given portentous significance – they become dramas in which identity is laid on the line for confirmation. Every encounter turns into an opportunity for weaving meaning out of confusion, so that the encounter itself becomes a way of reaffirming the social bond. Without this incessant process of negotiation it would seem that social structure is impossible. Hence, society exists in, and because of, communication. There is, in other words, a complete absorption of structure in culture. Human beings are completely encapsulated in systems of meaning.

How can we escape from meaning? If it is omnipresent, if all human action is circumvented by what Turner calls 'forest of symbols', then is it ever possible to get outside this forest?[9] Taken literally, the claim that identity, everyday life and social structure are constituted by communication and language is fragile – nevertheless, it is not easily overthrown by counter-arguments. Take, for example, the literature of motive attribution which has come to dominate versions of deviancy theory. Instead of motives, we now talk about accounts, reasons, narratives, plots, etc., etc. What is suggested by this literature is an almost unbelievable capacity for the construction, elaboration and the selling of identity in the motive market. Everyday life is, by this token, a game of make-believe, of masks and mirrors, in which it is impossible to tease out the real living person. And there is the suspicion that this is all there is, that behind the masks there is nothing, or perhaps some nasty brutish being. Moreover, social structure is treated as if it is an epiphenomenon of culture, as though it is completely dependent on symbolic construction. Of course, all this begs a whole host of questions about the nature of the symbol and its relationship to the world, which cannot be handled here, although the question of the dualism of culture and structure is a crucial one for social theory.

Now, I realise that the foregoing is a caricature of various rhetorical approaches to everyday life in which meaning is the sole topic of concern. I still remain convinced that this kind of approach is of great value, especially in the format we owe to Kenneth Burke and Goffman, but it has obvious limitations. (Very crudely, it needs to be *plugged in* to some other broader historical frame – it needs to mesh with a Marxism which is prepared to meet it half way, a formidable project by any stretch of the imagination, and one which lends iteself to a spurious synthesis.) The trouble is that

37

we tend to lose sight of the world beyond the symbol, the world our interpretative procedures gloss over. It is unlikely that human beings cannot and do not distinguish between the meaning structures to which they pay allegiance, and the world which is host to those meaning structures. Certainly in everyday life people are often suspicious of the words they use, of the language they hear on the television screen, of the lies they suspect are being told by politicians, and they also know that language and ritual are consciously employed in order to secure political and economic goals. They do not necessarily believe the propaganda beamed at them. After all, in the post-Watergate era it is very difficult to rely completely on the surface structure of a political utterance.

Symbolic reality can be considered paramount if it is demonstrated that other levels of analysis are themselves *meaning structures* existing in the minds of men only – nowhere else – and this is pure idealism. Typically, in everyday life situations there is a delicate interplay between moments of complete absorption in symbolic interaction, and other moments when the world outside the symbolic context comes flooding in, overwhelming in its demands for immediate gratification. The visceral underground is not completely subject to symbolic 'mediation', neither are the emotions. We have become so indoctrinated with the language of motive attribution that when one makes such an elementary point one is greeted with cries of amazement. For example, take the phenomenon of hunger; there are countless monographs in physiology and psychology describing in the finest detail the physical and biological processes which enter into a scientific account of hunger as a state of the organism. Ingenious experiments have been constructed by animal behaviourists to measure and control the 'hunger' drive. Psychologists have studied the social shaping of hunger, and we have a veritable cross-cultural index which details the variation in food habits, eating patterns and the like. What remains constant is that humans and animals must eat in order to survive – there seems to be no problem about this, and yet, in the rhetoric of motives, hunger seems to be forgotten, except as an occasion for social ritual. Whatever symbolic construction we may put on hunger, it is not invented, nor, for that matter, is sex.

There is another associated strategy in formulating a sociology of meaning – this is Wittgenstein's postulate about the grammatical rules of a language generating a separate social existence or form of life. While it is not completely clear what Wittgenstein meant by a language game, this has not prevented the notion entering social theory as if its meaning is self evident. Conceivably we could describe 'everyday life' as a mosaic of language games which are

38

constantly flowing into each other, modifying each other and, in general, reflecting and influencing the forms of social existence to which they are attached. As Albrecht Wellmer has remarked:

> In other words, it is now apparent that the explication of ordinary languages is possible only in the dimensions of that language itself. This circle, in which any understanding and any explication of language is comprised, is bound up with the acquisition of a form of existence: language is part of an activity, or form, of life. The grammatical rules of language constitute a form of social reality; in other words, the grammatical rules are necessary more than mere grammatical rules; inasmuch as they govern a *praxis*, they are also rules of training in a social form of a life.[10]

What is not immediately clear is whether the grammatical rules constitute the reality, or does the reality constitute the grammatical rules, or, alternatively, do they mutually constitute each other? In the first and third alternatives we are giving assent to a commitment which finds the ultimate stuff of social existence to be a set of rules which hold good for particular forms of life at particular moments in time. Forms of life are, by this token, only understandable in their uniqueness – they do not provide the grounds for a general social science, or for historical analysis. Accordingly, all that can be hoped for is the detailed analysis of various 'forms of life' as they present themselves to practitioners. At best, we might be able to chart the ebb and flow of different language games as they cross each other's path, and perhaps at the metaphorical level *only*, talk about a structure (possibly we might want to assert along with Harvey Sacks[11] that we obtain our knowledge of structure through talk. But that is another story). The examination of meaning and language in everyday life is such a complicated and controversial area of discourse that one constantly gets the impression of walking around in a vast minefield in which nearly everybody is busy burying mines. What is peculiar is that while practitioners are intrigued by language games they tend to lose sight of the fact that their own language games about language games often give the impression of being too analytical. In other words, the 'lived' reality of language is lost in the intricacies of analysis.

IV The problem of fragmentation

In most contemporary discussion about everyday life, fragmentation themes occur with monotonous regularity. If it is not fragmentation, then it is alienation, or estrangement. The empirical formulation of the fragmentation thesis does not provide any major difficulties. Life is fragmented; there is a social division of labour; there is a continuous splitting of role functions at the personal and public levels – all this is documented in most introductory texts in sociology; it is not news. Looming large in this discussion is the problem of privatisation. The privatisation thesis assumes that industrial society is becoming more and more middle class, more and more consumer-oriented. Consequently, the working class is doomed to absorption into an ever-increasing amorphous mass of middle-class strata whose sole commitment is to current consumer lifestyles. (Embourgeoisement was a common enough topic in British sociology in the 1960s, and the idea of the Post-Industrial Society is even more common now that Daniel Bell has caught the attention of a large non-sociological audience.) The image we have of modern industrial society is of a plurality of privatised spheres in conflict with a monolithic bureaucracy. Privatisation involves intense emotional involvement in the family; in one's friends, in one's hobbies, etc., etc. More importantly, the world of work is believed to be completely insulated from private life, leading to a split between the private and public self. Hence the private self becomes the focus of gratification.

Behind the standard picture of affluence and the multiplicity of routes to private gratification, there is a peculiar tendency to treat privatisation as though it were the only way in which human beings can get away from the nastiness of the world. What remains of the integrity of the 'self' is not to be found in the public world of politics, factory floor and the like, but in an extended trip into sensual and emotional gratification. Such a journey is no longer the prerogative of the privileged few, or the traditional citizens of Bohemia – it is a journey now undertaken by millions. For some commentators, this spectacle of affluence and private experience is a confirmation of the promise of capitalism. Capitalism has delivered the goods – 'look how its abundance is enriching the lives of millions who in past ages would have been confined to the deadening experience of the factory bench and the boredom of office routine.' For other commentators, this is a spurious optimism which has no real justification. Their reading of fragmentation is pessimistic and apocalyptic. Not only is 'everyday life' a cesspool of emptiness, but the estrangement of private troubles from public issues is linked to the crisis of industrial-isation, and more specifically to the crisis of capitalism. Nowhere is this fragmentation more evident than in the family, at least this is what the literature keeps on telling us. The privatised nuclear family becomes a microcosm of hate, envy, power struggles and sexual angst, in which husband, wife and children are engaged in a war of mutual self destruction. This is a theme which keeps occurring time and time again in the modern novel and drama. But more than this, it seems to suggest that this is the final fate of the private life – it is the logical outcome of the forces set in motion by the elaboration of the social division of labour; the family turns inward for emotional strength, but ends up as a privatised hell. Whatever the truth of this grim picture, it is a view shared by a great many people who now identify the family as *the enemy*. At a less spectacular level, we find these anxieties expressed by sociologists and social workers, who point to the exponential increase in marital problems leading to divorce and emotional bankruptcy. In other words, the proliferation of 'private troubles' tends to overwhelm the literary and sociological imagination.

In his profoundly depressing novel, *Something Happened*, Joseph Heller describes in merciless clinical detail the disintegration of a family into a group of isolated and anguished individuals who are bound together only by the mutuality of their hatred, and their inability to locate identity in the public world. Slocum, the protagonist of the novel, works in a nameless organisation in which he performs his function in an atmosphere of fear and compliance – a normal routine for the young executive on the 'make'. Whatever identity he projects is tied to the demands of the 'arse-licking' syndrome. At home, Slocum's self is employed with a vengeance in a crusade against his wife, his daughter and his son. No holds are barred in his joyless search for love and dominance, and in the end the tragic futility of it all is climaxed by the death of his son. The family is an exercise in futility, but it is the only place that Slocum can point to his own existence, no matter what the price is for others. His wife is the receptacle of his own distorted self, and because of this she is a symbol of his trajectory to complete nothingness:

> I want to get free of her before her health fails. I see an ailing wife in my future. There are eloquent forerunners now of chronic invalidism. (She is sure she has, is getting, will get, cancer, and maybe she will.) I know her health will degenerate before mine does. She's better at it. I don't want to be tied to her by sickness (hers, that is). I will. I'll get battered by continuing hurricane warnings of bursitis, arthritis, rheumatism, diabetes, varicose veins, dizziness, nausea, tumors, cysts, angina, polups, the whole fucking shebang of physical dissolution. (I can do without everyone else's but my own.) I'll be caught on that barb. And my grown up children will keep me there.[12]

Something has certainly happened, but what the nature of this something is is anybody's guess. In the enclaves of private

41

experience the family is not a refuge, but a prison in which the inmates slowly devour each other. Do we really recognise ourselves in this lens? The blurb on the book says it is about 'the malaise of modern America', and by extension, western industrial civilisation. Malaise suggests a surface condition of some deep underlying cause which must be treated if the symptom itself is to disappear. There is the implication that private troubles exist only because there is something rotten in the body politic. Dropping out is no solution, neither are drugs, nor middle-class spouse-swapping games in Hampstead and the suburbs – these are frenetic attempts to avoid coming to terms with the real world. Yet, such a view has an element of 'moralism' built into it. How do human beings come to terms with reality? In what way can one demonstrate that there is an alternative or better way? How can one condemn the primacy of the private sphere in the consciousness and actions of people in a society which is premised on the continued production of goods and services for a consumer market?

The split of contemporary consciousness into the private and public is explicable historically. There is no way in which we can understand the fragmentation process except in a historical context. Fragmentation is a fact of life, but if this is so, then this must mean that the discontinuity between private trouble and public issues is not an invention of 'the modernist imagination' but reflects the actual distortion, disjunctions and contradictions of the capitalist mode of production. This is not to say that I am proposing a simple vulgar Marxism, but rather that there is no way in which we can afford to talk about privatisation as if it were a symptom of spiritual malaise, or a psychological problem. Private spheres are private only as long as there is no economic and social crisis impinging on the lives of those who deliberately set out to construct islands of gratification. All this can be ended by the threat of redundancy, inflation and the insidious possibility of civil violence! As John Rex writes:

> Did anyone think that Mill's private troubles referred only to middle-class Americans on psychiatrists' consulting couches? Such people may be in pain, for all suffering is ultimately mediated subjectively, but even more immediate than that sort of suffering is the actual fact of violence in the world.[13]

No doubt, one could see fragmentation as a highly desirable state of affairs, fitting nicely with a view of society as a balanced relationship between various autonomous groups who compete with each other to share the fruits of affluence, a sort of pluralist paradise in which fragmentation goes hand in hand with the growth of individual freedom and social mobility. Possibly we could read

42

Durkheim this way, who, in spite of his fundamental pessimism about the threat of anomie in industrial societies, has his optimistic moments. Optimism has not completely disappeared from sociology, although one would be hard pressed to justify it. Who are the contemporary optimists? Parsons? Daniel Bell? Marcuse?

One of the strange things about the discussion of fragmentation is that it is conducted in the context of a partial view of the world and its history. Does it make sense to speak of private trouble and public issues outside the European and American contexts? What are the private troubles of peasants in a small village in Bangladesh, faced with the problem of crop failure, the monsoon or the possibility of yet another civil war? It is unlikely that the victims of such disasters conceive of them as private troubles. They might try to explain their predicament in all kinds of way, including the possibility of religious defilement and the like, but they certainly would not see this predicament as a private event cut off from the private events of others. It might well be that the concept of privatisation is only applicable in those societies which have developed an elaborate division of labour. The key word here is 'troubles' *not* private. Troubles are universal: privatisation is not.

It is self evident that we face the world as subjective beings – that our pain is our own pain – there is no getting away from this. When a husband and wife are tearing each other to pieces they are not conducting an experiment in conflict theory, nor are they particularly concerned with the placing of their particular kind of hell on some private–public continuum. What the sociologist tries to do when coming to grips with personalised problems of this nature is to point to structural factors which impinge on the family as an institution – so we get statements of probability about the chances of marriages ending in divorce, as well as more radical statements about the family as a repressive institution. However, for the husband and wife who are locked in their act of mutual destruction this is completely irrelevant. Their 'troubles' are their own. How, then, can we reconcile 'troubles' with 'issues'?

The problems discussed above have as their central theme the difficulty of developing an adequate language to describe the relationship between social structure and the flow of everyday life. It might well be that it is impossible to do so – this remains to be seen. And for those practitioners who would like to see the emergence of a comprehensive 'theory' incorporating 'everyday life' and 'social structure' the prospect seems to be daunting, to say the least. It might well be that the solutions offered by the classic tradition and the 'new' sociology are incompatible, or the whole discussion may be irrelevant and not very interesting. This is not my position. It seems to be inconceivable that 'everyday life' is a

43

special category of analysis cut off from the structural concerns of a historically oriented sociology, but, equally, it is inconceivable that sociology can be a worth-while enterprise if it dismisses 'everyday life' as a trivial problem. Since Wright-Mills's time, the political dimensions of everyday life and private troubles have increasingly forced their way into the foreground of social theory. Everyday life has become politicised, but this is not really epoch-making – it always has been politicised. In the next chapter both the political and sociological implications of the 'split' between private troubles and public issues will be discussed in terms of everyday and global processes which various practitioners believe to typify contemporary social reality.

3 Privatisation and fragmentation

Recently, we have been bombarded by texts which have attempted to document the apparent split in consciousness between private and public spheres. It is now taken for granted that such a split has occurred, and can be empirically tested in our observation of everyday life. Privatisation is described as being endemic to modernisation, and frequently it is given a moral evaluation. The privatised human being is an alienated human being who is so divorced from involvement in political and social issues that it becomes impossible to think of him as a conscious political actor. Outside the private spheres of family, friends, leisure interests etc., the worlds of work and bureaucracy loom large as impersonal forces from which individuals somehow need to escape.

In addition to the split between private and public spheres, there is a tendency for the social world to split, to fragment. Fragmentation is a multi-dimensional process in which both the private and public spheres are themselves split into relatively autonomous compartments. Reality is pluralised – the 'pluralisation of life-worlds' is perceived as being the 'normal' condition of contemporary existence. In phenomenological accounts, the social division of consciousness is treated as the logical accompaniment to the social division of labour, but more significantly, consciousness is given equal status with institutional determinants. Hence, both consciousness and institutions are subject to fragmentation, at least, this seems to be the case for individuals caught up in the modernisation process.

In other words, privatisation and fragmentation, while having objective correlates in the social division of labour, are defined as subjective phenomena. They constitute the root metaphors for an entire vocabulary of moral terms which articulate what Berger *et al.*[1] call 'homelessness'. There is no 'home' to be found in the political

45

and social structures of modern society, because these structures have become 'things' outside the subjective understanding and control of individual persons. The implication of this being that with the breakdown of the medieval synthesis and the growth of industrialism, there is no longer an institutional source from which individuals can draw their values and locate their identity. It is in the private sphere that an individual finds meaning and identity, not in the bureaucratised world of work. While there are romantic undertones to this picture of a rootless and homeless world in which meaning is sought in the frantic excesses of the drug culture, or Zen Buddhism or whatever, there can be no doubt the phenomenon of privatisation is a real one, and not simply a figment of the sociological imagination. Paradoxically, while structuralism reacts against subjectivity in social theory, phenomenological sociology discerns an excess of subjectivity in the modern world:

> Inevitably the individual is thrown back upon himself, on his own subjectivity, from which he must dredge up the meaning and the stability that he requires to exist. Precisely because of man's intrinsic sociality, this is a very unsatisfactory condition. Stable identities (and this also means identities that will be subjectively plausible) can only emerge in reciprocity with stable social contexts (and this means contexts that are structured by stable institutions). Therefore, there is a deep uncertainty about contemporary identity. Put differently, there is a built-in identity crisis in the contemporary situation.[2]

Contemporary institutions are by this token incapable of supplying the identity needs of the vast majority of human beings exposed to modernisation. Not only are the old gods dead, but there is also an abandonment of belief in the efficacy of political institutions. In this kind of social and moral climate, it is readily understandable why privatisation is regarded, not simply as an escape from 'reality', but as a process actualising an alternative reality. Accordingly, it must be stressed that privatisation, although implying a split in consciousness, does not necessarily have a moralistic connotation. One might not approve of the individual and social consequences of privatisation, but one can hardly avoid recognising its actuality.

After all, the concept of privacy has been around for a long time. Is it simply a direct result of the inexorable movement of technological and industrial forces, or does it specifically relate to the emergence of the bourgeoisie and the middle class as the dominant source of ideological legitimation? Privacy, in a sense, is a very bourgeois virtue. The slogan 'an Englishman's home is his castle' is resonant of a bourgeois style of life, it does not have working-class origins. It is only in the decades after the Second World War that 'embourgeoisement' became a fashionable topic in the discussion of class in this country, although revisionists like Bernstein had already pointed to the same phenomenon in Western Europe as long ago as 1899.[3] Privatisation, in this context, is associated with the emergence of a consumer orientation in western capitalism, and with the ideological commitment to the welfare state. Given the apparent successes of American and European capitalism in the post-war period, privatisation was no longer an aspect of the bourgeois lifestyle – it permeated the entire fabric of western society. For some it seemed to be a measure of capitalism's success – it was identified with affluence and with the triumph of the consumer ethic. But for others, affluence and privatisation were seen as involving frightening social costs. Galbraith, for example, articulated this anxiety in his claim that personal consumption was increasing at the expense of public squalor. Be that as it may, privatisation had, by the 1960s, become a topic of concern for social scientists. Whether or not we consider privatisation to be a temporary problem of industrial capitalism, the fact remains that the split between the private and public spheres engages the attention of a great many social theorists who formerly would have dismissed this split as armchair speculation.

The private individual

The concept of privacy is intimately connected to the concept of the individual in western thought, especially to the bourgeois individual and his property rights. Property and privacy are terms which undergird the vocabulary of bourgeois individualism. In practice, it meant the privacy of the *few* who were in a position to enjoy the fruits of property. Certainly, the bourgeoisie were the only group, apart from the old landed aristocracy, who could afford the luxury of a private life. Hence, the private individual purchased privacy by his expropriation of an economic surplus. Even though there were differing styles of privacy, ranging from frugality to conspicuous consumption, private life was generally an aspect of the dominance of the bourgeoisie as a class. The workers and peasants of nineteenth-century Europe did not partake in this process, and it is only when we can discern the effects of the mass production of goods for a mass market that we can speak of the privatisation of the working class.

It is not all that easy to come to grips with the subjective dimension involved in privacy. At a very simplistic level, the private sphere is a hidden dimension of individual being, hidden in the murky depths of the self. Indeed, the self is conceived of as the core element of a system of defences against the encroachment of the hostile outside world. It is hidden from the inquisitive gaze of others – and constitutes a psychological refuge from the pressures of the world. The uniqueness and privacy of the self are recurring themes in European thought; the conception of the solitary ego pitted against overwhelming odds appealed to the romantic imagination of generations of intellectuals who saw in industrialisation the complete immersion of the individual in society. But exactly what is it that must remain hidden and private? If the experience of the self is a private game, then what is it in this game which is experienced as belonging to a separate and inviolable world? What goes on in my head or your head is private, it could be claimed, provided it is not available to anybody else, and also provided a deliberate attempt is made to conceal one's thoughts, emotions and fantasies from the other, but this seems to be a not too interesting way of describing the 'felt' dichotomy between 'the private' and 'the public'.

Moreover, what if the apparent discrepancy between private and public worlds is not demonstrable in other societies not exposed to the influence of industrialisation? Or, to put the question in a different way, is the distinction between the inner world of the private self, and the outer world of social and natural forces, confirmed for all humans, in all societies? Anthropologists, sociologists and other practitioners have no doubt that the 'self' is a social invention, that is, a social construction which appears only in certain historical and cultural contexts. The fact that the distinction between self and world is a commonplace of contemporary thought must not blind us to the evidence from alternative social structures where the 'self' may, or may not be, differentiated from the tribe, extended family or kinship group. This point is made nicely by Roy Willis in commenting on Godfrey Lienhardt's ethnography on the Dinka:

> Godfrey Lienhardt, the ethnographer of the Dinka, has emphasised how profoundly Dinka conceptions of the self differ from our Western ideas. 'The Dinka have no conception which at all corresponds to our popular conception of the "mind" as mediating and, as it were, storing up the experience of the self'. . . .
>
> Dr Lienhardt quotes the case of a Dinka man who has been imprisoned in Khartoum, who called one of his children 'Khartoum' in memory of the place, 'but also to turn aside any possible harmful influence of that place upon him in later life'. What Western man would call a 'memory', related to a past

experience, Dinka conceive as an exterior agency still potent to act upon them. Where the individual in Western culture encapsulates his personal past within himself, Dinka experiences what Western man would regard as interior psychic phenomena as features of a timeless external world. Both the boundaries of the self and the nature of the external world are differently conceived and experienced, by Dinka and Western man.[4]

In a society in which the individual is made the focus of political and ideological commitment, it seems impossible to envisage other cultural frames in which privacy and the self are not taken for granted. The belief in the interiorisation of a world of meaning and uniqueness of experience is embedded in the language and literature of western society, particularly the language and literature of bourgeois society. Privacy is not only taken for granted, it is elevated to a moral category. The violation of an individual's privacy is viewed in the same way as the desecration of the sacred by the unfaithful. Today this horror is expressed by the 'menace' of bureaucratic encroachment, by the belief that the state is insidiously eating into the last vestiges of individual freedom and privacy. Moreover, this perennial fear of the intrusion of the state into the private affairs of the individual is accompanied by the contradictory description of everyday life in industrialised societies as becoming more and more privatised. Presumably, there could be no such a contradiction in Dinka society, for the simple reason that the notion of the separate autonomous individual has no meaning for participants. The implication of all this is that individuality and privacy are only experienced in those societies which have undergone, or are undergoing, modernisation.

The liberation of modernity has been, above all, that of the individual. Modern social structures have provided the context for the socialisation of highly individuated persons. Concomitantly, modern society has given birth to ideologies and ethical systems of intense individualism. Indeed, it has been suggested that the theme of individual autonomy is perhaps the most important theme in the world view of modernity. The experience of 'alienation' is the symmetrical correlate of the same individuation. Put simply, alienation is the price of individuation. Quite logically, therefore, an important theme in demodernising movements is the protest against the allegedly excessive individualism of modern society. The individual is to be liberated from this individualism to the solidarity of either old or new collective structures.[5]

49

The private individual in western society, then, is a compound of contradictions. On the one hand, autonomy is positively evaluated as a moral principle, and on the other hand it is equated with 'alienation' and 'possessive individualism'. In the classic liberal bourgeois view, the private individual is a person who can only fully realise himself if he is not fettered by the constraints of the 'public sphere', that is, he is free to accumulate property without too much state interference. Privacy, in this context, relates not only to the individual person, but also to the exclusive rights to property. To respect a person's privacy, therefore, entails respecting his right to property. What I own, and what I lay claim to, limits the extent of my privacy. Hence, as an individual, I demonstrate my autonomy to the extent that my ownership of property allows me to pursue my own interests. From the radical point of view, the private individual is an alienated being, atomised by the exploitative nature of social relationships, cut off from other human beings in enclaves of rootless subjectivity. The privacy of capitalism is the privacy of alienation.

While the foregoing might typify views of privacy appropriate to the situation of nineteenth-century capitalism, there are other emphases which have become predominant today, especially the emergence of the 'counter-culture' and the discovery of psychedelic politics.

The secret individual

The private individual in western society is in a sense a product of a socio-historic situation. Given a radical transformation of social structures in the west, it is conceivable that the phenomenon of privatisation could be modified, and perhaps disappear altogether, but this assumes that we want it to disappear, or that it really is a problem. What appears to be a problem to sociologists is often differently perceived by participants. The nostalgia for a lost past in which community relationships were paramount is usually found in highly articulate members of the intelligentsia, or amongst politicians who see in modernisation the complete disintegration of traditional legitimations. Privatisation is not necessarily seen in these terms by its supposed victims (we might want to call this false consciousness).

One of the confusions emanating from any discussion of the nature of privatisation is the fact that it is often taken to be equivalent to secrecy. True, we talk of privacy and secrecy in the same context and, I suppose, it would be reasonable to see the private individual as the secret individual, but this implies that privacy is a deliberate intention to conceal and hide. It would be more appropriate to say that one needs privacy in order to conceal one's secrets. However, the secretive person is not necessarily bound by a context or a situation. He or she may act secretively in all situations; the world may be defined as a hostile or potentially dangerous place in which it is foolhardy to reveal to others the true nature of our feelings and attitudes. This is not to describe some paranoic condition in which everybody is desperately attempting to hide away from the prying eyes of some imaginary 'Big Brother'; rather it perhaps exemplifies a principle of social organisation found in a variety of cultures and societies, namely the bifurcation of reality into the sacred and the profane. Just as there seems to be an element of social life which is vested with the mystery of secrecy and taboo, whether it be a totem or the belief in mysterious happenings taking place in the White House or Number 10 Downing Street, so the individual has secrets, rituals and taboos which he must camouflage and mask. Until recently, for example, the open demonstration of homosexuality was liable to be subject to the severest legal penalties. Homosexual behaviour could only be carried out in the privacy of some well-hidden and secret venue. For the practising homosexual the planned secrecy of his assignations, plus the continued effort to disguise his 'everyday' (profane) conduct, entailed a cleavage between his 'real' nature and the 'artificial' reality of the straight world. To survive in such circumstances one has to lead a secret life, just as the spy had to lead a secret life in the various espionage capitals of Europe during the last war. On a more mundane level, everybody finds it difficult to operate in a completely 'open' atmosphere. The 'cliché' that everybody has something to hide may not suggest the profundity of sociological insight, but it does reflect any everyday insight into everyday behaviour. It may well be that such an aphorism is culturally specific, in the sense that it refers to everyday life in a consumer society in which the values of the market place force individuals to 'mask' their real emotions etc., but I would have thought its relevance is far broader.

Secrecy tends to have some associated nastiness built into it. To be secretive suggests what one is hiding is somehow shameful and disgraceful. Hence, it becomes imperative that secrecy is maintained, because to reveal one's secrets could lead to undesirable social consequences. Certainly, there is no advantage in boasting of the number of times one has broken the law if such boasting lands one in prison, but, more importantly, if the temptation to reveal *all* has psychological consequences which generate unbearable psychic pain, then obviously this is too great a price to pay. When politicians are accused of sexual deviance (whatever that might mean) they move heaven and earth to deny these accusations. They operate on the premise that the open perusal of their sex lives diminishes their stature as serious public figures – it is as if the open recognition of a secret sexual identity will precipitate personality disintegration. Even in the supposedly permissive climate of current sexual discourse, the exposure by the media or one's political enemies of one's sexual secrets could mean the end of a political career.

Nevertheless, in spite of the stigma attached to aspects of an individual's secret life, there is also the possibility that what is hidden and masked is felt to be 'valuable and desirable', as though it defined his true existence. Sexual deviance does not have to be negatively stigmatised – on the contrary, it may be the central component of identity. Accordingly, instead of guilt, the appropriate tactic could be the ability to play the social game of concealment and deception without giving away secrets. There is an element of excitement in the chance to subvert the official straight world by the attempt to get away with something under the noses of disapproving others. Such a tactic (beautifully documented in Goffman's work) enables the individual to enjoy his secrets – he is getting away with blue murder – he is indulging his particular need in a dangerous manner. The archetypical 'lover' in the classic French novel lives dangerously precisely because he believes he is managing to deceive the husband. His secret is a source of continuous enjoyment at the expense of a poor benighted cuckold. In everyday life, deception and contrivance are far more difficult to arrange, but even so 'infidelity' is a common enough occurrence for it to be part of the mythology of sexual adventures.

From the insider's perspective, a secret life, or a repertoire of secrets, is not something one shares with others, except perhaps in some conspiratorial fashion. For the outsider (observer, interpreter) the secretive individual is open to the accusations of deceit and dubious motives. Secrets are, by definition, reprehensible and suspect – furthermore, there are typical vocabularies of dubious motives that can be invoked to pigeon-hole the suspected secret ('he seemed such a quiet and timid person, but I always suspected that he was a dark horse' and so on and so on). When, for example, the McCarthy witch-hunt was at its peak, Americans began to see subversive implications in the most ordinary mundane behaviour; it was not uncommon for the victims of such accusations to act in such a way that their behaviour was construed as expressing their guilt. In front of the glaring spotlights of congressional inquiry, it was easy enough for the most innocent statement to be construed as evidence of a damaging political secret. In such a climate of suspicion it is taken for granted that you are guilty, unless you can overwhelmingly demonstrate your innocence.

One of the peculiar consequences of privatisation is the spectacular media presentation of suburban violence. Usually, the stories are of respectable middle-class homes behind the walls of which are found all the orgiastic rites of paganism, wife-swapping, drug addiction, hard porn. Suburbia is transformed into a Dionysian hothouse in which the pleasure-principle reigns supreme. Of course, nobody really believes this sort of script – it never happens in one's own suburb, it might sometimes happen in Hampstead or Chelsea, but never in Surbiton or Poppleton. It reflects a strange preoccupation with the 'believed in' mystery of other people's lives. Your next-door neighbours might be staid middle-class conservatives who never seem to put a foot wrong, but who knows what goes on in the privacy of their home? The assumption of hidden secrets does not necessarily have to assume the proportions of a Dionysian mystery; if things are not what they seem this is in keeping with the stock of everyday beliefs about the relationship between appearance and reality. Your neighbours need not be members of the 'mafia', but 'what about the state of their underwear' plainly visible from your upstairs landing? There are cues to be picked up, signs to be read which allow you to make an educated guess as to the nature of their private lives – at least, you think you know what these signs mean. Flippancy apart, everyday life in the suburbs, in spite of its apparent ordinariness, tends to excite the imagination of the media. Either it is pictured as a boring arena for routine mediocrity, or it is seen as a boiling cauldron of mass desire. For sociologists the problem is somehow to make sense of the media's image, and try to come to terms with the actuality of privatisation. But sociologists are also 'outsiders' who probe into the private lives of participants. They listen to talk, conduct surveys and discover a hidden universe of meaning behind suburban doors. They find secrets, perhaps write books about privatisation and alienation in the suburbs, and, in so doing, add to the general game of motive attribution. In finding out secrets, the sociologist is supposedly engaging in a job of demystification, and nothing excites the imagination more than the discovery of vast reservoirs of vice and sin in the suburban wasteland.

Simmel, more than anyone else, recognised the import of 'secrecy' for the sociological understanding of social interaction. A secret is a relational property. There can only be secrets from others (this excludes the possibility that one can hide something from oneself, in the Freudian sense). Hence, one hides one's sexual secrets from one's parents, affairs from one's wife, and law-breaking from the police. But secrets can also be shared with a privileged few – they carry with them the excitement of common danger, of 'us against them'. It is no use telling the world that you and your comrades are just about to blow up the Stock Exchange. Nor for that matter (in spite of media portraits of open marriages) do you broadcast your 'affair' with your best friend's wife. In a more general sense, the keeping of secrets is a requirement of group survival; if secrets are leaked to one's enemies then the entire structure could come tumbling down. The possibility of betrayal is a constant threat to the hegemony of the group, as well as to the self esteem of its individual members. At the same time, however, as Simmel has observed, there is a peculiar fascination in the anticipation of the act of betrayal – it is as if secrets are at their most potent when they become public knowledge.

> The secret contains a tension that is dissolved in the moment of its revelation. This moment constitutes the acme in the development of the secret; all its charms are once more gathered in it and brought to a climax – just as the moment of dissipation lets one enjoy with extreme intensity the value of the object: the feeling of power which accompanies the possession of money becomes concentrated for the dissipator, most completely and sensuously, in the very instant in which he lets the power out of his hands. The secret too, is full of the consciousness that it can be betrayed; that one holds the power of surprises, turns of fate, joy, destruction – if only, perhaps, of self destruction. For this reason, the secret is surrounded by the possibility and temptation of betrayal; and the external danger of being discovered is interwoven with the internal danger, which is like the fascination of an abyss, of giving oneself way.[6]

In Simmel's view secrecy is inversely related to the complexity of social structure, and in this respect his analysis is not at variance with other sociological accounts of the individuation process in western society. The more undifferentiated the society, the less likely is it that secrets can be kept from the gaze of inquisitive members of one's kinship group, or family. Privacy and secrecy are functions of the growth of complicated developments in the division of labour, as well as the elaboration of a market and money economy. The undifferentiated community keeps its stock of secrets in the form of the 'sacred', but this is vested in the community as a whole, not in individuals. With the emergence of large-scale industrial societies the process is reversed – complexity involves a separation of spheres in which the private becomes more secret, and the public becomes more open. In theory, this public openness is related to the democratisation of the polity which is open to inspection by everybody in the community. This, of course, depends on whether or not the public sphere is really open in the 'ideal' democratic fashion. Who, for example, would want to claim that contemporary nation states of both the eastern and western variety are open? Whatever one's views on the nature of the state and bureaucracy, it is evident that they operate in a climate of secrecy. The recent revelations about the CIA and its clandestine war against practically everybody does not inspire one with confidence about the nature of the 'open democratic society'. Although treason and betrayal are endemic in interpersonal relationships, the betrayal of one's friends is not subject to the same stringent sanctions as betrayal of one's country. In private life the 'fascination of betrayal' is part of the game of secrecy, a game which has individual consequences, but the betrayal of one's country is not an exercise in personal gamesmanship, rather it is to be seen as an act against the objective character of the public sphere:

> If, above all, individualistic interests, there has grown an objective governing structure which embodies certain aspects of these interests, the formal autonomy of the structure may very well entitle it to function secretly, without thereby belying its 'publicity' in the sense of a material consideration of the interests of all.[7]

In other words, the betrayal of the state can be perceived as an act of betrayal against the 'individualistic interests' embedded in its institutional structure. In giving away secrets, one is betraying 'everybody', not simply one's friends – or, it could be claimed, betrayal at this level is an act of resistance against particularised interests, especially when these are defined in terms of class interests. The point of all this is to distinguish between the separate spheres as they intersect with individual consciousness; that is, the way in which the secret life of the privatised individual confronts the depersonalised rationalised structure of the modern bureaucratic state. This separation of spheres is taken for granted in current discussion. Certainly in Simmel's case, the evidence for 'separation' is overwhelming. For Weber, the tension between individual and organisation is the theme of his pessimistic assessment of the future of industrial society. For Marxists, the separation of the private from the public can be traced to the shattering of the old feudal hegemony in which all spheres occupied a fixed position within a given set of production relations. The removal of economic production from the home to the factory meant that the family became the focus of personalised and privatised life, while simultaneously action as an extractor of surplus value from its key workers, 'women'. Hence, the breakdown of the old feudal order meant not only the separation of spheres, but also that the family became an emotional battleground in which women found themselves in an increasingly isolated and exploited situation, despite the liberal illusion that 'domesticity was beautiful'. There can be no doubt that the main victims of privatisation have been, and are, women. It is they, more than anyone else, who have been subject to the emotional, economic and ideological pressures arising out of their position in the family in capitalist society.

If privatisation is such a dominant theme both in contemporary social theory and in the 'women's movement', then perhaps it would be as well if we could spell out the dimensions of the process in a more ordered fashion. However, before doing this, I think it is essential to emphasise that privatisation is not an autonomous process, which, once set in motion, assumes all the characteristics of other social and economic forces. Privatisation is an unanticipated consequence of industrialisation – it is wrong to claim that the splitting of spheres was a voluntary commitment on the behalf of thousands of families to withdraw from community bonds. We cannot, therefore, assent to the proposition that states that the splitting of spheres is a direct result of a rational choice about the desirability of privacy. This is not necessarily to foreclose on any discussion of the influence of ideological and religious factors on the growth of 'individualism', but it is to stress the importance of what Berger *et al.* call the primary carriers of modernisation, namely the 'economic – technological' and 'bureaucratic'. Privatisation is not relevant in contexts in which social institutions have not been touched by modernisation. Hence, their thesis is that modernisation invariably sets in motion forces which produce the splitting of spheres, and the fragmentation of consciousness.

There are recurring themes in this process, some of which have been implicit in the early discussion. Broadly speaking they can be conceived of in the following way:

1 the dissolution of totality
2 consumerism and the insatiability assumption
3 embourgeoisement
4 famialism

1 The dissolution of totality

By the dissolution of totality is meant the break-up of the bonds of community. Nineteenth-century social and political thought was replete with metaphors of dissolution of the traditional world. It is not at all easy to document the differing strands of argument that have gone into the 'loss of community' theme, for the simple reason that there is no general consensus on what is meant by 'community', nor is there agreement on the historical evidence. For Nisbet, 'community' is the key unit-idea for sociology. In his typically elegant way he writes:

> Community is a fusion of feeling and thought, of tradition and commitment, of membership and volition. It may be found in, or be given symbolic expression by, locality, religion, nation, race, occupation, or crusade. Its archetype both historically and symbolically, is the family, and in almost every type of genuine community the nomenclature of family is prominent. Fundamental to the strength of bond of community is the real or imagined antithesis formed in the same social setting by non-communal relations of competition or conflict, utility or contractual assent. These, by their relative impersonality and anonymity, highlight the close personal ties of community.[8]

Nisbet discerns in nineteenth-century thought a nostalgia for the certainties of an earlier time, when everyday life was governed by the over-arching symbolism of the church, and the 'warmth' of the kinship group, or family. The fact that industrialisation had undermined the closed manorial system of feudal Europe, plus the increasing secularisation of life and thought, entailed an almost mystical commitment to a 'past' which was believed to have provided human beings with a cognitive and emotional 'home', a home which was stable and secure. In spite of evidence about the exploitative nature of the feudal relationship, the high death rate, the fantastically low standard of living and the debilitating devastation of disease and epidemics, the traditional order was given a retrospective gloss which contrasted favourably with the unpleasant realities of everyday life in a Europe which had suffered from the excesses of the industrial revolution. Not that any of the classic theorists believed that the clock could be turned back, or that this was desirable; rather, it was hoped that new communal ties would emerge, which possibly could replace the old religious sources of communal legitimation.

In other words, the actuality of community was thought to be not necessarily bound by the limits of a territory or place – its existence could also depend on the common recognition of a corporate identity, such as the 'nation', and so forth. Community, in this sense, could transcend the fragmentation of industrialism, it could make sense of the multiplicity of role relationships, and it could mitigate the effects of conflict amongst competing classes and groups. If the local community was no longer able to provide the framework for close interpersonal relationships, then the need for other sources of communal identification seemed to be an

57

urgent necessity. Hence, classic sociology saw the decline of community as an almost inevitable consequence of industrial-isation, and the rationalisation of social life (the evolutionary implications of all this is implicit in the proliferation of typologies like Gemeinschaft and Gesellschaft, mechanical and organic solidarity, folk and urban), yet this decline was never seen as final, for the simple reason that most theorists made an implicit assumption about the supposed need for meaning and significance in everyday life. They assumed that, without meaning, without a belief in the essential orderliness of the world, human beings find life intolerable, especially under conditions of extreme social change. The same assumption is made about the effects of modernisation in the third world. Everywhere community life is being dislocated and ravaged by new technologies, new forms of social organisation, and everywhere, these dislocations lead to a profound crisis in value orientation and identity. Indeed, for some commentators it is this dislocation which they see as the most pernicious consequence of modernisation. So, the central problem for all industrialised and industrialising societies is the establish-ment of some common focus, some source of community.

The opposite of community, is, by definition, an impersonal world of shallow instrumental role relationships, in which the individual is constantly driven into himself to quarry the last nugget of significance. There is only one possible setting for communality, and this is in the privatised setting of the family, the last resort of intimacy. Outside the family, the world is a harsh battleground of conflicting interests. The family, of course, always was the archetypical communal institution – it was the family which provided the language and rhetoric of community, from the kinship group to the nation, and although the importance of its associative and instrumental functions were never overlooked, this was, and is, played down in the emotional 'rhetoric of community' used by politicians, social workers, priests and other 'official' spokesmen. The splitting of the world into private and public spheres is, therefore, one way of looking at the decline of community. And it is at this juncture that the 'mass society' thesis becomes such an important element in social analysis, particularly for those practitioners who find it difficult to come to terms with Marxism. Mass society and its collective political and bureaucratic manifestations can be described as a modern attempt to find an answer to the problem of community; at least this is one inference to be drawn from the copious literature. The family in itself cannot do what the old traditional community did, that is, it cannot act as a complete repository of identity – all it can do at best is to provide a refuge from the nastiness of everyday life. The communal intimacy of the family is not enough to sustain emotional and cognitive significance; for this to happen, other forms of social organisation are needed which superficially resemble the old images of the traditional community.

The mass society thesis is partly premised on the proposition that human beings find it intolerable to stand alone, that they always need the self validation of confirming others. The fact that most of this literature is American should not surprise us – it is here, more than anywhere else, that the peak problems of an industrial society are evident. It is also in the USA that the rhetoric of individualism and community is invoked as a matter of course, no matter the reality behind the rhetoric. If traditional communities have disappeared, then the alternatives to them are the typical organisational structures of industrial society – namely, bureau-cracies; but obviously it is difficult to identify with ICI, British Leyland or Shell Petroleum, except in so far as one can identify with an occupational role. But the 'mass society' argument is not about identification with specific roles – it is concerned with the 'crisis of industrialisation', and the associated alienation of the masses. For neo-Freudians like Fromm, the problem of western industrial society is precisely the isolated situation of the individual who is continuously battered by the crises of capitalism (unemployment, inflation, war and the plethora of social problems constituting the reality of everyday life). Because there are no 'community' solutions to these crises, individuals join mass movements, political parties – they surrender their freedom of choice to a leader of an élite, and in so doing discover a 'new' community. Hence, the rediscovery of community is not in the neighbourhood, or in the local voluntary group, but in the embrace of mass social movements, like National Socialism, and it is in this context that Fromm's isolated and alienated human being finds his 'home'.

But, the notion of a 'mass society' is not solely social-psychological. For Kornhauser: 'Mass society is a situation in which the aggregate of individuals are related to one another only by way of their relations to a common authority, especially the state.'[9]

The situation described is obviously an extrapolation, an imaginary projection into the future of industrial society. It is the complete antithesis to community, positing a state of privatisation not to be found in the 'real' world. Kornhauser and other proponents of the 'mass society' thesis are obsessed with bureaucracy – they see the state and other bureaucratic organisations acting in such a way as to isolate completely individuals in encapsulated pockets of specialised roles. So, we have a picture of a *possible* society in which all mediating organisations between the state and the individual are weak, slowly losing whatever influence they might once have possessed. Even the family is no longer able to provide a shelter for the individual, because it, too, is subject to the increasing bureaucratisation process.

The inference to be drawn from this vision of the 'mass' society is that of complete atomisation and isolation – the ultimate alienated state of the bureaucratic nightmare; for the individual this implies a retreat into the self, a flight from all social commitment, while simultaneously surrendering moral and political autonomy to the 'state'. From this point of view, 'mass' democracy is an illusion, fostered on unsuspecting 'masses' by manipulating élites who use the media as the means of securing their own privileged domination. Although not necessarily explicit, some mass society conceptions are rooted in the belief that the 'masses' are an irrational conglomerate of anchorless individuals whose sole needs are maximising pleasure and emotional security. The breaking up of the old traditional community resulted in a frantic search for alternative forms of social organisation which could somehow satisfy these needs, but the persistence of irreconcilable tensions in industrial society makes it increasingly difficult for them to be assuaged. If unemployment, inflation, industrial and class conflict, pollution, environmental despoilation, war and the host of socially induced psychological problems constitute the backdrop against which human beings live out their lives in the contemporary world, then it follows that solutions which cannot meet these needs will not have much chance of success.

Hence, the failure of liberalism in Europe during the decades between the World Wars, is seen by Fromm and others as being symptomatic of a deep-rooted anxiety about the 'protective' nature of the traditional institutions of western society. Capitalism had smashed the community basis of social life, and, consequently, in the consciousness of men, it seemed that the only real alternative was the welcoming embrace of the corporate state and Fascism. The substitution of the 'volk', the 'nation', or 'state' for the bonds of community was a logical outcome of the process of fragmentation set in motion by the industrial revolution, a revolution which destroyed the 'wholeness' of individual and society.

While the mass society thesis is not primarily aimed at dissecting the structures of European totalitarianism, it exhibits, to a very large degree, a fear about the future of industrial society which is almost histrionic in tone, especially when this future is spelled out in terms of the frightening costs of bureaucracy and élitism. It is in this context that the assumption is made by 'mass society' theorists, that even under conditions of affluence, there is no way open to individuals to find community and identity, except in the narrow sense of role identification. Accordingly, the quest for community, for identity, for meaning, is conducted in the privatised spheres of individual experience, in the alternative realities of intense personal commitment. Community is no longer a total conception, it is now seen to be available only in personal relationships, and this means that the family itself is perceived as a repressive bureaucratic institution impinging on the freedom of the individual.

What the foregoing discussion ignores is the prior question about the actuality of community. It is all very well for Nisbet to argue that the idea of community was the central unit idea of nineteenth-century social thought; it is another thing to demonstrate the historical reality of community. The fact that a group of human beings shared the same territory, performed the same rituals and were enmeshed in a system of kinship relations, does not preclude the possibility that such an arrangement was exploitative. The idea of community assumed a degree of uniformity, both in behaviour and in belief, which, on further investigations, was far more complicated and divisive than originally thought by historians and anthropologists. Norman Birnbaum, commenting on Nisbet's regret for our beautiful communal past, writes:

> He depicts the epoch before the French revolution in terms which exaggerate its positive aspects. Community, in fact, brought with it a quite intolerable moral constriction, authority in its traditional form entailed quite an intolerable quantum of domination, the sentiment of sacredness was allied to a blind obscurantism. Class relations under the *ancient régime* were not clearly as fixed as Nisbet thinks, but having a fixed place in the social order meant, for most men, having an abominably minimal share of social product.[10]

Nevertheless, despite the romanticism of Nisbet's reconstruction of a community life which probably was harsh and desperate, there can be no doubt that the rhetoric and ideology of community still does have a powerful appeal to a great many people. Although the mass society thesis is, empirically, a non-starter, there are millions of young people in the west who literally believe that the societies in which they live do produce alienation, isolation and atomisation. It is in this climate that a new vocabulary of community is articulated in the journals and literature of the 'alternative society' and 'counter-culture'. What is Theodore Roszak's *Where The Wasteland Ends* if it is not a massive indictment of contemporary industrialisation and a cry for community?

In talking about the decline of the community, we are not necessarily talking about the dissolution of totality. The shattering of the old medieval synthesis into its constituent parts of church, polity, economy and society, was not simply a breakdown of community bonds; it was also the prime example of what Marx considered to be the development of a new totality – 'capitalism'. Hence, the dissolution of one totality, 'feudalism', did not entail an absolutely meaningless fragmentation process in which all constituent parts pulled in completely different directions; the fragmentation implicit in capitalism, from Marx's point of view, could only really be understood as a totality – that is, the tensions, ambiguities and contradictions of the capitalist mode of production were not random movements of economic and social forces; on the contrary, they were structurally related.[11]

It follows, that in talking about privatisation we can follow two lines of argument:

First, we can see privatisation as the direct consequence of processes set in motion by the growth of industrialisation, and the decline of community; or *second*, we can point to the false antithesis between the privatised and public spheres which contemporary social theory has supposedly established as part of its portrait of contemporary capitalist society. In taking the second line, Marxists do not so much deny the actuality of privatisation, rather they question the interpretation advanced by practitioners who give privatisation an almost autonomous status.

The notion that privatisation is a 'self-regulating' autonomous process is pertinent to some of the problems we shall be looking at in the next section.

2 Consumerism and the insatiability assumption

One of the pivots of the privatisation argument is the evidence offered about the transformation of capitalism from an economy of production into an economy of mass consumption. This process is believed to be accessible to analysis by a systematic consideration of the way in which capitalist society has changed during the last three or four decades. It is not my intention to document the arguments for or against this view of the transformation of capitalism. What I intend to do is to provide a sketch of strands of the controversy which are directly of interest to the discussion of privatisation.

For some economists and sociologists, the transformation of

capitalism is self evident. In this country, people like Crossland, Hugh Schonfeld, on the continent Ralf Dahrendorf, Raymond Aron, Touraine, in the United States Daniel Bell, Edward Shils and a host of others including Galbraith, have for a long time claimed that capitalism has been so radically transformed that it no longer makes any sense to talk about capitalism at all. This meant that we were exposed to a whole corpus of terms which tried to capture the flavour of the 'new' approach to industrial society. Post-capitalist, Post-industrial, The Affluent Society, the Consumer Society and so forth – these are only a few representative labels that have been variously employed by practitioners in their attempt to delineate this radically different kind of society, which they believe is discoverable by anybody willing to get rid of outdated ideological tools of analysis.

What all these diverse people are in fact saying is that, in the advanced societies of the industrialised west, the old problem of scarcity has been partly solved, and therefore the critical problem for these societies is no longer the distribution of the national product but the way in which this national product is consumed. At the same time, they believe that the classic problems of capitalism have been mitigated by a continuous rise in the standard of living for all strata. Hence although poverty has not been eliminated and class conflict has not completely disappeared, these sources of tension are presumed *not* to be the *characteristic* tensions of latter-day industrial society. For post-industrial theorists the crucial areas of conflict are those relating to the supposed debilitating effects of consumer affluence and the paramount role of bureaucracy. Put differently, the emphasis has passed to 'consumers', facing 'élites', and, by implication, this means that the kind of society described by earlier social commentators can no longer be designated 'capitalist'.

Consumerism also involves a psychology of insatiability. Once the broad masses of the population have been exposed to the benefits of mass production they develop a taste for consumer goods which is incapable of satisfaction. Starting with the usual household durables like the refrigerator, washing machine, television etc., the consumer demands a car, two cars, a holiday abroad and so on. Hence, we are presented with a society of privatised consumers who spend their lives trying to accumulate more and more goods; in other words, there seems to be a peculiar reversal of 'the law of diminishing returns'; instead, the 'law of increasing returns' seems to hold – the more one has, the more one wants. Such a notion of the insatiability of 'wants' is related to a dominating 'pleasure principle' which knows no bounds. Once the craving for consumer goods is stimulated, there is no way in which it can be held back.

Supporting the 'insatiability of wants' is a vast advertising industry. Advertisers sell privatisation – they sell the means whereby individuals isolate themselves from the demands and obligations of political and social relationships; they sell the glorious picture of the 'good life' lived by beautiful people in suburban utopias. What this conjures up is a model of society in which the divisions between classes are non-existent, because everybody is presumed to be a consumer with middle-class tastes. Conflict in this situation is not between sectional interests, but between a multiplicity of individuals competing for a larger and larger share of available resources; as long as there appears to be an illusion of availability there is no open conflict. Conflict occurs only when there is an interruption to the flow of goods and services occasioned by 'disturbing' influences such as a strike, war, inflation, etc. However, these disturbances are regarded as marginal, provided they do not threaten the actual existence of the 'consumer society'.

This is not the time or place to get involved in a dissection of the pleasure principle, except in so far as it illuminates the notion of the 'insatiability of wants'. To claim that participants exposed to the benefits of mass production automatically develop an auto-nomous set of self-sustaining motives which further fuels the original production process, is simply to describe an economy geared to the maximisation of profit. If manufacturers cannot sell their goods then, obviously, they search for new markets or they look for techniques which allow them to soften their previous market. It is in this context that a whole new industry has grown up in recent decades, which purports to study and analyse consumer motivation. Whether it is in such areas as 'market' or 'motivational' research, the fundamental strategy is to stimulate new consumer needs so that they are integrated into the individual's 'want' system. There may be no intrinsic need for a colour television or a tumble drier, but after being pressurised by advertising channels, what was once peripheral and outside your original stock of wants is now a central component of that stock. It could be argued, therefore, that this is precisely what is at stake when we speak of the insatiability of wants. We are really speaking about the way in which manufacturers endeavour to keep their markets alive.

However, it could be that the advertisers have done such a proficient exercise in stimulating 'needs' and 'wants' in individuals (consumers) that it may make sense to see this in terms of autonomous motivation. Hence there is, in all this, a tendency for 'consumerism' to be treated as if it is a form of addiction – an addiction leading directly to privatisation. The ultimate logic of this admittedly over-stated picture can be found in the image of late capitalism painted by a contemporary political philosopher, who writes:

> For the market system, based on and demanding competition and emulation, creates the wants which it satisfies. The tastes and wants which people learn to satisfy, as they rise above bare subsistence, are, as we have seen, tastes and wants created by the productive system itself. And as the system increasingly moves away from a pattern of widespread competition between many producers (when it was still possible to think of it in terms of consumer sovereignty) to a pattern of competition for power between fewer and larger corporate units and groupings, which are increasingly able to control prices and products, *the tendency of the system to create the wants which it satisfies will become stronger*. There is no reason to expect that the wants and tastes which it satisfies will reflect or permit that full development of the individual personality which is the liberal-democratic criterion of the good society.[12]

The so-called new sovereignty of the consumer is not, therefore, located in the autonomous sphere of individual motivation, but it is heavily dependent on the workings of the productive system. If 'consumerism' is to be regarded as a form of addiction, then it is an addiction which has more in common with false consciousness than with drugs. The selling of consumer goods which encapsulate individuals in their private spheres, is, in the last analysis, not a problem in individual psychology but is implicit in the logic of capitalism.

3 Embourgeoisement

Perhaps a more central dimension of privatisation is the one which tended to dominate discussions about class and class conflict in the late 1950s and 60s. It has appeared under many guises since 'class' became the focal element in sociological accounts of stratification. We are, of course, referring to the embourgeoisement thesis. Until the Goldthorpe *et al.* studies of the Affluent Worker, it is true to say that we did not have a comprehensive analysis of this phenomenon, although, in various ways, American sociologists had more or less accepted the actuality of the thesis in their standard treatment of the American working class. It would be pointless for me to rehearse all the relevant issues in this debate, except in so far as it is of relevance to privatisation.

In its extreme form, the embourgeoisement thesis suggests that

65

all classes, all social strata in the industrial west (and, increasingly so in the Soviet Union) are becoming more and more middle class in lifestyle, attitude, ideology and behaviour. In practice, this means the divisions between classes are believed to be disappearing, and, hence class consciousness is relegated to the realm of a mythical industrial past. One version of this thesis is optimistic (usually advanced by conservative theorists). If class divisions are disappearing then capitalism is beginning to live up to the expectations of all the great liberal democratic thinkers of the nineteenth century. The affluent society is the promised society in which the 'private' individual is free to retreat into the confines of his home and garden. A second version is pessimistic, seeing embourgeoisement as a surrender to the bribes of affluence. Both Marcuse and Wright-Mills have subscribed to this position, although in Marcuse's case this is in the context of his general disillusionment with working-class radicalism. There is a prior question to be answered before we can hope to reject or accept the embourgeoisement thesis, and that is the actual extent to which the middle class has become the dominant class in Europe and the United States.

Bottomore [13] has suggested that there have been three different interpretations of the middle class as the source of social power and domination.

First, there is the interpretation which sees the middle class as continuing to expand both horizontally and vertically, eventually incorporating the working class and defusing the ruling class. The main thrust of this interpretation was centred on the 'end of ideology debate' which saw the gradual elimination of class conflict and the emergence of a general consensus about the aims of public and economic policy. In the 1950s political scientists like Lipset were almost lyrical in their description of the 'good society' which they believed was in the process of becoming a reality (especially in the USA). Of course, this contrasted with the alternative views of Wright-Mills, who saw the explosion of middle-class occupations and values as an aspect of the polarisation of society into élites and masses. The effect of all this was presumed to be the mass internalisation of middle-class values in which the acquisiton of a consumer ethic was predominant.

Second, there is the interpretation which sees the middle class as a completely new ruling class. It is different from other ruling classes because its percentage of the total population tends to be far larger than those usually attributed to the classic ruling groups of nineteenth-century Europe. In the USA, this new dominant class is defined by its affiliations to the 'management' functions of industry and the state – what Galbraith calls the 'technistructure'.

In Europe, Dahrendorf, Touraine and others have discerned similar tendencies at work, although they conceptualise this class, not in terms of their non-ownership of the means of production, but in terms of their bureaucratic commitments and involvements. The new ruling class is a mixture of bureaucrats, technocrats and some members of the traditional bourgeoisie who believe the problems of an industrial society can be solved by application of rational procedures to problems of economic growth and political stability. However, this class is not necessarily dedicated to the public good, but is engaged in establishing its own collective interests at the expense of the rest of the population. Moreover, conflict is not contained or institutionalised – despite the fact that it is not the traditional form of class conflict described in standard sociological texts. The new focus of conflict is not centred on questions relating to the distribution of scarce resources; rather it is about the reaction of various groups in post-industrial (sic) society to the manipulative strategies of the new ruling class.

Privatisation, in the framework offered by this interpretation, is primarily equated with alienation. The vast impersonality of the new technocratic state entails an increasing feeling of powerlessness in the broad masses of the community. Indeed, this technocratic 'interpretation' is strongly connected to aspects of the 'mass society' thesis.

Third, Bottomore suggests that there is a radically different interpretation of the new middle class which defines it in terms of its relationship to the working class. This presupposes that the middle class in contemporary industrial society is a sub-section of the working class, or, to put it differently, the working class is no longer identified with manufacturing and extractive industries, but is considered to include the vast armies of professional and technical workers who have traditionally been associated with the middle class. The evidence for this is believed to be demonstrated by the increasing radicalisation of middle-class trade union movements and the politicisation of hundreds of thousands of students. It is argued that the vanguard of resistance to corporate capitalism now comes from these groups, and not from the 'old' working class (1968 is usually quoted as the significant date for this controversial development). While this interpretation derives mainly from continental theorists, particularly reflecting the French situation, it has found increasing favour amongst political groups with a strong university connection. Nevertheless, the slogan that 'we are all workers now' has not significantly penetrated the consciousness of 'the middle class' in Britain (although this may be altering now in the context of the unionisation of middle-class occupations).

Obviously these interpretations describe tendencies, not irreversible processes. In Bottomore's words:

> These diverse interpretations describe tendencies, all of which are present, none of which is clearly predominant, in the western European societies. The working class has not yet withered away, nor has it been absorbed fully into a traditional middle class; there is not yet an established technocratic bureaucratic ruling class, the new 'middle class' does not yet conceive itself as a working class, and it remains to be seen whether the students of the 1960s will actually bring about or sustain a new social awareness in their eventual professional occupations.[14]

In general terms the embourgeoisement thesis has not been confirmed as a master process. The Goldthorpe and Lockwood[15] studies scotched the idea that the emergence of a relatively affluent strata of workers automatically implies a wholesale adoption of middle-class attitudes by vast sections of the working class. Hence, the concomitant belief that a higher income, of necessity, implies a change of lifestyle and ideology, is not borne out by the evidence. The usual evidence advanced in support of the embourgeoisement thesis is largely made up of data relating to the consumption patterns associated with higher wages. It is assumed that these wages are spent on the 'goods' and 'services' which formerly were only within reach of the middle classes (although the term middle classes is frequently used ambiguously). The purchase of these goods is somehow regarded as symbolic of an entry into a new class situation, in which there is an almost automatic adoption of the values of the middle class. Accordingly, the consumer syndrome becomes the means whereby the old structure of class relationships is systematically eroded. The working class internalises the value orientation of the middle class, and retreats into the privatised sphere in which the consumer ethic reigns supreme, namely the family. The extent to which it is correct to identify embourgeoisement with privatisation will, therefore, depend on whether the family itself is simply a consumption unit geared to the needs of a volatile productive system, or whether it represents a sphere which is divorced and cut off from the sphere of production.

4 Familialism

The resurgence of interest in the family is to a large part due to the emergence of the women's movement as a formidable political force, especially in the United States. The standard sociological treatment of the family was dominated by a peculiar self-satisfied complacency which saw it in terms of 'structural differentiation'. It had suffered from the shocks of the industrial revolution and was in the process of coming to terms with the increasing rate of social change in the twentieth century. True, there were sexual and emotional tensions in the family situation, but these were considered to be problems of adjustment which were capable of solution by wise counselling and therapy. The idealised image of the nuclear family as the sphere of emotional security and individuality, as the primary civilising agency of society, has run into a veritable chorus of derision and cynicism. Twenty years ago it is unlikely that the following passage would have appeared in a standard sociological text:

> The essential similarity between the family and more complex political systems is, that, in both, relations of dominance and submission rest in the last analysis on violence or threat of violence. Father can out-whack mother, who in turn can out-whack the children, at least until adolescence, when parental authority becomes challenged. Power is not automatically received and unquestioningly accepted. It is in the nature of power to be resented and challenged by those at the receiving end of the stick, and to be retained and defended by those who hold it. Violence, or the threat of violence, is the ultimate argument in a power contest. The average family is no more exempt from violence than the average state, though our ideology concerning the family makes us reluctant to accept the fact.[16]

Our reluctance to accept the fact of violence and coercion in the family is partly explained by the almost taboo-like status it has had in social theory. Although the fact of the pattern of dominance and submission has been implicit in diverse descriptions of the family in industrialised society, it always tended to be regarded as not being of any profound significance, especially when the statistics demonstrated that more and more people were getting married (what the divorce rate implied was not the breakdown of an institution, but the normal wastage to be found in any institutionalised relationship). At the same time, the tendency for the family to withdraw and isolate itself from the main political and economic currents of the time was perceived as an inevitable, and even welcome, consequence of industrialisation. The family was the place where you found a haven from the exacting world of work, from the 'rat-race' of the factory floor and the 'status differentials' of office. And there was your wife – 'the little woman' – waiting for you, with your meal prepared, your socks washed and your children disciplined.

The sheer smugness of this picture is beyond the bounds of credulity. What the women's movement has done, more than anything else, is to point to the unreality of the official definition of the family as the epitome of harmony and social order. The romantic gloss of so much commentary on the family is understandable, when it is seen in the context of a system of beliefs which extol the virtues of individuality and privacy, so that the actual nature of the family relationship is obscured. The family might have been a haven and retreat for men, but it was not necessarily a haven for the vast majority of women. I am not arguing that the family is of necessity an exploitative relationship in which men 'use' women in order to satisfy their security and sex needs, but I am saying that the family in industrial (capitalist) society is the crucible of privatisation, and that women are in this sense pushed outside the so-called essential productive and public dimensions of economic and social life. There is a tendency, therefore, to regard the work that women do in the family situation as being non-economic and personal. Furthermore, this tendency is reinforced by socialisation and education procedures which legitimate the sexual division of labour as being in the nature of things.

But, the split into private and public spheres is *not* in the nature of things. Before the industrial revolution, economic and personal life were not split into separate autonomous spheres, because the family was both the unit of production and the unit of reproduction. This is not to deny the evidence which purports to demonstrate that even in this context, women were exploited, but it is to specify the way in which industrialisation institutionalised the private sphere as *the* domain of the family, so that personal life seemed to exist independently of the outside world of economic and political events. In a sense, therefore, the proletariat consisted of the workers who manned the production lines of capitalism, and the women who remained behind in the home to minister to the needs of the 'male' workers. With the changing nature of capitalist society, the role of the women workers at home was influenced by the opportunities of employment made possible by the increasing demand for labour, but this in itself did not change the actual pattern of relationships within the family. What did change was the intensity of the personal life, especially in the USA:

By the twentieth century, a sphere of 'personal' life emerged among the proletariat itself. In the absence of a political movement that sought to transform both personal life and production, personal life was characterised by subjectivity – the search for personal identity outside the social division of labour. Having no private property to uphold, contemporary individualism upholds the self as an 'autonomous' realm outside society. This new emphasis on 'one's' personal feelings and inner needs, one's 'head' or 'life-style', to use contemporary formulations, gives a continued meaning to family life and at the same time threatens to blow it apart.[17]

It was on women more than anybody else on whom the full weight of privatisation fell. Whether working or middle-class, relative affluence did not make much difference to their encapsulation in private worlds. On the contrary, it could be argued that the development of 'mass consumption society' made it far easier to be isolated in the forests of suburbia and in the barracks of high-rise estates. One of the popular themes of the sociological critique of industrialisation is the assumed superficiality and impersonality of relationships in both middle-class and working-class areas of cities, especially those areas inhabited by uprooted and mobile populations. In these areas we get a picture of privatisation which sometimes borders on the horrific. Granted that descriptions of suburban privatisation are often highly coloured, there is enough hard evidence around which supports the claims made by 'victims' (women) that privatisation, boredom and monotony are the basic ingredients of contemporary domestic life.

There is an additional by-product of family privatisation, and this is the growth of an entire new industry of counselling services which caters for the proliferation of personal troubles that continuously erupt in the family situation. In the United States the 'upper middle class' resolves its marital problems by divorce, or by making use of the multitude of depth psychologists who specialise in 'reality adjustment techniques'. For the working classes in the USA and Europe, social workers of all kinds are employed to bolster up and solve marital problems. Indeed, one could almost construct a measure of privatisation in terms of the density of counselling services available. In other words, there is still a strong commitment to the belief that the 'family' *per se* is *the* basic social institution, and that ultimately all other institutional spheres are dependent upon the family infrastructure (strangely enough this is the basis of Shulamith Firestone's [18] analysis of the biological roots of sexism in all cultures). If the family's problems can be alleviated by counselling and psychoanalysis, then it follows that the dependent institutions will themselves be influenced by action taken at the family level.

However, whatever the ultimate fate of the family (including Firestone's technological solution for ending male biological domination) it still remains true that it is in the family that the individual man or woman articulates his or her typical response to the demands of consumerism. The illusion of the beautiful private life might be something to be found in the pages of glossy magazines, or on the television screen, but it is an illusion which is not readily shattered, despite the statistical evidence of the marriage breakdown rate coming out of California and other western societies. The rhetoric which emphasises 'the home', 'companionship', 'motherhood', 'equal partnership', 'personal fulfilment', 'self-expression', etc., has a curiously hollow ring, but it still has an emotional force which the 'counselling services' use as one of their main weapons in their attempt to defuse marital tension and conflict. All such attempts are premised, or at least until recently were premised, on the belief that the family can be doctored back to health by therapeutic techniques. But, all this is done within the parameters of a set of cognitions and practices which tacitly accept the *status quo* of male domination. The object of these techniques, therefore, is to make the everyday lives of housewives more tolerable by investing their 'housework' with an aura of glamour and social significance. 'Women, too, are doing a job of work' – 'they are the mothers of future generations of workers' – and various other sickening clichés have for long been the standard repertoire of counselling ideology. Moreover, most of the literature dealing with the family has seemed to operate on the associated proposition, that the family is an institution with a number of problems, which in principle are solvable, provided the participants in a marriage are willing to take the advice of those who claim to be qualified to give this advice. So, we arrive at a state of affairs in which the privatisation process is reinforced by the creation of a network of counselling services which allow families to 'adjust' to the excessive demands made on them by the encroachment of the 'bureaucratic state' and the imperatives of consumer insatiability.

But, as theorists in the women's movement have reminded us, this view of the family as a 'sick institution' ignores the way in which it has mirrored the power and exploitative nature of other social relationships. If women are a deprived and disadvantaged group, then this must be due to broader patterns of exploitation and domination implicit in the institutional structures of late capitalism. It is all very well for male sociologists to dispute and deny the implications of this claim as being the ideology of a 'new' political movement, it is another thing to examine the way in which sociology itself has treated women as an object of study. In a sense, the sociological study of the family has been attenuated by a whole corpus of literature which somehow leaves women out, except in so far as they are carriers of roles. Not only are women hidden from history, but they do not appear in sociology until the 'women's movement' began to challenge some of the assumptions of the previously male-dominated discipline. Indeed, the way women appear in standard texts on the family is as beneficiaries. (Even Marxists leave out the privatised housewife from their general approach to exploitation.). Ann Oakley argues that the 'concealment of women' is a reflection of the male orientation of sociology. The one sociological sub-division which is supposedly about 'women' is the family, and as she writes:

> Where are the women in all this? They appear to occupy the centre of the stage, but in what guise? A favourite word is 'role', and the dramaturgical metaphor is highly appropriate. In family and marriage literature, women are highly encapsulated within the feminine role. The psychoanalytic view has been very influential, leading to an implicit definition of women as wives and mothers to the virtual exclusion of any other life-area. In addition, the literature has a definite 'social problem' orientation, which is shown most clearly in the vast number of studies of the 'working mother'. The focus on child-rearing implications of women's employment has led to such detailed consideration as the relation between the employment status of mothers and their children's health, and the possibility of an association between employment and the nutritional adequacy of preschool children's diets. . . .
>
> Almost none of this literature is woman-focused. While considering the advantages and disadvantages to other family members of new patterns of domestic life, the consequences for the woman are often omitted. 'Role conflict' is talked about, but this is not necessarily the same thing.[19]

In a nutshell, we have a situation in sociology in which 'the privatisation of women' is taken for granted, because they do not appear on the historical and sociological stages constructed by male sociologists. Women are concealed, both in theory and practice. Their privatisation takes place in the context of structural forces which pushes the family in to itself. And, as Berger *et al.* have observed, this process repeats itself in those parts of the world which have only lately been affected by 'modernisation'. The fact the family is at the receiving end of so much propaganda, and is geared into the 'consumption ethic', makes it the key area for the study of privatisation, but unfortunately the sociological account of all this has been from the outside, from the point of view of the detached observer concerned with the incidence of divorce and marriage rates. The interior life of the family has been left to psychologists and psychoanalysts, who either see it as a quagmire of emotional conflict, or as the crucible of identity crisis. What is missing from both sociological and psychological accounts is a feeling for the 'structure' of the privatised sphere.

The rise of a 'mass consumption' society, and the associated access to areas of experience previously reserved for the upper reaches of the middle class, has meant, literally, that millions of people are *theoretically* in a position to articulate their privatisation. That they do not do so is a key problem in any discussion of ideology and false consciousness. Like 'class consciousness', the articulation of the concrete actuality of life in the family and the elaboration of a language to describe the privatised existence of women, depends largely on the emergence of a self conscious group of women who are able to politicise their experience of the family, as well as the broader implications of that experience. The women's movement has been relatively successful in the United States in 'raising consciousness', but it is too early to say whether the long-term consequences of this will be global. More important is the possibility that the whole discussion of privatisation is rooted in a middle-class view of the family as a repressive institution, While we might want to talk about privatisation as though it is a universal process transforming both middle-class and working-class families into apolitical retreats from the world of work, we cannot assume this. To claim that working-class families are privatised is to assent to the argument that the working class *per se* is becoming more middle-class. (Also, we cannot assume that the American experience is necessarily the 'model' which all other societies automatically emulate.)

In summing up, I would like to suggest that privatisation is not an imaginary phenomenon, although it is almost impossible to obtain accurate information about the extent to which 'consumerism' is in fact a dominant aspect of contemporary consciousness. Certainly, for practitioners like Lefebvre, consumerism is not a peripheral problem. It defines the reality of millions of people in the industrialised world. However, this is not necessarily equivalent to asserting that consumerism and embourgeoisement demonstrate the inevitability of privatisation. The working class has not disappeared, and is not, disappearing into the middle class, but at the same time there appears to be some evidence for the belief that the family operates as *the* primary ideological focus of consumer ideology. In a sense, as I have argued, it is women who have been particularly exposed to privatisation pressures, despite the fundamental change in the employment patterns of industrial societies during the last few decades. The fact that more women are employed in full-time occupations, and the corresponding economic independence this entails, does not mean that we have witnessed a major structural change in the pattern of relationships between men and women. In general, the dice are still heavily loaded against women, even in those advanced capitalist societies in which the 'liberation' movement has come to be perceived as having potential political significance.

At another level, it seems to be difficult to deny the reality and seductive influence of the private sphere. Personal, private life looms large in the consciousness of so many people, because it is experienced as being more satisfying and rewarding than the world of work. That this may be an illusion is beside the point. For women, the illusion of personal fulfilment in the family may prove to be the stumbling block to their liberation; for workers, the illusion of affluence has often been the means whereby they have been conned by the manipulators of mass opinion, but, illusions or not, the private sphere is a primal element of contemporary consciousness.

In an earlier chapter I discussed the way in which subjective humanism has been submitted to trenchant criticism from a group of theorists who reject the humanist obsession with the self and consciousness. Their critique of contemporary social theory is based on a rejection of what they regard as a reification of subjectivity in social analysis. Nevertheless, even though some practitioners treat the private sphere as though it was autonomous and mysterious, it makes no sense to ignore it. Personal life does exist and, just like the public sphere, it needs to be transformed. Such a transformation is problematic, given the problem of false consciousness. In this connection a recurring theme in the discussion of privatisation is the influence which the media are supposed to have on the consciousness of individuals, in the way in which language itself lends itself to the distortions of the market, as mediated through advertising. A consequence of this is believed to be the emergence of a passive citizenry who has lost the ability to engage in criticism and political action. The private sphere is apolitical, because it is dominated by a language of make-believe in which participants define themselves as being happy and contented. Thus, participants who pride themselves on their personalised lifestyles, and the implicit autonomy which this is supposed to entail, will not be impressed by arguments which purport to show that privatisation is a form of false consciousness. For Henri Lefebvre, this state of affairs is a measure of the hold of the language of make-believe on the consciousness of the populations of capitalist societies, including intellectuals, academics and sociologists.

For the intellectual, make-believe, flowing with the waters of rhetoric, language and metalanguage, is the permanent substitute for experience that allows him to ignore the mediocrity of his condition, his lack of power, of money and the humiliating fact of having to submit to compulsions and myths in order to climb a few rungs of the social ladder, and become a popular writer, a famous journalist, an eminent technician or government adviser, etc.[20]

If 'make believe' is the permanent substitute for experience then: 'An individual who sees through this cobweb is little better off, for he remains captive of the relations in which the actions and delusions of others have left him.'[21]

Perhaps this is no more evident than in the enclosed world in which most social scientists live out their lives. Here, we can discern both fragmentation and privatisation themes at work. Although practitioners are acutely aware of the encapsulated and make-believe nature of their everyday existence in this or that department of sociology or politics, what is more depressing is the realisation that what they say and do is not generally noticed outside a small coterie of like-minded practitioners. Sociologists are in the peculiar situation of believing their work is of direct relevance to the 'world' out there, and yet they discover that the only people who read their books and research reports are other sociologists and students.

Part two

4 The biographical self

In previous chapters I have been concerned with the supposed split of consciousness into private and public spheres. I say 'supposed' because it is not clear whether this split should not be described in terms of the social division of labour, that is, as part of the forces set in motion by the growth of a capitalist society. Nevertheless, from the point of view of the individual who divides his or her life between 'the world of work' and the 'world of private life', it would be difficult to maintain that there is no subjective discontinuity between the two spheres. For Berger *et al.*, this private sphere is 'under-institutionalised' and over-subjectivised, while the 'public sphere', in the form of bureaucracy and the technological system, is impersonal, cold and rational. Hence, the self can find no resting place or home in the work world, the bureaucratic world or in the political structure. Instead it searches for 'meaning' in the private personal world, but this search is hazardous – there are no certain signposts, no established rules, except those provided by discredited institutions. The individual has literally got to invent 'meaning' and significance: 'The individual is given enormous latitude in fabricating his own particular life – a kind of "do-it-yourself" universe'. . . .[1]

Inventing a do-it-yourself universe imposes incredible strains on the individual – there is no way in which this can be done without some sort of reliance on systems of meaning. The intensity of personal relationships, the intoxicating immersion in new sexual experience, the discovery of new forms of religious ecstasy, indeed the entire fabric of meanings discoverable in the private sphere, are ultimately grounded in the need for institutional support. They cannot survive the uncertainty of standing alone against the monster institutions of contemporary society: 'Social life abhors a vacuum, probably for profound anthropological reasons. Human beings are not capable of tolerating the continuous uncertainty (or, if you will, freedom) of existing without institutional supports.'[2]

What is being asserted here is *the* fundamental premise of the sociological account of individuality, namely, the commitment to the social production of the self. In the Durkheimian scheme, the concept 'individual' of necessity has a social determination, just as the self has a social origin in Mead's 'conversation of gestures'. Take away the social underpinning of the self, and all that is left is a vessel emptied of meaning, a vacuous entity of confused emotions. The implication of all this is that participants cannot bear too much subjectivity. The structures of modernity are, by this token, found to be wanting, because they do not, and cannot, provide a focus for subjectivity. Accordingly, there is a frantic search for alternative kinds of identification in the 'private sphere', in the family, drugs, leisure pursuits, sexual adventures, communes, etc., etc. In the end, however, all this frenetic activity seems to be futile, because it comes into direct conflict with the public sphere, and with the *functional rationality* implicit in this sphere. The self itself is in danger of being incorporated into the rationalised world of 'everyday life', and even the most assertive declaration of freedom from the demands of 'straight' society, is ultimately doomed to failure because it cannot resist the pressures of rationalisation. Communes are set up by persons intent on carving out a new life for themselves away from the commercialism and exploitation of everyday life, but they too, after the initial moment of revolutionary elation, are forced to make compromises, until the weight of compromise produces a duplicate version of straight society.

In talking about the 'self', the 'individual', 'subjectivity', 'consciousness', we are, of course, presuming a great deal. Indeed, for various practitioners, as we saw in the first chapter, these concepts are useless, non-scientific and expressions of ideological discourse. Also, it is true that most of these terms may have no meaning outside the western context, and even in the western context are historically specific. Does this mean that we should abandon this kind of language altogether as being too self-indulgent and too romanticised? Certainly, in the pheno-menological description of consciousness employed by Berger *et al.*, it would completely emasculate the entire point of their analysis of modernisation if we decided that the use of terms like 'life-world', 'identity', and 'consciousness' were meaningless and arbitrary. It would mean that the only valid way of examining social processes would be to do without the self altogether. Can we do without the self?

Perhaps it would be as well to look at the status of the self concept in social theory before we decide to relegate it to the ideological scrap-heap. For a great many sociologists, social psychologists and other practitioners, there are a number of competing definitions of the individual and the self which are at variance with the standard socialisation model (although these definitions have played a part in the construction of this model).

1 Separation and difference

Most notions of the individual argue for the separation of the individual from others. Crudely, this means we all have different genetic endowments and, hence, different bodies. Thus, the individual can be seen as a body occupying a distinct physiological and psychological space. Sociological accounts of individuality take this for granted without too much difficulty. Nevertheless, bodily space is ultimately seen to be dependent on the social definition of the body as separate and different from other bodies. Such a definition is rooted in common-sensical interpretations of reality prevalent in western societies – the body is perceived and experienced as having desires, needs, pains, that is, as possessing the entire repertoire of visceral and muscular pleasures and tensions which inform everyday life. Each individual body is, by this token, the final arbiter of its own experience. It alone 'knows' its own pain and pleasures.

At the heart of this view of the 'individuated' body is its supposed relationship to the self. In western thought, since Descartes's time, the 'self' and the 'body' have been in a state of armed belligerency. This 'uneasy dualism' has had the unfortunate consequence of bifurcating experience and, until very recently, demoting the body to an inferior status. However, the rediscovery of the body has not necessarily redressed the balance – on the contrary, contemporary views of the significance of bodily experience have bordered on the mystical. Phenomenologists have insisted that the dualism in western thought of body and self is due to a complete misunderstanding of the nature of the body, or, to put it another way, they have argued that the 'body' is not a 'thing among things'. From their point of view, it is wrong to talk about the body in terms of ownership – 'my body', 'your body', etc., are phrases in common usage which apparently demonstrate the ingrained dualism of western notions of the self and body. The separation of self and body, then, does violence to the actuality of experience. The idea of ownership of the body, as a thing apart from the self, is reminiscent of the social relationship of slavery in which other bodies are disposable on the market. Everyday discourse is replete with this kind of dualism, yet in experiencing

81

the world no such bifurcation takes place. Ultimately, the way in which we confront this world is grounded in the indistinguishable unity of self and body.

Whether or not we agree with the phenomenological assertion that the body is the human species' basic mode of being in the world – what they call embodied consciousness – there can be no doubt that in traditional sociological discussions of the 'body', there has been a tendency to take it for granted as an object or a thing which is a universal adjunct to social conduct. It is there, and it is not there – it is assumed to have fixed and invariable features which are experienced as such:

> Salient among the assumptions made about the body by social scientists and others is what may be called a *radical equalisation of the social significance of the human body*. That is, they have assumed that since the body is composed of universal features, it necessarily is experienced as such; furthermore, given this 'universality', it need not be accounted for within any special system of propositions bearing on the explanation of human behaviour. Put in more direct fashion, the attributes of the body equalise its social significance; any of its properties may be assumed to vary randomly and are, therefore, relatively unimportant in empirical analysis. Review of the literature discloses that sociologists have generally attended to the body only when its state or appearance has deviated significantly. Attention to the body under these conditions implies that under ordinary circumstances its characteristics can be taken for granted.[3]

Certainly 'the individuated body' has been taken for granted by sociologists. This is surprising, particularly when there is a great deal of evidence from anthropological literature which questions the belief in the solitary self imprisoned in a body. Moreover, as Manning and Fabrega point out, instead of the unity of self and body, we are presented with a disembodied self in the sociological literature, despite the fact that for Mead, the self was a bio-social phenomenon. Thus, not only is the notion of separation of body from body important in western thought, but, also, the simultaneous separation of self and body is implicit in the reification of social processes which underpins so much socialisation theory.

2 Temporal consistency

Whatever uniqueness is attributed to the individual as a body, or as a self, this means that it is invariably defined in terms of 'time'. The

82

individual sees himself as exhibiting consistency over a given time-span. In romanticised versions consistency is perceived as being valuable and private. At a more prosaic level, consistency is located in the routinisation of everyday behaviour. In the past *others* have responded to my existence by the performance of routines which reinforce my own self perception as an individual with a biography. What this implies (again at a common-sensical level) is that individuals can comment on their own conduct, not simply as a number of unrelated and haphazard episodes, but as a historical process. They have histories, which, in the orthodox western view, are developmental. The 'child is the father of the man' in more senses than one. Not only is he supposed to recognise himself as the product of past experience, but, in the Freudian model, he is living proof of the past masquerading as the present.

If individuals have developmental histories, then it is not surprising that in everyday life we expect individuals to manifest some kind of consistency of behaviour. When we say that a particular act is typical of the way in which Joan X behaves, what we are really saying is that in the past she has been observed to act in a similar fashion. Moreover, we assume that consistency of behaviour is indicative of permanence of personality character-istics. Piaget[4] has argued that the individual (Joan X) sees herself as existing over time when she learns that there are permanences or continuities in the external world. The self is thus experienced as the source from which all other continuities are defined (that is, once a degree of permanence is attributed to the outside world, the self becomes the arbiter of continuities).

It is difficult to challenge such an orthodox account of temporal consistency. In everyday life we expect consistency over time. We do not expect our friends, lovers and colleagues to engage in conduct completely at variance with our expectations deriving from our knowledge of them as being relatively predictable human beings. We do not expect them to engage in behaviour which produces ambiguity and anxiety. Their characters are 'taken for granted', because we tacitly assume that what has gone before must be the same as is happening now. True, friendships are broken, lovers turn cold and colleagues betray us, but this does not necessarily mean that we are entitled to believe in the randomness of everyday conduct.

Psychologists, personality theorists and various sociologists therefore find it difficult to operate on some watered-down *in-determinacy principle*. Hence, in versions of Freudian charactero-logy, the manifestation of symptoms or behaviour idiosyncracies are analysed *as if* they pointed to the overwhelming presence of a dark instinctual past. Similarly, reinforcement psychology articulates a view of human biography completely at the mercy of control factors – 'men are what they are conditioned to be'; in addition, socialisation theory sees individual development as the process of the accumulative acquisition of salient role identities. In these various formulations everything is perceived as having a logical story, with a beginning and an end. Of course, there are problems when all such academic accounts are matched with subjective definitions of the situation. For a great many people, the idea of their individual biographies showing any kind of logical consistency is laughable. There is nothing tidy and logical about the day-to-day problems of copying with visceral imperatives and economic necessities. Social science tends to posit logic and clarity, but all such postulations are usually from the point of view of the outside observer's commitment to regularity and order in social and individual life. We are so used to the traditional idea of biography having a beginning, a middle and an end, that we readily suppose that most human beings (at least in western societies) have the same commitment to this pattern. Accordingly, although the self may have a history which somehow conforms to the standard formulation, it is conceivable that this history is an invention – an imaginative construction which defines the past in terms of the present. Hence the notion of temporal consistency could depend on the current involvements of the self. In inventing a history of intellectual achievement, one might not be doing anything more than bolstering up a shattered sense of self esteem. Put another way, our knowledge of the permanence of some of our personality characteristics is a function of the ongoing interaction situation. The past is invented in order to defuse the explosiveness of the present. We sell this version of the past to those whom we need to confirm the reality of our contemporary existence. It is as though there is a need to propagandise and broadcast our right to our own biography.

For individuals socialised in societies in which the notion of temporal sequence is predominant, where there is a complete absorption into 'clock-time', it is almost impossible to break the ingrained habit of defining one's uniqueness in terms of temporal continuity. The fact that there are other societies which do not possess 'clock-time' is of no importance to the person caught up in the urgencies of everyday life. Western subjectivity is always geared to the demands of the clock – there are very few western institutions which can handle the kind of time so dear to Bergson and Proust. The factory system does not lend itself to the subjectivisation of time, except in so far as it precipitates the development of a fantasy life to counter the deadening weight of repetitive manipulative tasks and office routine. Fantasy provides a prime means of escape from 'temporal consistency' but it does not in any way subvert it's actual dominance of mundane reality. In escaping from the clock some individuals manage to invent alternative imaginary universes in which reality is overturned, but they do not thereby make the world over.

For instance, in Luke Rhinehart's *Diceman*[5] the 'self' is put up for auction by the use of dice. Socialisation is negated by the 'gamester's' construction of a new self for every situation. By throwing the dice, today I can be symbolic interactionist, tomorrow a Marxist, and on Sunday an ethnomethodologist. Perhaps I can alternate between sexual athlete on Tuesday, and Trappist monk on Saturday. Anything is possible. Now, of course, Rhinehart is not suggesting that the world is actually like a vast game of chance, in which each individual decides who he is going to be in a completely random and undetermined way, but he is explicitly arguing against the idea of 'character' and 'self' being rooted in the past. He is, in effect, saying that what we call the 'self' is merely a description of the 'action' at a particular moment of time. Tomorrow's self might well be the exact opposite of today's self, because circumstances have altered, or I have decided to behave differently. In everyday life the self is buffeted from one set of circumstances to the next, from accident to accident. Temporal consistency is an illusion, partly fostered by a tradition in philosophy and social science, which lodges the self at the centre of reality.

One of the dominant themes of the recent resurgence of interest in mysticism and the emergence of a psychedelic culture, is the *apparent* rediscovery of forms of consciousness which transcend the limits of the social self and which negate the consequences of the past. Psychedelic culture asserts the mystical unity of self and experience by acts of self negation – that is, it dissolves the bounds of the self into a sea of communal feeling buttressed by the euphoria of 'dope' and 'sexual discovery'. In a sense, what has been rediscovered is the pantheism of nineteenth-century romanticism, although I doubt whether Wordsworth would recognise himself in current versions of psychedelic thinking. Be that as it may, we are faced with a peculiar contemporary paradox, namely that while the focus of liberal ideology is still firmly based on such values as the freedom of the individual, freedom of choice and so forth, there is, simultaneously, a revulsion against the 'burden of self', especially the burden of self which is directly attributable to socialisation and indoctrination.

It is the 'socialised self' which is seen as the enemy of spontaneity and authenticity by the counter-culture, and it is the socialised self which is questioned by such writers as Rhinehart and Genet, but not only writers. The whole thrust of Foucault's and Althusser's attack on subjective humanism is also an attack on the sociological image of the 'self' (although this onslaught is not in the name of spontaneity). If the self is considered to be both the enemy of spontaneity and the ideological repository of subjective humanism, then it follows that we are dealing with a concept which is resonant with ambiguities. Are we then to suppose that the notion of consistency over time is meaningless, because of the difficulties encountered in trying to make sense of a self which is constantly negated by others?

To an extent we might want to say that the entire discussion about self consistency only takes place in an academic framework and that, in actuality, there is no such problem for the proverbial 'common man'. Although in 'everyday life' participants often expect unexpected behaviour from other participants, they do not usually expect complete reversals of this behaviour on a day-to-day basis. Their expectations about other people are generally confirmed over time. Of course, it is true that they may observe 'Fred' in action in unfamiliar contexts – instead of the mild non-assertive person they have learned to like in the office, they might discover him behaving aggressively towards his wife and children at home. Yet these reversals are allowed for in the taken-for-granted implicit personality theories which constitute part of the stock of everyday knowledge. It is assumed that people will behave differently in different situations, but it is not thereby implied that such variability is indicative of personality disintegration. In spite of Fred's authoritarianism at home, there is usually no doubt that it is, in fact, the same Fred from the office.

What is taken for granted in everyday life becomes an intractable problem for a number of psychological and social psychological accounts of behaviour. I say intractable because the temptation is always present in social science to treat consistency as if it were similar in kind to the invariants found in natural science. What is it that is supposed to remain consistent? Is it behaviour? Is it disposition? Or is it the self? Also, if the outsider (observer) claims that he knows Fred is a 'changed man', but Fred persists in his belief in the image that he has of himself as being a certain kind of person, does this mean consistency can only be defined from the point of view of the participant? Accordingly, consistency may depend on the perspective of either the observer, or the participant, and this makes it difficult to talk about invariants in human behaviour, or rather, it makes it difficult to conceive of temporal consistency simply in terms of an outsider's viewpoint.

From the outside, it is very easy to assume that behaviour must be accounted for by external factors or internal pushes. If we observe consistency, then we are supposed to look for 'controlling conditions'. As Harré and Secord write:

> The Humean positivist methodology makes an investigator
> look for the explanation of human behaviour in the
> 'controlling conditions', and to make two important identity
> assumptions about the people involved. One is that persons in
> experiments are identical to one another except for individual
> differences which are regarded as 'error' or unexplained,
> uninteresting, idiosyncratic variance. The other is an identity of
> the single person over time, a continuity of his behaviour. *In
> this second identity, the invariant, which is necessary to any
> science, becomes something like a person's character, or
> personality.* This choice of invariant encourages the application
> of concepts like consistency to all the thoughts, beliefs,
> emotions, acts and actions of a person, and the use of
> associated concepts like dissonance, in the explanation of
> changes in any of these items. So long as a person's behaviour,
> including verbal behaviour, is seen as an assemblage of
> responses to stimuli, however subtly these are differentiated
> and sophisticatedly distinguished, any attempt to introduce
> concepts such as agency into the scientific conception of man
> seems to be gratuitous. For an agent is apt to be considered
> capricious and unpredictable, quite unlike a robot. And it
> seems likely that we can develop 'laws' of behaviour without
> this concept of man as an agent.[6]

If we are not like 'robots', then the problem of consistency becomes much more interesting. For Harré and Secord this problem is partly resolved by describing human beings as 'rule-following, self-monitoring agents'. While I am in sympathy with this, it is precisely such a formulation which would be ruled out of court by Foucault *et al*. Nevertheless, unless one wants to declare a moratorium on the use of such terms as the self and consciousness, there would seem to be no alternative to the notion of a self monitoring agent who can act consistently in terms of the application of appropriate rules in this or that situation.

3 Memory

In talking of temporal consistency from the perspective of the participant, we assume that he or she can comment on past and future behaviour. For William James,[7] 'memory' was the one psychological faculty which guaranteed the individual's perception of himself as a being who existed in time and who recognised himself as the same person from one time period to the next. Now, while memory has been an important topic in psychology, it has never really been of much interest to sociologists (with the possible exception of Maurice Halbwachs). It has been taken for granted in much the same way as the 'body' has been taken for granted. What has been emphasised more than anything else is the contents of memory, that is, the way in which cultural patterns are internalised to provide the individual with a sense of structural location. Memory, in this sense, is a social construction – it relates to cultural prescriptions and norms which define biographical continuity.

It would not be too far off the mark to say that for sociologists memory is nothing more than the 're-enactment' of role scripts. Hence an individual 'knows' who he is in terms of his ability to symbolise past role experiences. An individual's memories are, therefore, a consequence of the dual operation of language and roles. For symbolic interactionists, the past is defined by the multiplicity of role encounters and the interpretative (symbolic) procedures which underpin individual and social processes. Just as the self is regarded as a social process, so is memory. When we remember ourselves at a certain stage in our lives, perhaps as children, what is remembered is the self in action with others, and imaginary others. Our past is recaptured in a social context – hence, past happiness is remembered in terms of experiences in which others contribute toward a definition of a shared reality. The question remains, of course, whether or not memories of childhood are simply glosses, distortions and selective reconstructions of a past which never existed. The remembered happy childhood may be an exercise – an escape from the horror of the present. In Freudian terms, the flight from reality, which is implicit in the memory of a happy childhood, simply reflects the individual's inability to cope with the contemporary 'adult' world.

What would happen if we were to argue there is no stable sense of self, no memory of the same self over a given span of an individual's life? This would imply that the continuities we discern and the events and processes we remember, are always aspects of practical consciousness in the here and now. Such a purely situational view of the self as infinitely volatile, as being entirely at the mercy of context, is not speculation; it can readily be found in role and labelling theory literature. Accordingly, what is fundamentally an attempt to locate the roots of deviancy in societal processes, can also be construed as an argument for the 'self' as situation.

This means that memory is situated. An individual will use 'memory language' to the extent to which a situation allows him to construct his past. Every social situation is, therefore, an opportunity for a person to construe himself as an individual with a biography – a biography located in routines of the present. For example, the routines typical of a white-collar existence which revolves around the home, family, office, pub, cleaning the car, watching television and so on, will not be shaken by trivial interruptions. The situated self simply 'performs' in a standard fashion for each occasion. Put in a different way, the roles of 'family man', 'office manager' and 'extrovert drinker' tend to be reconfirmed on a day-to-day basis, provided nothing happens to disturb established procedures. As long as others help me to construe my memory of myself as a person who regularly does this sort of thing, then there is no problem, but what happens if, in the pub, you come across somebody who 'remembers' you from a different time and context? His memories of you do not fit with the beautiful equilibrium informing your current life. He remembers you as a teetotaller, as a dedicated revolutionary and as an opponent of a 'settled' bourgeois life. You might want to reject his account of your past as inaccurate or distorted, you might claim that he is lying, or you could shrug it off with some folk-aphorism such as 'we all make mistakes in our youth' etc. Whatever tactic you employ, the past will be doctored to meet the requirements of the present.

Memory, for a number of sociologists, is thus (especially in symbolic-interactionist terms) a function of context. One remembers a past seduced by the present. For other sociologists, memory depends on what has been put there by society in the first place. One remembers the contents of social experience. For psychologists of a behaviourist persuasion, memory is an aspect of the learning process. For orthodox Freudians, memory is severely limited by defence mechanisms which distort, and frequently 'repress' past experience. Psychological accounts differ from sociological accounts in their tendency to treat the social factor as one variable among many which influence memory. Hence, psychologists have studied the relationship of memory to motives, culture, class, emotion, language, etc. Sociologists, on the other hand, have moved away from seeing memory as an intrinsic psychological process. This is in keeping with the (often unstated) premise that psychological states can be translated into sociological vocabularies. It is rooted in their classic suspicion of reductionist statements about human behaviour. Yet, to assert an un-compromising sociological point of view is to ignore an enormous amount of evidence accumulated by hundreds of other practi-tioners. Psychological approaches to memory are not subsumed under the aegis of behaviourism – the contribution of cognitive psychology in this respect places memory into a 'constructionist' framework, for example, both Piaget and Bruner, from different starting points, have described cognition in terms of dynamic psychological processes, and, earlier, gestalt and field theory reacted strongly to mechanistic accounts of cognition.

In this connection, perhaps the most important development in recent years has been the amount of attention paid to 'symbolic' processes as biosocial phenomena. 'Language' is now firmly at the centre of discourse for practitioners from different disciplines, and there can be no denying its critical relationship to such psychological processes like memory, perception and emotion. Language, in the final analysis, is the only means we have for locating the self in a biographical or historical matrix:

> The formative element of biographical memory is verbal conception. I doubt that any creature without some sort of speech has a sequential memory of its own life, or the possibility of constructing its own past. Language, propositional thinking and everything that goes with speech is such a special development of the hominid brain that it is not surprising to find verbal memory exhibiting quite different forms and procedures from any other type of recollection.[8]

Apart from the fact that 'memory' is not an exclusive human characteristic, it is certainly true (as far as we know) that no other animal has a sense of autobiography or a sense of self (biographical memory seems to be species-specific). The trouble is that sociologists tend to go far beyond the parameters set by a naturalistic view of human functioning. 'Self other' relationships are very often treated as if they are aspects of a negotiating process in which anything is possible. It is as though the self is reconstituted from moment to moment into patterns which bear no resemblance to any previous pattern. Admittedly, the foregoing is an exaggeration, but it is an exaggeration based on a consideration of a 'too' literal application of role theory to every conceivable social and individual context − not only role theory, but also labelling theory posits an infinitely malleable human being with an infinitely malleable memory.

4 Psychological organisation

Holistic models of personality are legion in the literature. Very crudely, they claim personality is an organised system in which different elements contribute to the integrity of the whole. Despite the varieties of formulation, most of them assume that there is a central core to personality which acts as an organising principle. For Allport,[9] for example, this principle is the self (proprium). For others, the core is defined in biological terms, while for some practitioners the notion of self development is cardinal.

They stress the idea of the 'uniqueness of personality', a uniqueness which, in their view, is always in danger of being overwhelmed by external forces. Hence, their belief that neurosis is merely an expression of stunted personality growth occasioned by the frustration of 'needs' by cultural and social determinants. Of course, these approaches have a long and venerable history in western thought, particularly in relation to the growth of romanticism in the eighteenth and nineteenth centuries. Certainly, from Rousseau onward, the belief in an unspoiled individual 'core' of personality has been a dominant theme of European romanticism. As Steven Lukes has observed, self development is implicit in the romantic movement as well as in the liberal tradition mediated through John Stuart Mill:

> The notion of self development thus specifies an ideal for the lives of individuals – an ideal whose content varies with different ideas of the self on a continuum from pure egoism to strong communitarianism. It is either anti-social, with the individual set apart from and hostile to society (as among some of the early Romantics), or extra-social, when the individual pursues his own path, free of social pressures (as with Mill), or highly social, where the individual's self development is achieved through community with others (as with Marx, or Kropotkin). In general, it has the status of an ultimate value, an end-in-itself.[10]

While 'romanticism' stresses self fulfilment as value, personality theory tends to see it as a requirement for individual integration. Practitioners like Maslow, Rogers, Allport and perhaps Fromm, have all pointed to some kind of core need to actualise potentiality. As such, they have been criticised by tough-minded experimental psychologists as being far too vague and subjective. Yet, there are other emphases within the broader field of cognitive psychology which define integration in terms of the assumed need for consistency and meaning. Whether one accepts or rejects the claims made by proponents of the various kinds of cognitive consistency theory which dominated attitude research in the 1950s and 60s, there can be no doubt their appeal was partly due to their apparent ability to explain individual behaviour in 'core' terms. Indeed, 'Festinger's Cognitive Dissonance'[11] is fundamentally concerned with the motivation underpinning an individual's attempt to come to grips with behavioural ambiguity. While all these theories made allowances for the operation of interpersonal factors, it is true to say that their focus of interest was with the 'internal' organisation of the psychological system.

91

Internal organisation implies a system with boundaries – it therefore involves a degree of co-ordination of a whole complex set of biological and psychological processes. In theory, boundaries are supposed to demarcate the self from non-self, ego from alter, individual from society. Thus, as an organised entity, the individual strives to maintain the integrity of his or her boundaries. But how can we be sure that we know what we mean when we speak about boundaries? At a very obvious level, we might want to say that boundaries are defined by the body; more specifically, by the skin. However, this presumes all self-referring processes can be conceptualised in terms of the limits set by biological and physiological boundaries, limits which are described in different ways in different cultures. Alternatively, the idea of limits may be specified as an aspect of an individual's psychological space. For some people this would include the entire range of experiences from the interpersonal to the cold world of matter. A self which incorporates everything into its psychological space is impossible to understand as a simple case of internal organisation.[12]

The idea of a boundary within which individuals isolate themselves from the encroachment of the external world, or from the demands of others is not congenial to sociological thought. It assumes that individuals are atoms, self regarding monads who come into random contact with each other in order to form loose social relationships – social relationships subject to the arbitrary whims and preferences of this or that individual. Since Durkheim's time atomistic conceptions of human behaviour have been ruled out of court for sociologists. Interactionists, in particular, are almost obsessive about atomistic formulations. They emphasise the 'permeability' of boundaries rather than personality organisation. Nothing is static – everything is in a state of flux – the self flows into the other, and back again in a constant reciprocal interchange of perspectives, commitments and feelings. Over a period of time, the self is transformed – it assumes the clothing or the camouflage of countless others – it literally becomes synonymous with society, or, alternatively, fragments into multiplicity. Accordingly, the 'interactionist' view of self as process makes it almost impossible to postulate a unified core, or an integrated personality system with recognised boundaries.

If we take this to its logical ending point, this means that the whole idea of the self as the primary unit of personality integration is an illusion. Ideas of self development and self actualisation are, therefore, archaic leftovers from a more primitive mode of analysis. Certainly the tendency has been to veer away from 'essentialism' and 'coherence' in sociological accounts of self other processes (except in so far as 'role' and socialisation theory have

92

substituted the notion of 'internalisation' for psychological 'organisation'). Accordingly, self theory (in sociology) is not concerned with 'Global' internal processes, and indeed finds it difficult to find an adequate vocabulary to articulate such processes.

Nevertheless, if the essentialist view is dead in the literature, we have to ask ourselves whether it is dead in the everyday consciousness of participants? In addition, the dissemination of terms reflecting some of the concerns of those practitioners who have discovered identity as an alternative to the self is no longer confined to the pages of academic journals and monographs, but is now part of normal discourse on the mass-media. It is conceivable that, while various practitioners are busy burying the self as a topic for serious analysis, it remains a critical commitment for those participants who have to cope with everyday life.

5 Self determination

In trying to identify some of the problems related to defining the 'individual', we have concentrated on dimensions which have been taken to specify 'separation' of the individual from other individuals, and as an entity manifesting biographical continuity. In western thought all of these dimensions have been invoked in the age-old controversy about the nature of the individual as a free agent. The philosophical discussions about the relationship between free will and determinism have been so internecine and fierce that they have tended to lose their meaning. In positing individual autonomy, it is no longer fashionable to talk of a disembodied self which acts as an energiser of behaviour, although there are still practitioners and participants who subscribe to a belief in the reality of moral choice.

Granted that it is not easy to spell out what precisely is meant by the social determination of individuality, I do not think that there is any real difficulty in finding 'determinism' in social theory. If you take, as an example, some of the assumptions built into the role model of socialisation, then it is evident that the individual is explained at all levels by the operation of the social system. His sense of separation is given by his society, his belief in consistency over time is traced to society, his memory is merely a reflection of what has happened to social contexts, his sense of integration is merely the internalisation of values and norms, and his feeling of freedom of action is defined as the merest illusion. Indeed, individuality, freedom and choice are often described as if they were catch-words of a non-scientific ideology. So, instead of a view of human behaviour as being under the control of the individual himself,[13] we have in sociology a view which seems to opt for complete social encapsulation. In contrast, in everyday life there is a limited consciousness of autonomy, a common-sensical formulation of the self in conflict with the other, especially when the other is given the status of a powerful, but fallible, being. This is not to say that the self is a product of strife and conflict, or that it emerges out of a social matrix in order to pose as a 'freedom fighter' – rather, it is to take issue with the view that human beings exhibit self consciousness as a mere reflection of social institutions. To do so is to fall into the trap of 'abstract individualism', except that instead of the old notion of an abstract essence which somehow universalises human nature, we are faced with a monumental sociological abstraction which de-natures human reality. The abstract individual[14] of nineteenth-century economic theory has been replaced by the abstract individual of social theory. Both these 'individuals' are theoretically capable of self determination, provided they do not stray too far from the limits imposed by the original theoretical formulation. Put another way, it is easy to *invent* situations in which they can be put to work. Hence, in sociology, the individual as a carrier of roles is described going about his everyday life as though contradictory role expectations forced him to choose between alternatives.

If we cannot dismiss autonomy from an analysis of social reality, or from everyday life, then on what grounds can we claim autonomy? There are practitioners who would say we can make such a claim only if we locate human action within a historical context in which 'human nature' is *produced*. In other words, we are in territory travelled by Hegel, the young Marx and by Sartre – a territory in which 'Praxis' is the dominating feature of the landscape. In Sartre's case, it is history which displays 'man's' autonomy and self creation. In a famous passage he writes:

Man is, for himself and others, a signifying being, since one can never understand the slightest of his gestures without going beyond the pure present and explaining it by the future. Furthermore he is a creator of signs to the degree that – always ahead of himself – he employs certain objects to designate other absent or future objects. But both operations are reduced to a pure and simple surpassing. To surpass present conditions toward their later change and to surpass the present object toward an absence are one and the same thing. Man constructs signs because in his very reality he is signifying; and he is signifying because he is a dialectical surpassing of all that is simply given. *What we call freedom is the irreducibility of the cultural order to the natural order.*[15]

In surpassing 'all that is simply given' man can literally create himself; he can control his future by radically transforming the present. Of course, this view of the nature of praxis is subject to all sorts of difficulty, particulary when it is seen in the context of a view of the 'cultural order' as an autonomous sphere of self-contained meanings. The question of reduction to the biological, or the economic, or the social for that matter, haunts Sartre, and in his debate with Lévi-Strauss he accuses the structuralist of reducing the study of humanity to the status of a study of ants.

Such a stark presentation of the individual who chooses himself, who continuously creates himself anew, would seem to be patently absurd to hard-minded empiricists and self-declared determinists. Moreover, there is the strange way in which 'social nature' is cut off from biology, from the body and from its fabric of feeling states and tensions. It is possible Sartre is too obsessed by his attempt to find historical truth as the 'totality' of the individual life and historical processes. The individual who chooses himself, chooses himself as the 'subject' of history, and it is precisely this promotion of the choosing 'subject' which is anathema to practitioners like Lévi-Strauss and Althusser, and which leads them to stringent opposition to 'humanism' and 'subjectivity' in the social sciences. Indeed, as Althusser has argued, it is only when we can speak of Marx's theoretical anti-humanism that we can begin to think about the transformation of the world:

Strictly in respect to theory, therefore, one can and must speak openly of Marx's *theoretical anti-humanism*, and see in this *theoretical anti-humanism* the absolute (negative) pre-condition of the (positive) knowledge of the human world itself, and of its practical transformation. It is impossible to *know* anything about men except on the absolute pre-condition that the philosophical (theoretical) myth of man is reduced to ashes. So any thought that appeals to Marx for any kind of restoration of a theoretical anthropology or humanism is no more than ashes, *theoretically*. But in practice it could pile up a monument of pre-Marxist ideology that would weigh down on real history and threaten to lead it into blind alleys.[16]

Althusser goes on to argue that even when we know that an ideology is an ideology, this does not mean that it automatically disappears. It follows, therefore, that the multiplicity of humanisms, of which existentialism is one, do not fold up when they are exposed to the full blast of a scientific analysis. They exist as historical forms, as ideologies which are imposed on men, not as aspects of consciousness:

> They are perceived-accepted-suffered cultural objects and they act functionally on men via a process that escapes them. Men live their ideologies . . . not at all as a form of consciousness, but as an object of their 'world' – as their 'world' itself . . . it follows that this action can never be purely instrumental; the men who would use an ideology purely as a means of action, as a tool, find that they have been caught by it, just when they are using it and believe themselves to be absolute masters of it.[17]

This certainly sounds ominous for the idea of autonomy, especially if we accept Althusser's view that 'ideology' is profoundly unconscious in the way it expresses itself in the lived relation between men and the world. From this perspective, the entire discussion of the nature of self consciousness and self determination has no scientific status, because it is simply a manifestation of ideological discourse. This means that if we take Althusser's argument to its logical conclusion, then most standard sociological discussions are ideological, especially those which are rooted in attempts to formulate a 'sociology of the individual'. All such projects must fail in the end because ideology is not equivalent to the real relationship between men – it is an 'over-determination of the real by the imaginary'.

In everyday life, such an 'over-determination' is so commonplace that it constitutes the 'lived relation' of human beings in bourgeois society. Accordingly, when participants ascribe freedom to their own actions they constitute themselves ideologically. Also, in speaking of biography, temporal consistency, memory, the body, psychological organisation, we are engaging in ideological discourse, because ultimately all these dimensions are premised on the individual as a subject (conscious or unconscious). Not only is the 'abstract' individual thrown out, but the 'concrete' individual implicit in a humanistic reading of Marx is dismissed in the same way.

How then are we to account for the continued interest in consciousness among practitioners when it is argued that this is purely an ideological interest? When, for example, Berger *et al.* discern an excessive amount of subjectivity and individualism in the 'modernised world', are they reporting an actual phenomenon, or are they distorting the world by being unconscious spokesmen of a 'lived ideology'? Or, does their phenomenological account of everyday consciousness in industrial society really help us to understand the manner in which concrete individuals cope with real social forces? The answer to these questions is not simply one of academic interest, but is of vital concern to the way in which so-called emancipatory themes enter into social theory.

If, as Berger *et al.* have maintained, the structures of modern society (late capitalism) cannot tolerate an excess of subjectivity without some kind of institutional support, then this must imply that the relationship between the individual and society is highly attenuated under conditions in which there is no secure basis for the development of an integrated self. Yet, at the same time, they claim that because of the lack of institutional support, subjectivity reigns supreme in the lives of millions of people in advanced capitalist societies. There is the implication that it is industrialisation which inevitably creates the conditions for the divorce of self from society, and there is the further implication that only a radical transformation of the structures of society will ensure their remarriage. Furthermore, the splitting of consciousness into private and public spheres at an ever-increasing rate, means that, for all practical purposes, the self comes to be defined as a refuge from the intrusive demands of the public sphere. Hence, what is secured for the private self comes to be perceived as intrinsically valuable and desirable. Each affirmation of the self's separation from others is marked off as a major victory of individualism over the brutish institutional order. What becomes dominant in the consciousness of men caught up in the search for some kind of *private* stake in their individuality, is a new language which articulates such concepts like 'identity' and 'identity crisis'. Introduction of terms like alienation, anomie and identity into everyday language is a symptom of the polarisation of the world into mutually exclusive spheres; at least this is what is implied in the type of cultural diagnosis offered by Berger *et al.*

In this chapter I have been concerned with providing an impressionistic overview of the self as presented in various kinds of psychological and social perspectives. *Two* critical problems emerge from this overview: *first*, the problem of limits. By this I mean the existence or non-existence of boundaries which cut off or divide the self from non-self, and from others. Sociologically, the tendency has been to treat the self as permeable, as being in a state of flux. The self-as-process is a 'domain assumption' of the symbolic interactionist approach to socialisation. This is opposed to the 'integumented' view of personality which informs the theorising of practitioners devoted to self actualisation and the like.

The *second* problem relates to the *reality* of the self. By this I mean its reality for the individual, and as a *topic* for social science. As a reality for the individual is meant the 'taken-for-granted' aspect of self processes as they manifest themselves in language and conduct. In western societies the 'taken-for-granted' self is not a problem for participants – it only becomes problematic for those concerned with formulating a strategy to 'theorise' about the self. In other societies there are alternative formulations of self–other processes, ranging from a complete absence of the self concept to its complete immersion in the cultural milieu.

As a *topic* for social science, the 'self' is fraught with ambiguity. Not only is it deemed to be an unsatisfactory 'intervening variable' by behavioural psychologists, but its status is questioned by a whole army of practitioners who see it as an example of a kind of essentialism which has no place in social science. Moreover, in the strongest sense, it is considered to be precisely the kind of non-scientific concept which contaminates the entire social science enterprise. At best, it might have some utility in the explanation of interpersonal behaviour, but this utility is severely curtailed in 'structural' and 'historical' analysis. Accordingly, the reality of the self as a topic for sociology is problematic, especially in the context of far more *pressing* business. So we are faced with a situation in which self theory is relegated to prescientific ideology as a typical example of prescientific discourse.

However, no matter the strength of the case against the self, there is no indication that its actual demise has taken place. On the contrary, the self remains a critical element in the discussion of social reality; this is no more evident than in the attention paid to 'identity' by practitioners who have been nurtured on a diet of symbolic interactionism and dramatism: it is also evident in the proliferation of 'phenomenonological' accounts of reflexivity as demonstrated by the development of a phenomenological sociology.

In the following chapter I hope to examine some of the dimensions of identity in social theory, with particular reference to their implications for a sociology which defines itself both as a means of social transformation and social understanding.

5 Identity and illusion

The opposition of body and self is an old theme in European thought. This opposition has led to strong counter-blasts from those who see in dualism an obstacle to any real progress in the formulation of a social science. However, various practitioners have tried to give a naturalistic explanation for the apparent dominance of dualistic conceptions, both in everyday life and in academic accounts of individual and social processes. For instance, the emphasis Mead and Dewey put on biosocial processes meant that the 'self' was conceived of as a natural phenomenon arising out of a natural communicative matrix. Hence, for Mead, and later symbolic interactionists, there was no doubt in their minds that they had established the 'self' as a central aspect of social processes. Moreover, the inference to be drawn from their work was that sociology could not do without the 'self', or without reflexivity!

Of course, when we talk about 'the self' we are in danger of reification – symbolic interactionists are very careful to point out that the self is a process, and not some substantive energising principle, but this does not prevent enthusiastic devotees in going about their sociological work as if the 'self' were immediately available for inspection.

In Mead's terminology, the self is nothing more than the reflexiveness of the human organism – Mead used the notion of self to stress the cognitive capacity of humans to reflect upon their own actions, their own faculties and powers as if they were 'at a distance' so to speak, from their agents. Generally, the human organism acts towards others with the background knowledge that such others are also possessed of the capacity for reflexiveness (this is perhaps what is intended by the notion

99

of the 'self of the other'). Despite some of the unfortunate formulations of his more metaphysical followers, it is clear that Mead intended nothing mysterious in his use of the concept of self.[1]

The self, then, is a natural process grounded in the reflexivity of the human organism. Yet, this has not hampered the growth of an *as-if* conception of self which ascribes reality to an inner world of meaning. While the 'self' cannot be located as an object of empirical inquiry, its reality is attested to by the reification of this *as-if* quality. In everyday talk the *as-if* self is taken for granted, reflecting linguistic practice which appears to be so normal that it requires a major shift in imagination to distinguish between 'practice' and the 'self' which it presupposes. Hence, at the linguistic level participants do not usually question the status of the self referring concepts they employ. Such a questioning only comes when practitioners use analytical tools to dissect 'everyday language'. However, this questioning cannot do anything more than attempt to explicate the grounds on which we invoke self language – it does not banish the self from everyday life. The *as-if* self may be an illusion, but it is an illusion which is pretty commonplace, although there is always the temptation to give everyday practice ontological status. Ontological status or not, what is certain is that terms which 'show' the *as-if* self appear historically in the context of the development of a society, or group of societies. Consequently, an examination of these terms is of some significance in grasping the 'feel' of the *as-if* self as it manifests itself across time and cross-culturally.[2]

Any discussion of the self involves a veritable quagmire of confusion, especially when self is confused with person, and both are confused with identity. Undoubtedly, all three terms are interdependent and complementary, but what are we to make of terms like 'self-identity'? Or 'personal identity'? Is the situated self equivalent to situated identity, etc.? Problems like these are not solved by semantic tricks – they represent genuine conceptual bewilderment and, perhaps more importantly, they reflect stresses and strains in social reality. In recent years, it is 'identity' which has moved to the centre of the stage (in a sense, Goffman writes about 'identity' more than anything else). At the same time, the sociological discussion of identity has been accompanied by the discovery of absurdity. By this I mean identity is given an existential flavour – the search for identity becomes the search for meaning. If meaning goes out of the world then the presumption is that individual life dissolves into absurdity – identity is, by this token, always in danger of being overwhelmed.

Just as the self has been subject to misinterpretation by practitioners who have reified it, so has identity been contaminated by the burden of excessive metaphysics. For some practitioners, the 'search for identity' is the prime rationale for human existence – the image that this conjures is of millions of people conducting their everyday lives for the sole purpose of carving significance from an obdurate reality. The quest for significance, in this view, looms larger than the quest for bread. Hence, 'identity', which at one level is simply a term associated with the individual's interpretation of himself or herself as a particular kind of person, is, at another level, elevated to the status of a metaphysical crusade, the defeat of which leads to the absolute degradation of personality. Moreover, in contemporary formulations, defeat is more probable than not – industrial society by its very nature is not conducive to a climate of consensual significance in which the individual may find a 'home', or stake an identity claim.

However, we are told by other practitioners (Berger *et al.*) that the imperatives of industrialisation lead not to absurdity, but to privatisation, to withdrawal into the self. The implication to be drawn from this is that 'identity' becomes more and more important in inverse relation to the complexity of social relationships. There is a hidden image of community lurking behind the frantic rush to don new identity – if society has moved beyond the control of the broad masses of people in industrial societies, then the one alternative to the classic quest for community is a journey into the self, to a valued identity. Putting together a new identity to exist in such an unfriendly environment entails assembling a diverse set of cognitive, behavioural and cultural items into some form of package which enables the individual to perceive himself as standing in a significant relationship to others. In constructing an identity, or in assembling an 'identity kit', the individual finds a means of facing up to the world in an imaginary symbolic universe where the cardinal value is the private self.

The mixture of metaphysics and speculative social theorising about 'identity' means it is particularly difficult to know exactly what is really at stake. It might well be that nothing is at stake – simply another example of misdirected obscurantism masquerading as a genuine topic of inquiry. There is undoubtedly an aura of uncertainty about the way in which identity is, and should be, used. This derives, I suspect, from the suspicion that it is basically a term with a mental health connotation, and, indeed, in the social work context, identity is one of a battery of terms employed by practitioners in their attempt to highlight personality and social deprivation problems. (There is a belief that personality integration

101

has something to do with the attainment of a stable sense of identity.) In whatever way the term is used, one underlying theme is located in the presumed ability of human beings to interpret their own behaviour. This is echoed in Mead's notion of self indication, and in the general reflexiveness of the human organism.

Horrocks and Jackson define identity in the following way, and in so doing differentiate between self concept and identity:

> An identity is a result of a *dynamic cognitive process of selecting meaning components* of various self-concepts to form an assembly of self-meanings. In this manner identities emerge from combinations of self-concepts. The self-process produces an identity hypothesis with the result that the individual is able to verbalise to himself and to others who and what he is. . . . A separation of self-concept and identity poses a situation in which an organism is postulated as perceiving itself through its own self-concepts and expressing the perception as a series of identity hypotheses to be tested in the form of role behaviour. This reasoning obliges us to assume a self-process, but it does not lead to the further assumption that the self-process is infallible, since one of its products, identities, are only hypotheses growing out of self-concepts held and, like all hypotheses, may prove to be untenable when tested against reality.[3]

Translated, the foregoing means that 'identity' can be conceived of as a product of self processes – it has no permanent status – it has to be tested against reality, a reality which frequently does not confirm the view that the individual has of himself or herself, at a given moment in time. Identity is, thus, a symbolic interpretation of the individual as he believes himself to be, and as he hopes to be. The fact that there may be a discrepancy between these two aspects of identity has exercised a great deal of comment in the literature, particularly in accounts of the reported discrepancy between self and ideal self, but this is a problem in personality dynamics beyond the scope of our present discussions.[4] For our purposes, we are concerned with identity as a self defining picture subject to all kinds of pressure, and which, in certain circumstances, loses contact with 'reality'. Hence, identity is, from this perspective, infinitely volatile because it is located in a communication matrix in a state of constant flux. Thus, in considering identity, it is difficult to understand how we can speak of continuity over time because of the emphasis on the 'situation'. However, if an identity is an hypothesis which is tested or rejected by exposure to 'reality', that is, exposure to others, then continuity may well be dependent on the relative stability of the others' reactions. This would be to situate identity in a completely social framework, except that when we postulate identity as an hypothesis, this implies the active participation of a 'dynamic cognitive process'. Put differently, reflexiveness ensures that identity is not simply the automatic process of 'taking the role of the other' in a random mechanical manner, but is rather an expression of the individual's active cognitive capacities.

Nevertheless, the impression remains from an examination of the various sociological approaches to identity, that it is usually regarded as a 'mirror' which either reflects or distorts the social world of which it is part. If this is all there is to identity we might as well dispense with it altogether, because it adds nothing to our understanding of individual and social processes. Indeed, it could be argued that all we need is an appropriate language to describe the way in which human beings behave in this or that situation – such a language would not need to take recognisance of the self and identity at all, provided it could specify the actual situational determinant at work. Early behaviourism attempted to do just this, but not only behaviourism – there are other 'movements' which find it difficult to specify the reality of self processes, and consequently are contented with denying their reality or relevance (I have partly dealt with one such attempt in an earlier section of this book). Despite all this opposition, 'identity' will not lie down, and, as I have suggested, has become a highly charged philosophical and metaphysical concept while simultaneously securing a foothold in social theory. Richard Robbins[5] suggests that three dominant models of identity have engaged the attention of practitioners – (1) the identity health model; (2) the identity interaction model; (3) the identity world view model. I shall be concerned with the first and second only. Of course, this classification tends to simplify and demarcate topics which, in the nature of things, should be treated as unitary conception.

1 The identity–health model

The identity health model has close connections with some of the self actualisation theories which we touched upon in the last chapter. Its most important and influential practitioner is Erik Erikson,[6] who, I suppose, has become associated in most people's eyes with the identity concept.

A dominant assumption in this model is the belief that a stable and integrated identity is a fundamental requirement of mental and physical health. The fact that so many people have identity problems in western society is seen to be a function of the way in which critical experiences in the individual's developmental history

103

are influenced, helped, hampered or distorted by institutional and organismic factors. The operation of these factors can either have positive or negative results. If positive, then identity will approximate to the image of 'wholeness' and 'integration' which seems to be so much a part of the vision of mental health in psychiatric practice – and, if negative, identity will be fragmented, disassociated and subject to temporal disorientation.

Hence, one important aspect of this model is the belief that a secure sense of identity is a requirement of a successful biography. The absence of identity, therefore, is a sure indication of depersonalisation and alienation. Indeed, the mental health literature is replete with metaphors which purport to demonstrate that the self and identity are in constant danger of being 'overwhelmed' by forces over which they have no control, the most dangerous of which is usually depicted as the intrusion of the 'other' into the private world of the 'self'.

When Laing,[7] for example, talks about 'ontological insecurity' he is expressing in a vivid phrase the anxiety that inner actuality is an illusion or, if not an illusion, as being subject to the threat of external engulfment. While Laing spells this out in terms of his discussion of schizophrenia, the original rooting of his position is existential phenomenology is explicit. What this entails for a formulation of identity is an unequivocal assertion of what Sartre called 'existential commitment' – the belief that identity is the centre of sentience, that is, the notion of identity existing across time. However, this sense of identity cannot be predicated, except at a very subjective level – it cannot be demonstrated because it does not fit into the limits set by clock-time or other conventional personality parameters.

So, when Laing and other practitioners, such as Binswanger,[8] point to the threat to identity as being the most horrific of all psychic disasters, they are attempting to situate human actuality in what they are certain is the area in which human beings are most human, in their sense of continuity and sameness. But a sense of continuity is predicated on existence – on the certainty of the self existing before it is defined and categorised. Whatever empirical objections one might have to such a formulation, it does undoubtedly provide the rationale for the theory and practice of many practitioners who have rejected both the formulations of orthodox psychoanalysis and behaviourism. In other words, the mental health of individuals is presumed to depend very much on the way in which their sense of existential location has, or has not, been disturbed by the impingement of a hostile reality.

Implicit in this kind of thinking is the idea that it is the contemporary social milieu which has posed the most cogent threat to identity. This has been occasioned by the sheer complexity of industrial society. It is duplicated in the critique of industrialisation which we considered when we looked at the mass society thesis, but it is also tied into those diagnoses of western capitalism which employ concepts like alienation and estrangement. In other words, there is a marked overlap in the kind of vocabulary used by cultural diagnosticians who see signs of structural disintegration everywhere around them, and the vocabulary used by clinical diagnosticians who see evidence of that disintegration in their consulting rooms and clinics. In practice, of course, such a vocabulary constitutes a relatively limited universe of discourse. It is used by social workers, psychiatrists, clinical psychologists, and even in some cases by religious practitioners. Yet, if one looks at representative texts the prominence of the identity vocabulary is very marked: for example, Ralph Ruddock writes:

> It is the concept of identity that is most likely to provide the golden thread to lead through the labyrinth [that is, in interpreting the client's behaviour]. It has long been recognised that the best practice in casework involves waiting upon the free choice made by the client as his understanding grows, as opposed to such techniques as persuasion or manipulating his unconscious feelings by way of 'transference'. The choices that come to be made will depend largely upon the client's changing sense of himself.[9]

Ruddock goes on to suggest that it might not be enough simply to change a person's concept of himself by changing one role identification for another role identification. He seems to imply that the caseworker may have to go beyond roles to discover the 'real' identity problem of the client. This going 'beyond' leads straight into existential and phenomenological positions in which the concept of role is defined in terms of its invitation to act 'inauthentically' or in 'bad faith'. In the now famous passage from Sartre's *Being and Nothingness*, in which he describes the *waiter* as being imprisoned in his role,[10] we are asked to assent to the argument that the 'role' of the waiter, the grocer – in fact, all socially defined and internalised roles – are examples of the way in which human beings deceive themselves about their capacity for moral choice. This means that when social workers, psychiatrists and others endeavour to reformulate a person's role identifications, all they are really doing is to substitute one form of self deception for another. Ultimately, the inference would seem to be, mental health is not a matter of adjustment to the demands of reality, or the attainment of some peaceful balance between competing role expectations; rather, it is a process in which clients abandon their self imposed prisons. The teasing out of 'true identity', the 'real self', then comes to be seen as the prime task of both client and clinician.

The same concern for 'true identity' is to be found in various statements of political commitment in which true liberation is often equated with the discovery of identity. So much of the rhetoric of the psychedelic left has been concerned with 'levels of reality' and 'authenticity' that it is almost impossible to disentangle the various threads of influence which has gone into its political stance. Certainly, no matter the source of their belief in self liberation, whether it derives from a western version of eastern mysticism and religion, or from a romantic interpretation of 'existentialism' and the like, there is a belief that the structure of rationality has imprisoned the self in an artificial world of rules and regulations. The overwhelming commitment for the psychedelic left is personal liberation, which is seen to be just as important as social liberation. Without such personal liberation the revolution will degenerate into bureaucracy and authoritarianism. But personal liberation is not necessarily equated with the discovery of a lost identity − more frequently such a liberation is to be found in the reassertion of the 'body' − in the delights of sexuality, stifled by repressive social institutions. Hence, true identity, from this point of view, is a recognition of the 'reality' of the body. When Reich[11] wrote the *Sexual Revolution* his image of a revolutionary future as a realisable possibility was dependent on the prior liberation of the body, but such a liberation was a chimera because of the decades of sexual repression which had 'de-natured' the masses of western Europe, making them such easy targets for Fascism.

In contemporary terms, the idea of personal liberation is therefore a compound of differing perspectives about the nature of the 'true self'. Whether the self is defined as 'the body', or as 'identity', or as the 'soul', there is the same emphasis on the way in which social institutions have all combined to distort and coerce the individual into some kind of fraudulent and inauthentic posture. From the point of view of the diagnosticians of mental health, the problem is an individual one which is best handled in therapeutic situations, but from the viewpoint of psychedelic politics, the very idea of a therapist helping the individual to articulate 'true identity' is a contradiction in terms, because the therapist is defined as both a victim and agent of 'straight society'. However, in either case, both the mental health and psychedelic images of identity are premised on the assumption that there is something wrong with social reality. The clinician cannot do much about society − all he can do is to induce an acceptance of the value of the person to himself − in other words, despite the therapeutic vocabulary which is resonant with admonitions 'to know yourself'; 'to accept yourself', 'to come to terms with reality', and more daringly, 'to express yourself' etc., etc., there is no way in which such admonitions constitute a radical challenge to that society; at least there is no evidence available that would suggest that the search for identity has profound political consequences. Nor, for that matter, is it easy to assess the real significance of the new 'body politics' which has emerged in recent years – all that can be safely said is that the body is now receiving the kind of rapt attention previously reserved for 'class' and 'power'.

Be that as it may, we are confronted with the problem of the grounding of the kind of language employed by clinicians to pinpoint 'identity'. It can be argued that it is not enough to make an 'existential commitment' or an unavoidable assumption about the actuality of identity. What has to be demonstrated is the auspices under which it becomes possible to talk about identity in 'mental-health' discourse. For example, when Laing speaks about 'ontological insecurity', or when Erikson posits the crises and stresses implicit in the development of ego-identity (the Epigenetic crisis [12]), what grounds have we got for accepting this language as being representative of the phenomenon? Or, alternatively, how sure are we that there is indeed a 'phenomenon' to talk about? How are we to interpret the kind of statement which we often read in the reports of clinical interviews about the client's expressed inability to relate to other people? It may be that all such statements are context-bound, reflecting nothing more than the kind of conversational gambit usually expected in a clinical situation.

Moreover, in everyday life, when somebody takes you aside and tells you that she is lonely and depressed, one does not make ontological assumptions about the nature of identity, unless one has access to the specialised vocabulary of social workers and psychiatrists. Admittedly, the likelihood of access is much more probable among certain sections of western populations than among other populations (e.g. university graduates) – nevertheless, this is not to say that, even in this context, there is any necessarily agreed upon understanding of such terms as 'identity' and 'self'. Coming back to the woman who has told you that she is depressed, the range of responses open to you will depend on your linguistic resources, your experience of similar situations in the past, as well as your current interpretation as to what is actually going on. If you do have access to concepts like 'identity crisis', then to an extent you might satisfy yourself that you can successfully explain her behaviour, or at least provide a suitable stock of motive words to 'catch' her predicament. From her point of view, such an imputation of motives to her conduct might be completely irrelevant – all she might want from the situation is some advice, or your approval, or she might be employing 'sociability tactics' in the male/female situation.

All this is self evident, and it does not get us any further toward grasping identity as a datum of inquiry. It might well be that the mental health model is nothing more than a vague working hypothesis employed by a number of practitioners to understand experiences which are difficult to articulate linguistically. The point is, I suppose, whether it makes any sense to attempt to describe a phenomenon which does not appear to be available for inspection? Also, in view of the way in which self processes have been treated in sociology and psychology, as being fundamentally social in origin, as being subject to interpersonal negotiation, then does it not make sense to subsume all versions of identity under the rubric of interaction?

2 The identity–interaction model

The interaction model has been so pervasive in recent years that it is hard to remember a time when identity or the self were conceived of in any other way. I do not want to elaborate on the multiplicity of approaches to the 'social self' which have dominated symbolic interactionist thinking, nor do I want to go through the familiar literature on the pros and cons of labelling theory. My purpose is to state, as simply as possible, both the arguments for and against 'identity' being regarded as an interpersonal phenomenon.

At a very crude level, when we looked at the 'mental-health model' the difficulty we had was to account for an experience of self which apparently was beyond social influence. How can we account for the feeling of sameness, for memory, for unity – or lack of unity – in the day-to-day life of any human being? One way of doing this is to make some kind of unavoidable assumption about the 'transcendental ego' in Husserl's sense. The ego is transcendental because it is presumed to be given in experience – it cannot be thought away – it is 'alone' and *constitutive* of existence. This is put cogently by Maurice Natanson:

> The aloneness of the ego is both a means for the experiment [bracketing the world] and a result of it. As a means, a methodological procedure, radical suspension requires the solitary ego because all other bases presuppose the philosophical grounding at issue here: the constitution of self and world. For existential philosophy, the primordial aloneness of the individual is accompanied by the experience of anguish.[13]

What is being asserted here is a belief in the universality of human isolation. Isolation is thus a *given* of human existence, and accordingly all human beings are 'alone' in encountering each other and the world. The notion of the isolated and helpless individual imprisoned in the confines of 'ego' is a popular one in contemporary fiction and drama, but even more popular is the incommunicability of isolation. For example, in Pinter's plays we are continuously encountering situations in which the characters indulge in studied conversational emptiness, where conversation seems to be a desperate attempt to cover up 'nothingness' (this is even more true of the 'theatre of the absurd'). But it is not only literature which finds loneliness a seductive topic – its centrality is attested to by sociological and psychological statements about the aridity of urban existence, usually in 'mass society' formulations (Big City Blues). Thus there is an alternative, but associated, line of thinking which sees loneliness and isolation as a product of a particular kind of social existence. Isolation in this sense is nothing more than an unfortunate consequence of institutional complexity. By this token, 'identity' is a by-product, a reflection, of the situation of an individual in a society. Moreover, 'isolation' is a social concept, just as 'privacy' is a social concept. So this means, if we are to believe the literature, that the 'typical' human being situated in the urban wilderness of advanced industrialised societies, sees himself or herself as an isolated person, enmeshed in a network of other isolated persons. Typically, such self definitions are described as being 'normal' and 'general'; at least, this is assumed to be the case in western societies. In other words, the social genesis of the isolated self is taken for granted by sociologists in the same way as the 'transcendental ego' is taken for granted by phenomenologists. Of course, the phenomenological and socio-logical positions cannot by any stretch of the imagination be considered to belong to the same universe of discourse, except in their apprehension of the self as standing alone against the 'other'.

In standing alone against the other, we are claiming as sociologists that isolation can be given a social explanation. We are in effect saying that a person defines himself or herself as 'lonely' or 'alienated' in a social context in which privacy and isolation are not random phenomena, but are a direct consequence of the splitting of society into private and public spheres. The implication of this is that identity is always rooted in interaction. The isolated individual is isolated because of the pattern of relationships in which he finds himself. He does not choose isolation – it is forced upon him. From this point of view identity is a symbolic construction of the individual's perception of himself at a particular historical moment. There is the possibility that in other

109

times and places his view of himself would not necessarily be that of a solitary isolated being standing alone against other people.

Indeed, in some symbolic interactionist accounts, the very idea of a fixed isolated identity is ruled out of court. Identity is open to negotiation – it is seen as infinitely volatile (although in the literature there are a set of distinctions between 'situated', 'personal', and 'social' identity). Admittedly, for symbolic interactionists the assumption of infinite volatility is not easy to demonstrate, neither is it claimed, except as a statement of doctrinaire intent. What is claimed is a view of identity which locates it 'outside' the accepted boundaries of the body and self. Hence, whatever the situation or context, identity is regarded as interpersonal, as belonging to more than one person.

This seems to contradict the view that the 'private self' is not shared, but 'stands' against the 'other'. How can the 'I' that I value and affirm be a social process incorporating other identities? The typical answer to this is given in the standard socialisation literature in terms of the acquisiton of the ability to take the 'role of the other'. There is nothing private or esoteric about this – it is a natural process which generations of symbolic interactionists have taken for granted. The acquisition of identity is, therefore, the result of a long and continuous set of negotiations in which the person learns to define himself in a particular way; furthermore, negotiation does not simply entail the building up of a stable and static identity, but also the associated ability to conduct identity experiments – that is, to transform identity. At any moment in time, my self definition, my assuming an identity which I believe to be a measure 'of what and who I am', is subject to a complex pattern of negotiation, one offshoot of which is my belief in the complete 'privacy' of the 'self' (of course, this presumes that I have access to a vocabulary which differentiates between 'self' and the 'world'). From this perspective, the private self, is a social construction involving past, present and future 'others' who all contribute to the monitoring of my conduct.

There are superficial similarities between this 'sociological' account of private identity and the 'Private Language Argument' which periodically erupts among linguistic philosophers. When it is asserted that a 'language must have publically checkable rules'[14] and that, therefore, a private language is logically impossible, this could be another way of saying that identity can never be private for the simple reason that, in sociological terms, it is a symbolic construction which depends on language, and because language is a social activity, then it follows that identity must, in the final analysis, be a social construction. Such a position denies the possibility of 'privileged access' to a private world. While this may be an epistemological problem, its relevance to our understanding of identity could be critical, provided one accepts the argument that identity is a linguistic phenomenon. But even if we do accept this, does this mean that what we are doing when we talk about identity in the sociological sense, is to specify the rules of a language game, namely the rules appertaining to the use of self referring terms? If we say that identity has no explication outside an interpersonal framework, then at any moment in time the individual is not directly in control of his own participation in the world. He is always an arena for competing 'definitions of the situation'. In deciding on who or what he will be, in this or that context, he will not be acting as an agent, but as a product of a multiplicity of 'internalised others', as well as the 'others' directly involved in the ongoing interaction episode. His valued, private identity is, by this token, simply one of a number of possible identities available for use. In other words, what is revered as being secret and inviolable is, in reality, a symbolic formula for a special kind of reflexive relationship.

In conceiving of identity as interaction, the role of the 'other' becomes crucial, because in more senses than one the 'other' is essential to self definition. Hence, to make identity claims about the special kind of person you are, is to select an identity from a whole spectrum of possibilities. Presenting myself as one who has suffered great anguish and pain to an audience I have defined as sympathetic, may involve me in a deliberate attempt to produce the appropriate symptoms of suffering which I believe my audience expects. Thus, in a very crude sense, it could be said that I have convinced my audience about the genuineness of my symptoms and the reality of my pain. But, it might well be that I have convinced myself as well. Now the question arises, does this mean that I am, in fact, experiencing what I have sold to my audience? Put differently, in presenting myself as a suffering victim, does this mean I am a suffering victim? The way I have asked this question is, of course, not likely to produce a satisfactory answer, because it assumes that there is a one-to-one relationship between internal definitions and external conditions. It assumes that if I claim that I am a suffering victim my audience will validate this claim, or, alternatively, that if I am so defined by my audience, I will automatically accept the label. In either case, this is a far too mechanistic formulation of the interaction between self and other.

It must be remembered that the interaction model is not only about self other relationships, but also about the way in which participants organise their identities in order to negotiate the 'nastiness' of everyday life. In my earlier book, *Meanings and Situations*,[15] I subsumed this notion of interaction under 'the norm of cynicism'. In my reading of Goffman, I took him to be advancing a picture of social relationships in capitalist society which defined every encounter between self and other as an exercise in deceit. Hence, identity can never be taken at its face value, except in so far as there is an attempt to present the self as a mask. If the mask is mistaken for identity, then the 'actor' successfully manages to convince his audience about the sincerity of his performance. Identity, in these circumstances, is always suspect; it is believed to be masquerading under false credentials. The problem of identity, then, becomes not so much knowing who one is, but in constructing a role which enables you to maximise the benefits to be obtained from social encounters. It follows that, even if you know yourself to be a cynical self-seeker, this will not matter because you can project an image of yourself which 'masks' the reality lurking below the surface. It seemed to me that Goffman's image of human nature was nicely adapted to the workings of a society in which all social relationships were market-oriented. However, this was qualified by the observation that similar forms of self presentation seemed to be endemic in non-industrial societies. Despite this, it is in capitalist society in which 'masking' is the prevalent mode of relating to others. Goffman, of course, does not make any explicit political statement – for him, this is how the world is, and as such it is an interesting source for quarrying the almost infinite variety of social gambits to be found in interpersonal contexts. Hence, it was my contention that Goffman was an explorer of the 'micro-world' who unintentionally exposed the extent to which human beings were caught up in the 'artificial' and 'reified' world of the market.

Other commentators[16] have pointed to the ideological, ahistorical and apolitical nature of Goffman's analysis of interaction, and have tended to conclude that the 'dramaturgical' approach is a middle-class 'cop-out'. All this might be true, but it does not necessarily mean that the reality to which Goffman addresses himself is an illusion (except that 'reality' itself is problematic for Goffman)[17]. In everyday life situations, while I might not now want to make too much of the 'norm of cynicism' as the bedrock on which human beings encounter each other, there can be no doubt such a norm has become part and parcel of the lingua franca of the world of advertising, public relations and political disclosure. Thus, in the apparent open discussion on television about public issues, we are cued to expect the worst of the protagonists.

In other words, when, for example, it is said about a particular politician that he exudes insincerity, we expect to be able to 'see' behind the mask. Every utterance, every facial expression, every gesture, is scanned for evidence of subterfuge. Once the code is broken, we can say that his 'mask' was nothing more than an elaborate defence. We knew right from the very beginning that he was, indeed, not what he claimed to be. The question is, if his mask is simply a device to hide behind, what then is it that is hidden? Also, what are the implications for the individual who begins to suspect that he has been found out? In the case of the politician we might subsequently read in a newspaper that the reputation he has as an insincere man is not borne out by the evidence of his friends or his family. 'To know him is to love him' – 'he really is a wonderful husband, a kind father and a generous friend'. Are we to assume, then, that the impressions we have of the man as a scheming politician are incorrect, or is it that the 'role' of a politician itself is suspect? How, then, do we account for those politicians who are perceived as being 'sincere' and yet have been discovered to be 'wife-beaters'?

Admittedly, most of us do not directly interact with politicans – our picture of them is mediated through the mass-media, and it is therefore possible, that his identity projected on the television screen is a 'channel' effect or a deliberate distortion by his enemies. Nevertheless, whatever the complications, he will have an identity imputed to him which might, or might not, coincide with the identity he claims. How, then, are we to decide which is the real identity? If we do not accept his identity claims to be who he claims to be, then are we entitled to say that we know him better than he knows himself – and that in actuality he is a 'cynical self-seeking bastard'?

Both the interactionist and the dramaturgical models are highly suspicious of any attempt to attribute *primacy* to one aspect only of self other processes. Hence such concepts as the 'real self' are meaningless except as part of the ongoing process of symbolic negotiation, but this does not prevent practitioners from talking about the hidden and private self, although this does not necessarily imply that what is hidden is, as a consequence, central and significant. Nevertheless, even if it makes no sense to speak about 'real' identity, this does not mean that participants are bound by the same restrictions. The fact is, people do impute motives, they do make judgments about identity, and they often assume that others do the same. As Goffman writes:

> Whatever a participant 'really is', is not really the issue. His fellow participants are not likely to discover this if, indeed, it is discoverable. What is important is the sense he provides them through his dealings with them, of what sort of person he is behind the role he is in. In Gibson's terms, they are concerned

with the poet not the sonneteer. They are concerned with the author, not the writer, They are concerned with something that is generated in the contrasting streams of his immediate behaviour. What they discover from their gleanings will apparently point to what he is like beyond the current situation. But every situation he is in will provide his others with such an image. That is what situations can do for us. That is a reason why we find them (as we find novels) engrossing. But that is no reason to think that all these gleanings about himself that an individual makes available, all these pointings from his current situation to the way he is in his other occasions, have anything very much in common. Gleanings about an individual point beyond the situation to what, presumably, will be found in all other gleanings of him, but one cannot be sure that they point in the same direction, for it is their very nature to make themselves felt as pointing in a same direction.[18]

Does this mean that 'all these gleanings about himself that an individual makes available' cannot really be anchored down to provide a secure basis for saying anything about identity? Certainly, from the vantage point of the others, the 'gleanings' they have of the individual allow them to assume that they 'know' who and what he is. In practical terms, they are not concerned with the possibility that, in different situations, other participants might glean something else. But what about the individual who makes available those 'gleanings' about himself which he wants the others in a situation to catch? Does he possess a view of himself which cuts across situations, and which is capable of defending no matter what 'gleanings' others pick up? The phrase 'making available' suggests that there is an aspect of identity outside the 'situation' which the individual 'keeps back' from the interrogation of others. Are we to assume that in other situations he could conceivably reveal this 'private and hidden' dimension to those whom he regards as friends or confidants, etc.? If this is the case, then what criteria can we employ to decide whether such a convivial context is really a frame in which the 'private self' is displayed? It could be argued that such a display would be nothing more than one occasion among many in which a *version* of identity is offered for confirmation by others.

Accordingly, taking the 'interaction model' to its limits, we could say that there are as many identities as there are occasions, and, therefore, all self definitions are of equal value. Hence, when we speak of an individual 'keeping back' a valued private identity, all we are saying is that he is engaging in 'identity-work' appropriate to the situation. The politician who lets down his hair in private to his friends and reveals himself as a 'kind and generous human being' is, by this token, doing nothing more than participate in a shared situation, in which all the participants contribute to his view of himself. In other contexts, although he might endeavour to display these positive self evaluations, he might equally put as much identity-work into the cultivation of an image which he believes the occasion demands (provided the others allow him to get away with it); he might, for example, play the politician's role with what he considers to be the maximum insincerity, because somehow he believes that this is practical politics. It follows, if we accept this line of thought, that identity is context-bound – it can never transcend the parameters of time and place. There is no primary self or identity – only a multiplicity of situations in which 'identity' language is used.

There are obviously alternatives to such an extreme 'context-uality', especially when we look at the way in which other 'interactionists' have described 'deviance' and 'stigma'. For example, in Kenneth Plummer's excellent discussion of *Sexual Stigma*, we are given a description of the career stages of the homosexual. Here, the emphasis is not on identity as context-bound, but rather on the 'building-up' of a homosexual identity. 'Building-up' does not mean 'putting together' discreet elements of behaviour into some kind of consistent whole – a homosexual does not start out with a mish-mash of unrelated cues as to the nature of his homosexuality which he automatically translates into self awareness:

> One cannot see the individual 'automatically' and 'intrinsically' 'knowing' that he is a homosexual – as the simple interpretation of prior elements. Rather, one must analyse the social situations and interaction styles that lead to an individual building up a particular series of sexual meanings, a particular sexual identity. It is with those factors that create a potentiality for 'homosexual identification' that an interactionist analysis most suitably starts.[19]

Becoming a homosexual, therefore, involves a career through time in which others contribute to the quality of the homosexual's self perception and evaluation. The point is that this identity is not one among many. Given the nature of the societal reaction to sexual deviance, homosexuality becomes the most crucial aspect of a person's self definition – there can be no question of homosexuality being switched on and off – we are not talking about a 'Diceman' conception of identity in which one chooses the kind of 'mask' one is going to wear as though one is playing a game of lucky numbers. The 'mask' that the homosexual wears is a

115

prerequisite of his or her survival in 'straight' society. The fact that there are various strategies for coping with societal reaction to homosexuality means that it is difficult to talk about standard careers, so that it is wrong to speak of a *standard* homosexual identity. The processes involved in the construction of such an identity are beyond the scope of the present discussion – all I am concerned with is to articulate the biographical aspects of identity acquisition, that is, the notion that 'identity' can be conceived of as the result of a specific career, or, more accurately, as the historical view that a person has of himself or herself as 'standing alone against the other'. For homosexuals, standing alone is part and parcel of their definition of 'the taken-for-granted world'. As long as that world 'stigmatises' behaviour which it regards as threatening, immoral and so forth, then there is no way in which we can avoid making the distinction between private and public identity.

Interactionists do not, therefore, have to resort to the 'transcendental ego' to account for the 'self' hiding behind a mask, but we might want to ask whether such a complete social explanation is too cavalier? Earlier in the book we spoke of the ambiguity which several commentators have discovered in Mead's treatment of the self process. Both Natanson[20] and Douglas[21] have stressed the submergence of the phenomenological strand of Mead's thought by 'socialisation' themes which emphasise the 'generalised other'. In explaining the source of the private and public self in terms of interaction processes, there is nothing left over, except perhaps a residual quantity of energy which expresses itself in the antics of the 'I', and even this is under the control of the 'me'. For Mead the 'I' is engaged in a continuous struggle with the 'me' to assert 'selfhood', but it is a struggle which always ends up in the same way, that is, in the 'I's surrender to the 'generalised other' – in the submergence of the individual in a society which is taken-for-granted, never questioned. Mead, for various reasons, was never interested in the dynamics of society – he was not a sociologist, and this resulted in him seeing society as though it was a given (despite the evolutionary framework of his thought). It is not surprising that practitioners following him have found it difficult to describe 'self' and 'identity' other than in terms of static social formations – as Zygmunt Bauman puts it:

> Starting from existentialist assumptions, Mead went as far as it
> is humanly possible toward transcending the opposition
> between self and society and attaining a unified account of an
> apparently polarised experience. But the same assumptions set
> an unsurpassable limit to his achievement. The dialectics

disentangled within Meadian sociology inhered in the relationships between the ever-becoming self and a ready-made society. To expose the dynamics of the self, Mead had to leave in semi-shade the dynamics of society.[22]

There would seem to be two main difficulties for the 'interaction model'. *First*, despite its commitment to 'process', it tends to give priority to the notion of the self as being 'immanent' in social structure, so that identity can be derived retrospectively from a 'reading' of history, or from contemporary culture. *Second*, there is the associated problem of 'identity behind the mask'. If we accept that 'private identity' depends on the context in which it is invoked, and, therefore, is one identity among many, this still does not explain the persistent *rumour* of a presence behind the mask. The first difficulty may be partially resolved by remembering that when we talk of the self we are merely making explicit the 'reflexive' ability of human beings to monitor their own conduct, but this in itself cannot explain the 'illusion' of biographical continuity – an illusion which, to say the least, is pretty widespread, although there are some practitioners who prefer to speak of self deception. The mechanics of the relationships between identity and society are not perfectly understood. Nevertheless, one thing is reasonably certain, and that is both identity and society relate to each other through language, so that language is, to an extent, the critical dimension in any consideration of the interaction model.

The second difficulty is not so easily resolved – the 'rumour of a presence behind the mask' has, in the past, resulted in a whole host of formulations ranging from mysticism to mechanism – it has also precipitated the belief among various practitioners that such 'a presence' is, in fact, unknowable; it has to be taken for granted as the bedrock of self awareness – as a phenomenological 'given'. The trouble here is similar in kind to that indicated under the rubric of the 'mental health' model – there appears to be no way in which we can communicate self awareness except in terms of linguistic categories which possibly distort the experience. Moreover, it is precisely the vagueness of such attempts to articulate the 'inexpressible' which leads to the charge of mysticism and subjectivism. Nevertheless, I still do not know who it is that peers out from behind the masks so beautifully described in dramaturgical theory!

In this and the preceding chapter, I have been concerned with *sketching* an outline of various formulations of self and identity as they appear in practitioners' accounts. I have obviously left out a tremendous amount of relevant material, so in this last section I

117

would like to recapitulate some of my arguments in a more systematic manner, in order to prepare the ground for the next chapter.

I Multiple realities and multiple selves

Sociologists as a whole find it difficult to operate with 'global' concepts of self and identity processes. Consequently, what is stressed in the literature is the *dominance* of the situation. However, the difficulty with describing the 'self' solely in terms of situations is that it eliminates the actor who 'knows' that he or she is an entity with a body enduring over time. One way round this difficulty is to make a distinction between social and personal identity, as Goffman does in *Stigma*.[23] Or, alternatively, human beings are described as irrevocably split:

> we can observe two reductions applied to the double nature of man: abstract society, on the one hand, reduces the modern individual to a social functionary (a one-sided homo-externus), whereas this individual himself, on the other hand, exhibits the tendency to reduce his double nature into the opposite direction by either retreat or revolt, relying in both cases on irrational emotions and experiences, and longing for a social nirvana in which he can live as a 'pure' individual without any form of institutional alienation (a one-sided homo-internus).[24]

The splitting of the individual into a 'homo-duplex' is a common enough theme in the literature. In a sense, we could say that the split is taken for granted by participants and practitioners who distinguish between their inner private life and external public life. The fact that some participants cannot, or will not, make this distinction, is presumed to be the concern of psychiatry, not sociology (except in so far as it can be demonstrated that other societies do not make this distinction). If this was all there was to say about homo-duplex, there would be no problem. However, the thrust of contemporary argument is not about the relationship between 'inner' and 'outer' reality − rather, it is about the *disassociation* of these two realities. The 'split' is not simply taken as an anthropological 'given'. It is conceived of as multi-dimensional process in which both the self and society are continuously fragmenting. The reasons for this process are believed to be rooted in the dynamics of technological and economic change.

Hence, instead of homo-duplex we now have homo-multiplex. Homo-multiplex is context bound. There is no way in which he can locate his 'true identity', for the simple reason he is forced to display a different identity in different situations. The social division of labour has gone so far that the old dichotomy between homo-internus and homo-externus is fast becoming an historical curiosity. Obviously, such an extreme position makes it almost impossible to account for human behaviour in terms of self monitoring or reflexivity. One would be hard put to discover a 'living' example of homo-multiplex, despite psychiatric claims to the contrary. Nevertheless, when Berger *et al.*[25] speak of the pluralism of life-worlds they are not indulging in sociological fantasy – they are pointing to a phenomenon explicit in contemporary social existence.

From a different perspective, both homo-duplex and homo-multiplex can be described in linguistic terms, as exemplified in language games. The private, secretive self we value, or devalue, is, as a consequence, a language game we play in certain situations. Analytically, therefore, the distinction between private and public identity is one of degree, because both aspects of identity are language games. There is nothing mysterious about this, participants talk to themselves and they also talk to others. Hence, we do not necessarily have to throw up our hands in despair about the intricacies of the relationship between self and society, or the supposed iniquitous consequences of living out our lives in multiple realities. However, our problem is not merely to attempt to account for theoretical and academic ambiguities in the discussion of identity. We have to account for the fact that participants (including academics) conduct their lives as though there is a discontinuity between private and public spheres. It is no use demonstrating that this discontinuity is logically impossible, or that it can be explained in terms of symbolic and communicative processes – such a demonstration is of no relevance for participants who have to face up to everyday problems. In the earlier chapter on privatisation, the phenomenon of the split between private and public spheres was taken seriously. Homo-multiplex may have no real flesh and blood reality, but it is fair to say that in the discontinuities imposed upon our everyday organisation of experience by the social division of labour, it becomes increasingly difficult to find institutional support for identity.

2 The privatisation of the self

Daniel Bell writes:

> To the classic question of identity 'Who are you?' a traditional man would say 'I am the son of my father'. A person today says, 'I am I, I come out of myself, and in choice and action I

make myself'. This change of identity is the hallmark of our own modernity. For us, experience rather than tradition, authority, revealed utterance, or even reason, has become the source of understanding and identity. Experience is the great source of self consciousness, the confrontation of self with diverse others.

Insofar as one makes one's own experience the touchstone of truth, one seeks out those with whom one has common experience in order to find common meanings. To this extent, the rise of generations, and the sense of generation, is the distinct focus of modern identity. But this change is, also, the source of an 'identity crisis'. . . .

The sociological problem of reality in our time – in terms of social location and identity – arises because individuals have left old anchorages, no longer follow inherited ways, are constantly faced with problems of choice (the ability to choose careers, life styles, friends, or political representatives, is, for the mass of people, something new in social history), and no longer find authoritative standards or critics to guide them. The change from family to class to generation as the 'structural' source of confirmation thus creates new strains in identity.[26]

Daniel Bell is writing about American society. In his mind there is no doubt that the old 'identity-conferring institutions' are no longer capable of engaging individual commitment. Instead of the family and class, it is generation which provides a focus for identity, it is generation which answers the individual's need to locate himself in a system of significance. What strikes commentators like Bell is the apparent finality of the break from traditional sources of identity. The 'identity crises' of adolescence, explored by Erikson, are transformed into the identity crisis of an entire generation, and, by extrapolation, into the crisis of industrial society.

Two typical assumptions are made by Bell and other American post-industrial theorists. *First*, they assume 'class' does not enter into everyday consciousness in American society; and *second*, they assume that the family can no longer act as a crucible of identity. Both assumptions are believed to be partly true for other industrial societies, it being only a matter of time before all industrial societies approximate to the American model. The problems and conflicts of post-industrial society are different in kind from those traditionally associated with capitalism. One of the critical problems facing post-industrial society is the massive 'under-institutionalisation' of young people who no longer 'identify' with their country, their class, their families or their community. What this means is that there are literally millions of people who find it meaningless to define themselves in terms of traditional legitimations. Instead, they fabricate alternative kinds of identity – they experiment with drugs, sex, religious cults, communes and sometimes with 'radical' politics. In short, instead of individuals locating themselves on a sociological continuum, they delve into themselves and, more often than not, so it is argued, they find they are unable to cope with what they find there. However, the problem of unharnessed subjectivity does not only appear in post-industrial society literature. In one way or another, it has appeared in various forms and guises ever since the advent of industrialisation (after all, the nineteenth century saw the emergence of romanticism and the growth of the myth of the unbridled and authentic ego). But we are not concerned with this here. What we are concerned with is the validity of viewpoint which relegates the old identity-conferring institutions to a theoretical and empirical limbo. The point is, surely, not that we have entered a post-industrial age, but, rather, that the old institutions are themselves subject to fragmentation pressures which make it increasingly difficult for them to mobilise group participation. The contemporary family may not confer identity, but it is the institutional focus of privatisation. The privatised family is the breeding ground of subjectivity, especially middle-class subjectivity. Although at one level it might act as a recruiting agency for middle-class occupations, at another level it encourages the growth of dissent and free-floating subjectivity.

In a sense, therefore, the 'privatised self' is explicable in terms of developments in the class structures of western societies. It does not emerge as a result of the spontaneous choice of individuals. But the 'privatised self' is not a passive instrument. It looks for outlets, objects to which it can attach itself. It encapsulates itself in its own 'life-world'. The 'reality' of this life-world may be illusory, but it is the stage on which the self acts out its belief in its own potency. Accordingly, a remarkable consequence of the decline of official systems of public legitimation like the 'established church' and the 'traditional family' is the proliferation of thousands of alternative life-worlds in which individuals in western societies believe they have located their 'true' identity. The possibility exists, of course, that instead of the false consciousness of religion they have substituted the false consciousness of 'personal meaning', but such a consideration cannot alter the 'believed in' reality of this or that life-world. Moreover, as Stan Cohen and Laurie Taylor[27] have recently argued, we have underestimated and devalued the importance and intensity of these life-worlds, particularly in regard to the way in which participants organise great areas of their everyday experience as fantasy. While fantasy can be seen as one way of escaping from the exigencies of the present, or as an example of Freudian wish-fulfilment, its widespread generality among participants in western societies is not simply a form of indulgence – on the contrary, it represents 'reality' in the same way as public symbolic systems represent reality. Sexual fantasies are just as compelling as the institutionalised and public fantasies of religion or the state. Put differently, if we want to look for false consciousness in everyday life, it is no good simply examining the official ideological pronouncements of public spokesmen, we have to go to the 'grass roots' where participants try to cope with reality by constructing alternative realities.

3 The reality of the self

The previous discussion has centred on practitioners' accounts of self and identity processes. Privatisation is a sociological concept and is not usually part and parcel of participants' discourse. The two models of identity we discussed at the beginning of this chapter more or less take it for granted that self or identity is a central dimension of human experience, but do we really have any evidence that this is the case in everyday life? When, for example, Laing describes the anxieties of the ontologically insecure individual as being indicative of a real or imaginary threat to his or her sense of identity, does this mean we can generalise from Laing's clinical observations to the actuality of everyday life? While Laing became a cult figure in the 1960s, and his view of self processes was an everyday topic for students in and out of the counter-culture, this is not necessarily to say this was because he pointed to genuine everyday experience of identity.

Alternatively, when we talk about the meaning going out of the lives of the populations of industrialised societies, when we talk about a society of empty automatons going about their mundane activities in a routinised and fragmentary manner, does this mean that identity is infinitely variable, so that it becomes pointless even to talk about biographical continuity? Or, are we really saying that since the traditional identity-conferring institutions no longer provide frameworks for personal and social identity, it no longer makes any sense to speak about identity? How, then, are we to account for the persistence of the rumour of identity among participants and practitioners?

We might want to proceed, as we did earlier in this chapter, and speak of an 'as-if self' which participants acknowledge, for all practical purposes, but this still begs the question. Conceivably we might want to say, although in everyday life participants do ground

122

their activity in a common-sensical and pragmatic view of their own and other identities, that this does not entitle the practitioner to make any inferences about the reality of the self. Moreover, even if we do come to the conclusion that it does in fact make sense to impute identity to participants, the further objection may be raised which asserts that such an imputation is irrelevant for the purposes of social analysis.

It would seem to be a peculiar state of affairs which allows for an 'as-if self' in everyday life, and which simultaneously denies its theoretical and empirical relevance. Certainly, in some of the models we have been considering there is no such discrepancy. On the contrary, the difficulty here is to match theoretical language about the self with everyday conceptions. Both theoretical and everyday language are believed to have some kind of experiential basis – both languages are premised on the reality of self experiences. Nevertheless, the possibility remains that all such discourse is of no consequence to social science, except as an example of distorted communication, or false consciousness. If this is accepted, this means that the 'as-if' self cannot provide the ground for any kind of social theory.

Certainly, we do not find the privatised and subjectivised self in structuralist analyses of the relationship between cognition and society. There is no room in their formulations for a distinction between the as-if self and the self posited by social theory. Moreover, because of the structuralist opposition to phenomenological accounts of self experience, identity is treated as an aspect of cognition, as 'an image of the world which is already inherent in the structure of the mind'.[28] Consequently, when somebody imputes an identity to others, or makes an identity claim for himself, this is an irrelevance for structuralist analysis, except in so far as it can be used to decode unconscious structures. Identity, from this point of view, has a similar status to myth: it represents an opportunity for the practitioner to engage in a decoding exercise; it is not an exercise for the teasing out of personal meaning; the 'subject' has no privileged access to the interpretation to his, or other, identities.

What emerges from the structuralist denial of the knowing subject is a view of human action which does not allow participants to 'monitor' their own behaviour. Jacques Lacan in particular has advanced the view that it is not possible to discover 'the ego' because it is never available to consciousness:

> To Lacan, linguistics decentered the subject since the signifier represented a subject 'not for another subject but for another signifier'. The spoken I could never enunciate the actual I.

123

Hence: 'I am not in what I say; I am not where I think; I do not think where I am.' The level of language was so distinct from the level of the subject that the mediation of speaking did not unify the two. Worse still, there was a second level of structure, a second language: the unconscious was itself structured, enunciating the language of desire.[29]

To talk of true identity, the real self and so forth, is, for Lacan, a logical and empirical impossibility. All that participants are aware of is the fact that they speak and others listen, but speech does not reveal the self, all it reveals is speech. It is only through the help of a listener (structural psychoanalyst) that participants could conceivably partly understand themselves, but in everyday life very few listeners are psychoanalysts. In Lacan we again have a strong assertion of the idea that 'language constitutes man', but in a peculiar sense the shape and structure of this language is unconscious – it is not available for self reflection – it cannot reveal the self beneath the skin.

What then are we to make of the 'identity language' so prevalent in our culture? Is it language and nothing else? Who talks? Who argues? Who denies? The answer, presumably, is the 'unconscious', not as the reservoir of repressed instinctual energy, but as the source of language. When I ask 'who am I?', or 'who are you?', the responses are not in terms of a self monitoring consciousness, because by definition 'I' am not talking, 'you' are not talking. Yet, the everyday 'as-if' self will not lie down – it reappears from moment to moment, from situation to situation. Its reality is attested to by the pragmatic concerns of participants who have to negotiate with each other in order to establish some kind of coherence and consensus about the boundaries of the situation and the rules which apply within these boundaries. But negotiations are reflexive strategies involving a minimal degree of self consciousness. They presume that participants 'know', take for granted, that they speak when they speak, think when they think, feel when they feel. This is not a reassertion of the Descartean 'cogito' – all it implies is that everyday life participants do not usually have access to analytical tools which would allow them to question the 'auspices' under which they use 'identity language'. (We might want to ask 'what are the auspices which allow practitioners to dissect and demystify participants' "identity language"'?)

In discussing 'the reality of the self' and its relevance for social theory, we are, therefore, faced with three alternatives:

1 We can deny its theoretical significance: the 'as-if' self is seen as an aspect of everyday discourse. Hence, it cannot provide the grounds for the understanding of social action, because it assumes

that participants can act in terms of rules which they know how to apply in this or that situation. This is anathema for structuralists who are concerned with desubjectivising all views of human behaviour which posit a *knowing* active subject.

2 We can affirm its theoretical significance: the 'as-if' self is placed at the centre of discourse. Reflexivity is not only taken for granted, it is seen as the fundamental prerequisite for a sociological account of social reality. In other words, the self is not given 'as-if' status – it is accorded ontological priority. Some phenomenological and symbolic interactionist formulations come very near to positing a social world in which self processes underpin all social relationships. Although symbolic interactionists are very much concerned with the danger of 'reification' they themselves (sometimes) fall into the same trap.

> The desire to avoid the reification of concepts is noteworthy. Nonetheless, the *use* of concepts should not be confused with their reification. What epistemological principle gives us the right, let us ask, to employ the concept of self and to deny to others the use of the concept 'social class', 'impulse', etc.? Is the concept 'self' more empirically verifiable than the concept 'social class'?[30]

3 Participants can affirm the 'as-if' self: in the first two alternatives the reality of the self is denied or affirmed from the point of view of practitioners who are concerned with establishing the grounds for a description of social reality. In both cases, the 'as-if' self is not allowed to stand on its own. It is either demoted or promoted. The raw data, so to speak, of everyday interaction go through a conceptual sieve, and what emerges is either considered to be theoretically irrelevant, or it is elevated to over-arching significance. For participants themselves, identity and self are not theoretical problems. Everyday language is replete with linguistic terms which display self referring activity. In mundane discourse participants have no need to try to account for the way in which they define themselves and others, because there is no reason for them to do so. Participants, if you like, operate on their own implicit models of the self. But what is important, is that they do not attempt to deny the actuality of these models on the grounds that they are logically impossible. However, this is not to say that in everyday life participants do not question the reality of identity. On the contrary, identity is threatened by personal troubles and institutional pressures. Losing identity is an everyday possibility. At the psychological level, participants are continuously forced to expend time and energy to ward off the threats posed by

ambivalent personal relationships, while at the institutional level they are faced with the continuous threat of 'homelessness'.

4 Losing identity

When we talk about losing identity, we seem to imply that identity is grounded in supportive institutions, so that if they fail to provide such support then participants lose all sense of meaning and purpose. It follows that when, for example, colonisers undermine the indigenous institutions of their colonised subjects, they simultaneously erode their identity. Because it is believed such a condition is intolerable, it becomes imperative for the colonised to find an alternative source of meaning. The logic of this argument is taken for granted by practitioners who define modernisation in terms of the dislocation of traditional institutional ties. In addition, it informs the 'mass society' discussion of the rootlessness of industrial existence.

If we take this argument seriously, then if a society or community does not confer identity, if it does not allow individuals to see themselves as part of a larger system of significances, it follows it is in danger of disintegration. But can we take this argument seriously? If we do, this entails committing ourselves to a view of social and individual processes which does not tolerate ambiguity, conflict and dissent. It implies that individuals only function effectively in a social climate of consensually validated meanings, and this, to say the least, is a highly explosive issue in sociology. Yet, if we look at the 'mass society'[31] literature, one theme occurs time and time again, and that is the image of the isolated and alienated individual desperately attempting to find some kind of solution to his atomised existence. The old identity-conferring institutions, like the family, the school, the church, the workplace and the state, have lost their integrative capacity – they no longer provide a focus for self definition; instead, individuals find transitory meaning in personal relationships. In talking about the privatisation of the self and homo-multiplex, we are, therefore, using concepts and ideas which are strongly related to the theme of identity loss.

> Living between various institutional sectors, each requiring from him a behaviour that conforms to its autonomous norms and values, the individual will automatically develop a pluralistic identity. Naturally, the acquisition and maintenance of such a pluralistic identity puts a heavy burden upon him. Moving between the institutional sectors, the modern individual is compelled to change roles like the jackets of his wardrobe. A

distance grows between himself and his roles, and he experiences a loss of meaning and reality, which is usually called alienation.[32]

Losing identity, then, is equivalent to alienation (provided we are prepared to accept such a view of alienation). This presumes we have compelling evidence to demonstrate the relationship between institutions and self definitions: it presumes that an accelerated rate of social change has negative consequences for identity. Moreover, the implication here is that 'identity-loss' is *the* critical social and personal problem of our time – it is conceived of as a dominating aspect of the malaise of industrial society.

It is precisely this kind of formulation which appears to be so irrelevant to practitioners who are committed to examining and locating what they define as the 'real' forces at work in contemporary capitalist society. The question remains, whether or not identity, the self, consciousness, have any place in social theory, especially in a social theory which defines itself as fundamentally concerned with 'structure'. Is all such concern with consciousness simply to be dismissed as romanticism and ideology?

So we are faced with two critical problems for the next chapter of this book, namely:

1 Even if we grant that identity and self processes can be accounted for in social and linguistic terms, does this have any theoretical import for sociology?

2 Granting the reality of the split between the private and public spheres, between personal troubles and public issues, in what ways does this split have any relevance for a sociology which defines itself as emancipatory?

6 A concrete humanism?

Why should any sociologist concern himself with identity and consciousness when there are far more pressing and important claims on his time and energy?

It can be argued that to focus on the nature of personal experiencing – with the implication this can have for giving equally serious consideration to all matters that might momentarily concern the individual – is itself a standpoint with marked political implications, and that these are conservative ones. The analysis developed [i.e. in 'Frame – Analysis'] does not catch at the differences between the advantaged and disadvantaged classes and can be said to direct attention away from these matters. I think that is true. I can only suggest that he who would combat false consciousness and awaken people to their true interests has much to do, because the sleep is very deep. And I do not intend here to provide a lullaby but merely to sneak in and watch the way people snore.[1]

Goffman might have added that 'the sleep is very deep' for those who do the watching. Both practitioners and participants are asleep, if we are to believe the critics of subjective humanism. More importantly, they claim that even when practitioners believe they are fully awake, fully conscious, that this is an illusion. Certainly, from this point of view, the humanist project in sociology is self defeating, because it cannot transcend the limitations of its commitment to the autonomous self. Moreover, if this is what humanism implies for sociology, then there is not much point in defending it.

Now, of course, there are humanisms and humanisms. There is the humanism associated with the renaissance, there is the humanism associated with the enlightenment, there is the humanism associated with romanticism, and there is the ideological humanism associated with the rise of capitalism. The latter pays a great deal of attention to 'liberal' views of human nature which emphasise values such as 'freedom of choice' and the 'inviolability of the human personality'. The supreme moment of this *individualistic* humanism is embodied in the *laissez-faire* ideology of the classical economists and the English utilitarians. It assumed that only the free, untrammelled expression of the individual in the market-place, without interference from state and society, could guarantee the development of a free society. What it *did* guarantee was the unfettered movement toward economic and social exploitation. Indeed, when Spencer got into the act, *laissez-faire* ideology was translated into the excesses of social Darwinism.

It is this picture (often overdrawn) of the liberal view of individualism and humanism which has been instrumental in generating the belief that the individual has no place in Marxism, and that there is no such thing as Marxist humanism. The belief in a humanistic Marx is the result of a romantic reading of the *1844 Manuscripts* and the *Theses on Feuerbach*, but it may be argued that if Marxism did not have anything to say about human nature, if it did not have something to say about the individual, and if it did not have a humanistic commitment, then there are a lot of deluded people around. However, opponents of the humanistic reading of Marx do not deny that certain Marxist texts can be read this way — what they do deny is their relevance to a 'scientific' analysis of economic and social formations.

I am not attempting to get involved in problems relating to Marxist scholarship. What I am trying to do is to point to the ambiguities and doubts that any commitment to a particular reading of Marx implies for practitioners. These ambiguities are not resolved by arguing that the early Marx represents a prescientific stage of his theoretical development, whereas the mature Marx of *Grundisse* and *Capital* reflects the emergence of a scientific Marxism. It must be stressed that the early Marx does not defend the notion of the 'autonomous self' creating itself out of nothing. On the contrary, in the sixth thesis on Feuerbach the 'individual' Marx presupposes is social by virtue of being enmeshed in a network of social relations.[2]

However, this may be a tautology unless one can demonstrate the actual concrete rooting of human beings in a definite set of relationships. For example, when we talk about 'homo economicus', or 'homo psychologicus', or 'homo sociologicus' we are doing nothing more than 'abstracting' human nature. We are abstracting and, hence, 'reifying' particular aspects of human activity. Thus we can only talk of human nature if we are prepared

129

to concretise it. It is no use speaking of 'man' as the carrier of roles unless we can spell out the implications of such an assertion for the particular activities of particular men in particular situations. Accordingly, it is no use talking about the alienation of the worker unless we can point to the actual situation in which he is alienated. If workers are alienated, their alienation is not demonstrated by theoretical discussion – it can only be demonstrated by situating the worker in a system of relations in which he sells his labour for a wage. The parameters of alienation are, therefore, defined by the interplay of labour, wages and capital. Concretisation entails placing the worker in the 'here and now' of his everyday life in the factory, home and personal relationships. The point is that it is impossible to talk of the personal problems of the worker as though they originated in the recesses of his unconscious or in his autonomous ego.

What I am saying is this. Whatever we read into Marx, there can be no doubt that he is *not* concerned with the generation of a philosophical terminology to describe human nature. Accordingly, when we focus on the personal problems of the worker, or the housewife or the Black in Soweto, it makes no sense to treat them in isolation from the 'ensemble of real life processes'.[3] The postulation of a possible 'universal man' in the future depends on our understanding of human beings in everyday life situations. We can never know man in the future. We can only know real people in concrete relationships.

This means we can never ask the question 'what is man?' – it is unanswerable, but we can ask 'what is the nature of man *now* at this specific historical juncture?'. Freud, of course, thought the nature of man *now* is not all that different from the nature of man a thousand, or a hundred thousand years ago.[4] Marx could never have given this sort of answer. Human nature is demonstrated in the extant pattern of social relations. Hence, there is no way of going beyond the concrete particularity of everyday life. (Are we, then, to agree with those Marxists who argue that a concern with such things as individual suffering, pain and deprivation has no real significance in our consideration of the real world? Should we wait for the revolution to become humanists? Or should a humanistic commitment necessarily involve an undertaking to concrete individuals now? The problem of poverty, for example, is not an individual problem, but do we generally say 'let the people starve' because tomorrow the world is being made over. Or whatever theory of schizophrenia we accept or reject, do we simply assert that the attempt to particularise an individual's experience of schizophrenia or mental illness is simply a waste of time, because in the final analysis there is no possibility of eliminating the social determinants of mental illness until the social order itself is transformed?)

When we talk about the concrete individual we are not talking about the individual's encapsulation in the social world – he is not contained and shaped by monumental social forces. 'The essence of man is not an abstraction inherent in each particular individual. The real nature of Man *is* the totality of social relations.'[5] As Joachim Israel observes –

> We should observe that Marx does not state that man's nature is a consequence of his social relations, but that man's nature *is* the totality of social relations: this difference is of great importance. Marx does not consider Man's nature to be a system or a collection of characteristics, traits or other qualities, which in turn are shaped by his social relations. Man's nature is equal to those social relations: he is not an object shaped and influenced by the social relations he establishes but he *is* in relation to other men, with whom he interacts. Therefore man is both seen as an active subject when he interacts and a passive object when he is acted upon and these relations constitute him.[6]

The concrete individual, then, is constituted by the 'totality of social relations'. He knows, and defines himself as an active subject interacting with other men, but at the same time, other men act on him, often forcing him to act in ways which he believes are 'given' in the nature of things. Hence, some men 'know' that poverty is inevitable – they find it impossible to imagine alternative worlds in which it does not exist. Others know that poverty is not necessarily a permanent feature of social reality. Yet again, other men are far more concerned with the potency of their inner lives – poverty has no significance for them – their private world is the only reality to which they show allegiance.

However, poverty cannot be understood in isolation from the system of productive relations. Hence, those men who define poverty as immutable, and those who withdraw into the self, do not exist in different worlds. Their apparent insulation from each other is at the level of consciousness, not at the level of structure. But the point is, both groups of men are constituted by the extant ensemble of social relations. In other words, the so-called pluralisation of life-worlds is ultimately dependent on the social division of labour.

> Division of labour only becomes truly such from the moment when a division of material and mental labour appears (the first form of ideologists, priests is concurrent). From this moment onwards consciousness can really flatter itself that it is

131

something other than consciousness of existing practice, that it really represents something without representing something real: from now on consciousness is in a position to emancipate itself from the world and to proceed to the formation of 'pure' theory, theology, philosophy, ethics etc. . . .

The division of labour implies the possibility, nay the fact, that intellectual and material activity – enjoyment and labour, production and consumption – devolves on different individuals, and that the only possibility of their not coming into contradiction lies in its turn in the negation of the division of labour. It is self-evident, moreover, that 'spectres', 'bonds', 'the higher being', 'concept', are merely the idealistic, spiritual expression, the conception apparently of the isolated individual, the image of very empirical fetters and limitations, within which the mode of production of life and the form of intercourse coupled with it move. . . .[7]

When Marx argues for a view of consciousness as being intimately related to the social division of labour, he is not thereby claiming that consciousness is purely epiphenomenal. If this was the case he would not speak of the contradictions between material and mental labour. However, later interpretations of Marx have suggested that we should either treat consciousness as an illusion, or as possessing a limited degree of autonomy. In the former case this leads to a materialist and in the latter case to a humanist reading. Nevertheless, we must not forget that whatever interpretation we put on this or that passage from the corpus of Marx's writings, he is not concerned with explicating individual consciousness. Consciousness, for Marx, is always social consciousness, and the concrete individual cannot, and does not, have any significance outside the totality of social relations.

There is a distinction we can draw between Marx's view of the concrete individual, and his view of those theorists who overdo the autonomy of consciousness. The concrete individual experiences the world through his location in the social process – his personal troubles are not isolated from the personal troubles of others. His experience of poverty might be very personalised, but poverty is not a subjective phenomenon. The 'theorist', on the other hand, who claims 'autonomy' as a 'given', does so from the point of view of a 'consciousness' that 'can really flatter itself' into believing that it exists in and for itself. Such a 'theoretical individual' is more than likely to find reality in the autonomous self. This 'theoretical abstract individual' is enmeshed in an abstract humanism in which 'consciousness' is severed from its real foundations in social existence.

Does this mean that 'humanism' is simply an ideological ploy of academic social science and philosophy? When practitioners talk about 'identity loss' and 'privatisation' are they really engaging in ideological discourse? The answer must be in the affirmative if all humanist discourse is only about the problems of the 'solitary ego' and its estrangement from the world. But it could be that when practitioners concern themselves with 'personal troubles' they are not necessarily indulging in a fruitless search for the subjective springs of human action. Admittedly, when monographs are written on the 'Search for Meaning' and so forth, it is easy enough to see this kind of humanism as belonging to a romanticised middle-class view of the world. Yet, this does not mean that all such discourse is contaminated because it employs categories which are rooted in middle-class consciousness. The point surely is that when we talk about 'personal troubles' and 'privatisation' the intention is, presumably, to concretise and ground these concepts in the actuality of everyday life. If we talk about the privatisation of the housewife, we are not trying to romanticise her situation. On the contrary, privatisation like bureaucratisation, is a social and economic process, and consequently it can be described in terms of the social division of labour.

The real problem is not the appropriateness or inappropriateness of this or that concept – what is at stake is the very possibility of conceptualising subjective experience as a critical dimension of social theory. Now, it might well be that privatisation is a clumsy and irrelevant way of construing the experiences of housewives, consumers and so forth, but do we have any better way of doing so? It may be that some participants have access to a vocabulary or a conceptual system which enables them to make sense of their location in the world – they may, for example, know that privatisation is one term among many purporting to pinpoint social fragmentation – they may also believe that all terms and concepts which are supposed to articulate subjective experience have no place in a sociological discussion, or more realistically, in a Marxist discussion of social processes. However, having access to a theoretical framework which appears to explain one's position in the world does not of necessity negate one's subjective involvement in the world. There is no reason why a theory which claims to explain personal troubles should thereby make those personal troubles disappear.

Should we then say private troubles are simply the subjective reflection of objective institutional imperatives? There certainly is a temptation to do so. It is very easy to point to the relationship of personality disintegration to social disorganisation. From Durkheim onwards, academic sociology has been preoccupied with demonstrating the significance of suicide, marriage, divorce, crime, alcoholism and other rates, as measures of social integration. The usual inference to be drawn from the high incidence of a particular rate is that it is a social indicator – it tells us something about the degree to which a society is managing to cope with stresses and strains. Presumably, a high divorce rate is symptomatic of the decline of the family, and this in turn can be interpreted as providing a measure of individual pain and suffering in the marriage relationship. Although the foregoing is, perhaps, a caricature of some sociological approaches to social problems and private troubles, I think it is fair to say it is a reasonably accurate portrayal of the way in which practitioners have approached the analysis of social rates. While never explicit, there is a built-in mental health assumption in this kind of thinking. In a society in which divorce, crime and delinquency rates are 'low' it is easy enough to draw the conclusion that such a society is integrated and harmonious, and that, therefore, private troubles are at a minimum.

In general, the mental health model is deeply pessimistic. The increase and proliferation of private troubles and suffering is directly attributable to institutional complexity. Typical of such a view is Ruitenbeek's view of the disintegration of the traditional cohesiveness of western society, especially the United States.

One aspect of – crisis may be seen in the curious simultaneous movement away from intimacy and deep relationships – which are felt as threats to identity – and toward immersion in groups. Americans want to belong, yet there seems little worth belonging to. For social and religious bonds have been extended, blurred, disassociated from each other, and often weakened. Economic bonds have been strengthened, however; in many instances 'the company' has fallen heir to loyalties that once belonged to friends, family, church, or the state itself. 'What is good for General Motors is good for the country' might be spoken by many persons besides the person who was charged with having said it, and might apply to a broad range of social interests. Meanwhile, the individual is entangled in so many ties to so many organisations that he feels like an interchangeable part and less like a person. This is the situation that leads to a search for identity, for, entrapped in the web of organisation, man feels 'strange' isolated and alienated. Confronted by a freedom of a kind never known before, the person feels stripped of protection, fearful of being swept into 'the vastness swirling all around us'. And in the very organisational shelter the individual seeks and finds, he feels

134

swallowed up and alien.

And surrounded he is, for privacy is becoming more and more of an unknown quantity in American life. The absence of devices permitting a temporary retreat from society is in itself a sign of the completeness of the conquest of privacy. Americans live behind open doors in offices and dormitories. . . . They are not allowed to keep their names to themselves: the receptionist and the bank teller sits behind a little notice announcing his name to the world; even the waitress wears her name embroidered on her bosom. Fake personalisation, in the sociologist's phrase, has replaced a real regard for persons. Retirement into solitude has ceased to be opportunity offered by daily life. Where (beside the bathroom) can a man go to be by himself?[8]

I have quoted Ruitenbeek at length because I believe he illustrates the diagnostic viewpoint as well as anybody, a viewpoint which takes as its starting point the belief that industrial society is incapable of conferring identity. It is rooted in a view of anomie which is universalised for all industrial societies. But anomie is notoriously difficult to define and measure. The standard way to do so is to examine this or that 'rate'. The inferences to be drawn from the 'suicide' rate, for example, have occupied generations of sociologists ever since Durkheim attempted to provide a sociological explanation of integration.[9] The ambiguities implicit in any discussion of anomie are compounded by the confusion of psychological and sociological factors:

The normless condition – not individual responses to it – constitutes anomie. It cannot be defined independently of a group. Anomie represents a loss of pattern in the mutual expectations for social action. The various ways in which individuals react to a loss of pattern require different terms, *although different terms are not always used.*[10]

In the mental health model it is the psychological dimension of anomie (anomia) which is stressed. An extrapolation is made from the negative consequences of the division of labour to the psychological states of individuals. Industrial societies are anomic, hence individuals in these societies are anomic. Moreover, the focus of analysis shifts from normative integration to the individual's search for meaning. The breakdown of normative consensus supposedly leads to severe psychological disorientation, which in turn has negative implications for society. A whole battery of terms are employed in order somehow to 'display' the subjective experience of social disorganisation, the most important of which

135

are those relating to identity and its divorce from institutional legitimation. Thus, instead of private troubles being described in terms of the subjective feelings aroused by the experience of poverty, pain, disease, war, oppression, sexual deprivation and so forth, the mental health model is far more concerned with the loss of meaning.

The objections Marxists have to this view of industrial society as the forcing ground for identity problems are based on their argument that all such formulations are grounded in ideological categories deriving from middle-class conceptions of individual autonomy. They are grounded in a view of individual consciousness which distorts the 'real' concrete situation of the individual. Hence, while it might be feasible to speak of privatisation as a process which can be explained by the social division of labour, it cannot be explained as though it is simply the free choice of individuals to withdraw from their social commitments – such a choice is illusory – it is 'consciousness flattering itself'. Most Marxist critiques of mental health formulations stress the illusory character of the fragmented individual whose sole preoccupation seems to be the search for significance and essence.

> If one is to grasp the reality behind these illusory forms one must break with the idea of the human essence as 'substance'. This idea is the major obstacle to the materialist reversal of the whole conception of man and of history. It would seem, therefore, that one must give up the study of human individuals in order to study objective social relations. This break with the direct preoccupation with the human individual which was still to the forefront in the *1844 Manuscripts* is an essential and necessary moment in Marx's thought. All attempts to find a short cut to psychology by starting directly from the *1844 Manuscripts* are, therefore, based on illusion and lead us back to speculative humanism. However, this moment itself must not be separated from the whole movement in which it occurs. Such is the tendency of any anti-humanist interpretation according to which Marx rejected the concept of human essence once and for all.[11]

Thus against the abstract speculative humanism found in 'bourgeois' conceptions of the individual, Lucien Seve is arguing for a view of concrete individuality which rejects the illusion of the autonomous individual who confronts the world in a continuous state of despair. The despair and private agony of the individual are not rooted in the 'aloneness' of the 'ego' – they are ultimately dependent on the 'fundamental and immediate connection between men and the productive forces, in that men are themselves an integral part of those forces.'[12] Hence, if men describe their everyday problems in terms of 'identity crises', 'role conflict', 'existential despair', or if they see them as lying outside their control, as being determined by fate or biological necessity, then they are accepting at face value the illusory forms 'taken on by the products of work and by the producers themselves in capitalist society. These forms mystify men's immediate consciousness, just as more or less elaborated ideological systems also do.'[13]

Accordingly, the fact that individuals do tend to define their personal troubles as though they were immutable, as given by the nature of things, means that the task of demystifying is formidable indeed. Capitalist society produces both a fetishism of commodities, and a fetishism of personality. Mental health formulations are, by this token, ideological analyses of illusory forms of consciousness – they are ideological accounts of false consciousness. Furthermore, it is not only the fetishism of personality which comes under Lucien Seve's critical Marxist axe, but also the existentialist discussion of a 'human condition' which has no grounding in real social relationships:

> the logically monstrous thesis of an existence without an
> essence necessarily leads to attempts to base existence on the
> 'deus ex machina' of a metaphysical conception of the human
> essence. In fact existentialism turns out to be the mirror image
> of abstract essentialism. Neither of them can view the human
> essence as anything other than a general individual, whether
> this is in order to accept the idea or to reject it. Both are unable
> to break out from the vicious circle of these two
> complementary circles.[14]

Here, in a nutshell, we have the kernel of the Marxist rejection of abstract humanism. Both the essentialism of humanism, as well as 'implicit' metaphysical assumptions of existentialism are rejected because they fail to locate individuals in the nexus of production relations. Let us be clear about what is being rejected. Although Seve does not address himself to sociology and social psychology *per se*, it is evident that the sociological view of the social genesis of the self is also considered to be an example of abstract essentialism. This means that Durkheim's analysis of the acquisition of social nature, Mead's discussion of the communicative matrix of self and social processes, and the general symbolic interactionist position regarding the critical importance of the 'self' for social processes, are rejected because of their misleading emphasis on particularised and partial views of human behaviour. They are rejected primarily because they focus on man as social animal, not on man as

137

constituted by the 'ensemble of social relations'. The sociological model assumes a social world, which for all practical purposes seems to be cut off from economic and political realities. The political and the economic only enter into this world as disturbing influences, or as boundary conditions. Hence 'homo sociologicus' is just as much an abstraction as the abstract speculative humanism which Marx dissected in the nineteenth century. The crises which disturb homo sociologicus are not usually conceived of as deriving from outside the social world – they are *internal* crises. Homo sociologicus is faced with identity crises, he is faced with the continuous threat imposed upon his privacy, he is in continuous danger of losing himself in his roles, in the 'generalised other'. In short, sociological man is dominated by roles which define the parameters of his world.

It is not surprising that such a limited view of the 'social individual' lays itself open to charges of distortion and 'abstraction'. It is also not surprising that role theory has been criticised for its 'ahistoricity' and its tendency to reify both individual and social processes.[15] This brings us back to the question asked at the beginning of this chapter 'Why should any sociologist concern himself with identity and consciousness when there are far more pressing and important claims on his time and energy?' In addition, we might want to ask, in the light of the Marxist critique of abstract humanism, whether it makes any sense to defend humanism in social theory?

In this connection Horkheimer and Adorno write:

One might object that the sociological approach tends to again reduce man to a mere species-being, to make of him merely an impotent representative of society. This must be taken fully into account. The pure concept of society is just as abstract as the pure concept of the individual, and abstract, too, is the allegedly eternal antithesis between the two. Where the truth and falsity, justice and injustice, of these two moments lie, where the substance and where the appearance – this cannot be established once for all in terms of generalising definitions, but only by means of the analysis of concrete social relations and of the concrete forms the individual takes on within these relations.[16]

Horkheimer and Adorno go on to argue that the 'human being is capable of realising himself only within a just and humane society'.[17] The concrete individual in capitalist society is, by definition, not capable of 'realising himself' because he experiences himself as an alienated and fragmented being. It is only in the 'future' that the individual truly becomes himself, but this future depends on the prior condition that men actively work to transform the 'present'. If we are to talk of humanism therefore, then it can only be in the future, a future which constantly recedes as capitalism develops new strategies to retain its hold on the minds of individuals. In Marcuse's view this image of a humane future is problematic given the overwhelming power of the media as instruments of ideological domination.[18] For Lefebvre, the future is circumscribed by the ideology of consumerism.[19] And as Perry Anderson has observed, western Marxism in its recent theoretical formulations tends to be profoundly pessimistic about the future,[20] but this is even more true of those 'liberal' social science perspectives which define themselves as humanistic. However, my concern here is not so much in spelling out the reasons for pessimism, but rather, to examine the claim that a humanist approach to contemporary social existence must of necessity be an exercise in reification and abstract essentialism.

The criterion of concreteness

In talking about the concrete individual in concrete social relations we have to be very sure that we do not confuse the particular life of one individual with the concrete conditions in which the majority of individuals live out their lives. It may well be that we can describe a person's biography in the minutest detail, but this does not mean we have concretised his life. For example, we might write a biography of a black writer in the United States which stresses the influence other American authors have had on him, or we might concentrate on his childhood experience etc., but if we only do this, *and do not characterise his situation as a black writer in America*, then it is obvious that we have failed to concretise the world he lives in. Of course, this is an extreme and unfair example. The point I am making is that concretisation does not depend on the specification of an individual instance. Obviously each individual life is concretised in terms of a particular and unique experience of the world, but this does not tell us very much.

When we look at the typical concepts employed by practitioners to describe the individual's situation in the contemporary world, is there any way in which we can say that they concretise that situation? Can we concretise such concepts as the alienated individual, the anomic individual, the privatised individual, the fragmented individual, or are all such concepts examples of the abstract humanism which Marxists inevitably discover in the work of academic social scientists and philosophers?

Is it possible to concretise the position of a worker without having to resort to an interpretation of his subjective state, or does concretisation involve a total description of his situation? This question is not purely theoretical – because it is easy enough to point to specific conditions in this or that factory which demonstrate the concrete particulars of his work-life, but it is not so easy to concretise the totality of his life without introducing concepts like alienation. The alienated worker, in Marx's sense, is not only alienated at work – his alienation is total, encompassing all social relationships. Accordingly, the alienated worker can only be concretised in the context of a given set of social relations which enter into his subjective world as 'givens'. It is precisely the 'givenness' of his world of work, his family life and his personal relationships which constitutes both his subjective and objective reality. If we are to speak of the concrete individual, then this must of necessity entail the totality of his situation, including his experience of that situation – that is, his subjective definition of the reality of the world as having a degree of immutability. In short, the alienated worker in capitalist society cannot be described independently of his consciousness of that society. In concretising his situation we are saying something about his total environment in the total situation including his consciousness of this involvement. But alienation is also about false consciousness – hence, in concretising the individual, we are not merely saying that consciousness is an integral part of his life-situation, we are also saying that this consciousness is located in a historical situation in which his view of himself is false and distorted. Put differently, the concretisation of the worker in capitalist society logically necessitates taking into account the 'illusory forms' which 'mystify his consciousness'. [21]

If the foregoing approximates to a Marxist view of the 'concrete individual' in capitalist society, then in what way do humanistic formulations of the individual fail to meet the criterion of concreteness? If we talk about the alienated worker, then why not the privatised worker, the fragmented individual, the anomic individual and so forth? Are not all these concepts interchangeable? For example, in Ruitenbeek's description of the atomised and isolated human-being caught in the 'web of organisation' and pushed to the limits of his privacy by the ineluctable demands of the bureaucratic state, is this not simply a distorted version of alienation? Undoubtedly, there is a superficial resemblance between all these concepts, but the crucial difference is that Marxists insist that none of the humanistic concepts are grounded in concrete situations. Does this mean that all such concepts are ideological constructions of illusory forms? Is there no way that that which practitioners like Erikson, Laing, Goffman, Mead and humanists in general could defend themselves against such charges?

140

Humanist defences

One such defence may well be that concretisation does not commit the practitioner to a discussion of totality. There is no reason why we should not study individuals in specific contexts and, by so doing, concretise the seminal forces at work in their lives here and now. For example, while it is possible that the explanation of a high divorce rate in a society can be explained, in the last instance, by the contradictions of capitalism, or the dissolution of totality, this in itself is not decisive for explicating the situation at hand. If a husband, wife and their children are engaged in a mutual exercise of destroying each other emotionally, then their predicament is obviously one in which the concrete particulars are immediately available for investigation. While it is conceivable that the middle-class or working-class status of the participants is of direct relevance to the practitioner's understanding of this family's current situation, this in itself does not necessarily mean that they have grasped the reality of their everyday life as they express it in language, emotion, gesture and action. Consequently, concretisation may simply be a methodological stipulation about preserving the phenomenological present. (By this I mean taking the experiences of participants at their face value, both as a resource and topic of inquiry.) Thus, in the case of the family locked in its encapsulated emotional world, it is probable that their own explanation of their behaviour would be couched in the language of motive attribution, rather than in a vocabulary which 'totalises' or 'contextualises' their situation. From the practitioner's point of view the problem, therefore, is to ground or concretise his explanation in the participants' experiential world. As long as he has direct access to that world then it is conceivable that he may indeed manage to concretise their behaviour. (But, I suppose the question remains as to the validity and reliability of any technique claiming direct access to participants' definition of the situation.)

In very broad terms, therefore, humanists could defend themselves against the charge of abstract individualism and essentialism by maintaining that, on the contrary, their descriptions of individual and social life are genuinely grounded in the lived experiences of the participants themselves. There are a number of possible strands to this defence, two of which I shall consider below.

First, it could be argued, and is argued, that a concrete humanism starts with the body. The body is the fulcrum of experience – it is the most concrete of all our realities. A social science which ignores the body, therefore, is in danger of losing itself in pure abstract discourse –

The body is established as the final, and perhaps only, dense secure moral value in our world. Nothing else is shared as surely as it. In extreme situations, the body alone is left to signify with. When the situation makes verbal statement impossible or robs it of any meaning, the body can be used as an ultimate *non placet*.

The body is established as the locus of all ethical experience. Nothing happens to me which does not happen to my body. Insult the body and you insult the freedom within it. Attack the body, you attack the person. Torture the body, you mutilate the individual. Kill the body and you kill the spirit which inhabits it. For we are never in doubt as to where to place the wreath. The value has spoken and the body is dead. But with a sure hand we lay the wreath on the body itself, last shred and remnant of the spirit which worked with such powerful direct effect in the world.[22]

This theme of the ravaged and exploited body is a recurring one among humanists, but not only humanists. It is to be found in various radical analyses of the role of authoritarian morality in the suppression of sexuality. In addition, the body is seen as the prime symbol of resistance to technological rationality by the psychedelic left which imbues it with an almost mystical significance. While there are obvious excesses in current discussions, there can be no doubt that a concrete humanism stands or falls by its attitude towards the body. This is not simply to repeat phenomenological discussions about 'embodiment'; rather it is to point to the fact that social theory in general treats the body as if it has no existence outside the social world. This is an old story and it is not resolved by pious incantations about the centrality of bodily experience. In the final analysis, the body always pushes itself to the forefront of consciousness – it cannot be glossed over or rationalised away. Poverty might have a cultural connotation for some practitioners,[23] but its ultimate grounding is in the violence it does to the body. While it may be conceivable that 'homelessness' describes the subjective state of individuals in modernising societies who find that their old institutions no longer confer identity, it is also true that for the majority of individuals the world over, identity problems take second place to hunger. The violence done to the body by hunger, must to a great extent provide the rationale for any social theory which is both emancipatory and humanistic.

In saying that identity problems take second place to hunger and poverty we are not thereby advancing a 'full bellies' model of social behaviour. We are simply stating the fundamental belief of concrete or radical humanism, namely that to be human implies the right to a full belly. The fact that this belief is hidden behind elaborate theoretical language means that for a great part of the time radical humanists and Marxists lose themselves and their audiences in what could be called the 'false concreteness'[24] of everyday life. While it is evident that poverty is grounded in the relationship between capital, labour and wages, it is not enough to spell this out in terms of theoretical categories which stress the objective character of this relationship. Totality means nothing to hungry people unless they can understand its relevance to their actual situation.

A *second strand* in the humanist defence against the charge of essentialism and abstract individualism is to be found in the current attempt to ground the linguistic practices of the social sciences. The object of linguistic therapy is to bare the way in which both practitioners and participants reify the world, so that they lose sight of the common-sensical procedures which are believed to underpin all discourse. In achieving this object practitioners attempt to concretise language in everyday life situations – in a naturalistic framework in which participants accomplish their sense of social structure through talk and listening, etc.

The implicit premise of this exercise is the belief that language defines man and that everyday language is the ultimate ground on which all other discourse depends. In concretising speech, the practitioner concretises the individual and society. Accordingly, it is 'talk' which enables practitioners to concretise social activity:

> This concern has to do with the fact that talk is not merely sentence production, it is social exchange and social coordination. Talk is interactional. Instead of a model of language use and of language user we need to develop a model of interaction and of use of interactional abilities. Our concern here, therefore, is with interactional skills rather than linguistic ones. How is talk an interactional skill, one that enters into the organisation of everyday activities? How is it a regulative and a constitutive feature of that organisation?[25]

Concreteness therefore involves a notion of indexicality. While it is very hazardous to attempt to interpret ethnomethodological arguments, one thing seems certain, and that is the whole ethnomethodological project partly depends on whether or not practitioners can establish the ground rules for interactional competence. In concentrating on talk, ethnomethodologicians assume that: 'talk is experienced by participants as an ordered phenomenon. The ethnomethodological strategy is to explicate the *methods* by which glosses (talk) are produced and heard as ordered phenomena.'[26]

In 'explicating the methods by which talk is produced' the emphasis moves away from a view of the concrete individual as embedded in an institutional nexus, to one in which talk is a constitutive element of both individuality and institutions. The concreteness of the individual is exhibited in his interaction competence, that is in his ability to use talk as a means to establish his own sense of reality. In a sense, there is no reality outside the talk which produces it.

There are, of course, a number of problems associated with the view that talk concretises individual and social processes. These problems arise to a large degree because practitioners very often take as self evident some of the examples employed by linguistic philosophers. Marcuse, despite his pariah status for various English philosophers and social scientists, makes a very telling point about what he calls false concreteness:

> Throughout the work of the linguistic analysts, there is this familiarity with the chap on the street whose talk plays such a leading role in linguistic philosophy. The chumminess of speech is essential inasmuch as it excludes from the beginning the high-brow vocabulary of 'metaphysics'; it militates against intelligent non-conformity; it ridicules the egghead. The language of John Doe and Richard is the language which the man in the street actually speaks; it is therefore the token of concreteness. *However, it is also a token of a false concreteness.* The language which provides most of the material for the analysis is a purged language, purged not only of its 'unorthodox' vocabulary, but also of the means for expressing any other contents than those furnished to the individuals by their society. The linguistic analyst finds this purged language an accomplished fact, and he takes the impoverished language as he finds it, insulating it from that which is not expressed in it, although it enters the established universe of discourse as element and factor of meaning.[27]

Marcuse goes on to argue that linguistic analysis, by its abstraction from everyday ordinary language, sterilises and mutilates 'man and nature'. The trivial is elevated to the status of the 'real'. The accusation of trivialisation is a perennial one in the mutual slanging match between linguistic philosophy and its continental adversaries, but my concern here is not in stating the pros and cons of this debate; rather it is to examine Marcuse's assertion about the false concreteness of purged language.

If it can be demonstrated that practitioners do, in fact, operate in this way, then Marcuse's point is a valid one. But he is talking about linguistic philosophers, not about sociologists or ethnomethodologists. On the whole, it would seem to me that ethnomethodologists do not work with purged languages – on the contrary, their commitment to indexicality makes this highly unlikely (the attention they pay to the actuality of talk as it occurs means that they recognise the critical importance of the situation). While linguistic analysis endeavours to demystify speculative metaphysics, ethnomethodology engages in a similar exercise for sociological theory. It is in this context that I think we can claim that 'practitioners often take as self evident some of the procedures employed by linguistic analysis'. The techniques of linguistic analysis are transferred to the analysis of social reality. They become the methods which allow practitioners to demonstrate the way in which 'theorists' accomplish their theories. Hence, although it may be admissible to accept Marcuse's view of the false concreteness of linguistic philosophy, it is not admissible in the case of ethnomethodology, except for those practitioners who mistakenly believe that 'doing ethnomethodology' is equivalent to 'doing linguistic analysis'.

The point of the foregoing discussion is not to defend or attack the ethnomethodological position on indexicality, rather it is to highlight their insistence on talk as providing both the resource and topic of inquiry. Because ethnomethodology as a whole is concerned with the practical investigation of indexicality, this means that there is no way to the concrete individual except through talk. In other words, if we want to grasp the concrete individual in the actuality of his everyday life, we have to do this by discovering him in a situation, or a multiplicity of situations. The great danger in following this strategy is that it might encapsulate the individual in speech and language. Talk demonstrates concreteness, but it does not thereby incorporate all that can be said about an individual.

I have suggested that humanists can, and do, defend themselves against the charge of abstract individualism and essentialism by grounding their practice in the body and speech. But, such a defence may not be enough. Instead of abstract individualism, we could advance an *over-concretised* view of mundane behaviour divorced from the complexities of historical processes. My point is that we must be careful not to concretise individuals in abstract situations. This presumably is what happens when we talk about the suffering ego as the epicentre of individual and social existence. While the individual alone knows the true extent of his own pain and misery, this in itself does not enable us to make sense of the context or the grounding of his misery. Put differently, if we hear somebody speaking about the emptiness and meaninglessness of his life, it is almost impossible to let this stand alone. We simply

145

cannot take such 'speech' at its face value, unless we have some knowledge of the background conditions which have shaped his present psychological state. By background conditions I mean that we can situate the speaker – we know who he is – or we think we know that his speech is *typical* of a given category of persons in a given set of circumstances.

It is highly unlikely that concepts like meaninglessness, or identity crisis or alienation, would be part and parcel of the everyday language of participants who have not had access to the 'benefits' of a middle-class education. Accordingly, there are various kinds of speaker. There are different vocabularies rooted in different experiences of the world. While affluent intellectual craftsmen articulate their experience of misery and personal troubles in a self conscious language which confers reality to subjective states, there are those (the majority) who know that misery is concretised in the everyday world of scarcity and deprivation. It is difficult not to agree with Barrington-Moore when he writes that men in general are aware that misery is not merely subjective experience, but that it has its roots in the social world:

> If human beings find it difficult to agree upon the meaning and causes of happiness, they find it much easier to know when they are miserable. Presumably it requires no laboriously accumulated proof to demonstrate that they hardly ever really enjoyed (1) being tortured or slaughtered by a cruel enemy; (2) starvation and illness; (3) the exactions of ruthless authorities who carry off the fruits of prolonged labour; (4) the loss of beloved persons through the acts of others over which one has little or no control; (5) rotting in prison, being burned at the stake, or even simply losing the means of livelihood for the expression of heretical or unpopular beliefs. [28]

This listing of human miseries contrasts with those 'humanistic' perspectives which talk of the human condition as though it is immediately available as a resource and topic of inquiry. If humanism is to be defended, then this defence cannot be carried out in the name of such abstract categories as the 'condition of man' or 'ontological insecurity'.

The invasion of consciousness

In insisting that a humanist position involves concretising individuals in concrete situations, we are faced with a paradox. On the one hand, there is the hard political position which argues that personal troubles and private suffering are *not* remedied by *partial* solutions which enable individuals to escape and hide from the world, and on the other hand there are those practitioners who are concerned with the day-to-day miseries of individuals who cannot wait for the revolution. For those trapped in the everyday world, the promise of a humane future may not mean much when measured against the possibility of an immediate solution of their private misery. The experience of such misery is concrete even when there *appear* to be no real grounds for the experience. There is nothing abstract about sexual impotence, loneliness and the real (or imaginary) intrusion of the world into the private preserves of the self. It is true that the *expression* of such misery is usually located in academic analyses of middle-class people, but this it to point to the middle-class origins of certain kinds of private trouble – it does not deny their reality.

Moreover, to revert back to the discussion on the biographical self; if the self is experienced and described as fragmented, as though it is in full flight from the imperatives of the public sphere, then it is not too far-fetched to see this process as being symptomatic of the realities of late capitalism. Obviously, this is a deeply pessimistic point of view. It implies that we must ground our description of everyday life and the as-if self in the reality of the market-place or in the reality of the state.

In other words, private life is bureaucratised and commercialised. In retreating into the family, into the world of leisure (sport, hobbies, travel, sex), in retreating into fantasy, the individual discovers that he is caught by the very enemy he was supposed to have left behind on the factory floor and in the office. There is no escape from the insidious influence of the public sphere even in the privacy of one's bedroom. Indeed, what goes on in one's bedroom is generally available on the television screen.

Sexual privacy, supposedly an essential requirement of personal identity, is now subject to the dispassionate analysis of experts who comment on technique, performance and impotence, to a world-wide audience who suddenly discover their own sexual inadequacies. In addition, audiences are bombarded with images of sexual fulfilment which are presented as being immediately obtainable provided one rushes out and buys the latest car or smokes the right brand of cigar. Sexual privacy is, therefore, an illusion because each sexual episode is geared into a vast network of performance-requirements, which in turn generate anxiety about the sexual adequacy of the participants.

In essence, the privatisation of sex, and indeed privatisation in general, can be defined as the process whereby the subjective experience of individuals in industrialised and capitalist societies is distorted and influenced by the media and bureacracy. Instead of

147

privacy, therefore, privatisation involves the massive intrusion of the public world into the life of the individual. The retreat into the family, or the escape into fantasy, or the search for the true self, or the search for complete sexual fulfilment, are simply aspects of the invasion of consciousness by the instruments of technological and bureaucratic rationality. In a sense, privatisation is about the bureaucratisation of consciousness or, more appositely, in Hans Enzenberger's terms, 'the industrialisation of the mind'. There is no way in which human beings in the late twentieth century can really claim that they alone are responsible for the integrity of the self or the uniqueness of their biography.

Enzenberger argues that we have not fully accepted or comprehended the extent to which consciousness has been absorbed into the industrial world. We talk about the moral consequences of privatisation, but we still do not adequately understand the process whereby individuals become privatised. The standard treatment of privatisation is usually moralistic – it has strong mental health assumptions built into it. The media are seen as the means whereby the individual is estranged from himself and his society. Nevertheless, as Enzenberger points out, similar concepts appear in radical critiques of bourgeois culture, except that instead of mental health themes, *manipulation* is the name of the game.

Both in 'radical' and 'mental health' formulations the individual is pictured against a background of ideological and cultural forces which threaten to overwhelm him. Both positions emphasise the role of the media. In the mental health image, the media are a source for new forms of self definition and fantasy – they replace the old identity-conferring institutions by providing models of behaviour and morality which become universal criteria. So, for example, we are presented with the myth of a perfect sexuality ostensibly available to us all. Night after night on the television screen we witness simulated passion, which ten years ago would have provoked outcries of moral outrage, but which today is regarded as providing an honest account of free and uncontaminated sexuality. But, argue the mental health theorists, this is exactly what media-sex does not do – all it does is to raise expectations about sexual utopias which are not realisable, the net result being that individuals are left with a diffuse and generalised anxiety about the status of their sexuality. Instead of genuine sexual liberation, the media distort and emasculate the reality of bodily processes. Moreover, there is no indication that the so called 'eroticisation of everyday life' really represents a genuine shift towards the ideal of full sexual fulfilment. Mental health critiques, therefore, are concerned with culture and its erosion by the media.

148

The media are supposed to cheapen and devalue individual and social experience. In the case of sex, this is immediately apparent in the way in which it is used by the advertising industry to sell consumer durables and the like.

In radical formulations, the argument is not so much that the media misrepresent and distort reality, but that they are used by certain interests to manipulate reality. But as Hans Enzenberger argues:

> The New Left of the sixties has reduced the development of the media to a single concept – that of manipulation. This concept was originally extremely useful for heuristic purposes and has made possible a great many individual analytical investigations, but it now threatens to degenerate into a mere slogan which conceals more than it is able to illuminate, and therefore itself requires analysis.
>
> The current theory of manipulation on the left is essentially defensive; its effects can lead . . . to defeatism. . . .
> Objectively, it corresponds to the absolutely correct view that the decisive means of production are in enemy hands. But to react to this state of affairs with moral indignation is naive. There is in general an undertone of lamentation when people speak of manipulation which points to idealistic expectations as if the class enemy had ever stuck to the promises of fair play it occasionally utters. The liberal superstition that in political and social questions there is such a thing as pure, unmanipulated truth, seems to enjoy remarkable currency among the socialist Left. It is the unspoken basic premise of the manipulation thesis.[29]

It is not my intention to embark upon an analysis of the media. My concern here is to examine the plausibility of the argument which claims that contemporary consciousness is trapped and moulded by the media. This argument has in recent years dominated the thinking of the Frankfurt School (particularly Marcuse and Habermas), and this is in keeping with their general attitude to mass culture, as expressed by Max Horkheimer in the late 1930s:

> The so-called entertainments, which have taken over the heritage or art, are today nothing but popular tonics, like swimming or football. Popularity no longer has anything to do with the specific content or the truth of artistic productions. In the democratic countries, the final decision no longer lies with the educated but with the amusement industry. Popularity consists of the unrestricted accommodation of the people to

what the amusement industry thinks they like. For the
totalitarian countries, the final decision rests with the managers
of direct and indirect propaganda, which is by its nature
indifferent to truth.[30]

The fear of manipulation, the fear of being engulfed by the
cheapening and depersonalising world of mass culture, is very
much in the minds of those who equate technological rationality
with political and ideological domination. Technology is not
neutral – it is determined by structural forces typical of late
capitalism and state capitalism in Russia and Eastern Europe. The
media are, thus, simultaneously instruments of social control, and
sources of self definition. They are the means whereby the 'system
of domination' perpetuates itself in the consciousness of men.
Moreover, they are assumed to ensure the continuation of the
process whereby everyday life is bifurcated into private and public
spheres. The private sphere is ostensibly divorced and separate
from the world of work, but is linked to this world by the
instruments of mind control. Hence, the whole notion of privileged
access and control over one's mind and self processes is an illusion.
The very fantasies we indulge in are products of the media.
Subjectivity is dominated by images gleaned from the cinema,
television and the sportsfield.

In the mental health model 'fantasy' is regarded as being
symptomatic of the influence of 'sick' institutions on the psyches of
human beings in industrial societies. Sick institutions mirror
themselves in the fantasy life of millions of people who have lost
the ability to construe themselves as autonomous beings. The
mental health critique of the media and the communication
industry in general, is therefore complementary to the radical view
that argues that they are mere instruments of domination. In both
cases, the interior life of an individual is seen as being determined
and trapped by the media. The critical difference between mental
health and radical viewpoints, is that in the former the individual's
condition is attributed to mistakes in public policy or to the
misunderstanding of the consequences of technological advance,
whereas in the latter his condition is considered to be directly
attributable to ideological control.

The trouble with both the mental health and radical positions is
that it is difficult to gather evidence for or against their respective
positions. While it is easy enough to point to the broad institutional
parameters in which individuals live out their everyday lives, it is
far more difficult to specify the contents of their subjective lives. In
arguing for a concrete humanism, it is no use simply guessing that
everyday consciousness is distorted and controlled by the media.

Even at a very prosaic level such a claim is nonsensical. It assumes that human beings are completely subject to external control factors which make it impossible for them to ever act independently of the specifications implicit in the public sphere. At a simplistic level this cannot be the case. Although it appears to be impossible to conceive of contemporary consciousness as not being influenced by the media, this is not equivalent to saying that it is controlled by the media.

Nevertheless, despite the objections to the argument which encapsulates the 'mind' within the parameters of technological rationality, there is little doubt that a great many human beings experience and concretise the world in terms of their feeling of entrapment within the limits set by technology, bureaucracy and media control. The concretisation of this kind of response to technological rationality is the main task of the humanist and radical sociology. It is also my belief that it is one of the explicit tasks of emancipatory praxis whether it calls itself Marxist or not.

Recapitulation and conclusion

In the first chapter of this book I argued that the humanist position in sociology, as well as the other social sciences, is under attack from various quarters. In particular, 'structuralism' has questioned the apparent obsession with consciousness and the self which appears to dominate interpretative sociology and phenomenology. More specifically, this attack, especially from the point of view of Althusser and his associates, argues that contemporary sociology is ideological and hence incapable of coming to grips with the real problems of political economy. While I have sympathy with this point of view, this does not mean that humanism must be dismissed from the practice and theory of sociology. It depends ultimately on what is meant by humanism. If what is meant is speculative metaphysics or some vague commitment to 'the individual' and so forth, then humanism should obviously be relegated to the scrap heap. The trouble is, however, that the baby is thrown out with the bath water. Put differently, the negation of the self and the denial of the relevance of consciousness for the human and social sciences, entails an explicit denial of the reality and critical aspects of human *experience*. It would seem to me that when we argue for concretisation (that is, when we assert that individuals should only be specified in real concrete situations), this must also involve an argument for the concretisation of experience. Hence, it makes no sense to speak of exploitation without speaking of the experience of exploitation. It may well be that participants do not know that they are being exploited, but this is not equivalent to

151

asserting that they have no experiences at all which are significant for our understanding of exploitation.

The distinction that Wright-Mills[31] made between private troubles and public issues may not strike some practitioners as being theoretically fertile, but it seems to me that he clearly makes the point that private experiences are rooted in social reality. The problem, from the point of view of the practitioner, is somehow to relate experience to political, social and economic issues. Furthermore, not only must private troubles be contextualised in terms of historical and structural processes, but they must be concretised at the level of experience. Of course, difficulties arise when 'experience' is given priority over the public sphere so that all social processes are described as though they were appendages to private troubles. This presumably is why there has been such a sharp reaction to perspectives which emphasise psychic suffering or mental health problems. They appear to ignore the concrete situation in which suffering is located. Thus, when some practitioners talk about the 'search for identity' when a society is undergoing its worst unemployment crisis for decades, this does appear to be the grossest sort of romantic self indulgence. But again, this is not to say that concepts like identity-loss or alienation are merely illusory or mystical. If we accept that private troubles are not figments of romantic imagination then we must, of necessity, also accept that there is a language or vocabulary which articulates the experience of private troubles.

The real difficulty with private troubles is that they tend to be described as though they belonged exclusively to the middle class. Certainly the working class is described in terms of its deprived status, but in the main this description is couched in the language appropriate to the study of social problems, not private problems. It might well be, therefore, that when we speak of privatisation or homelessness, etc., we are in fact employing concepts which concretise experience in a middle-class world, which has no real relevance to working-class experience. Surely this is too far-fetched. Although privatisation is usually spelt out in terms of such dimensions as the decline of community, consumerism, embourgeoisement and familialism, the implication is, that as a phenomenon it is rooted in the experience of capitalist society, not merely the encapsulated experience of the middle classes. Consequently, it could be argued that while we may reject the embourgeoisement thesis as being grounded in a peculiarity optimistic liberal reading of the class structure of western society, we may not be able to reject the privatisation argument *en toto*, for the simple reason that its reality is attested to by the *apparent* increasing tendency for personal life to move away from the world of work.

It is precisely the divorce of private life from the factory, the office and the industrial world in general, which makes the language of privatisation so pervasive. Again, it must be emphasised, privatisation is not to be equated with embourgeoisement, nor is it a tendency which allows millions of people to withdraw from social ties. Rather, it is best described or defined as that process which commercialises and bureaucratises personal life. Thus, as a process, privatisation can be located in the elaboration of the social division of labour. What makes for confusion is not the process of privatisation *per se*, but the *language* which both practitioners and participants use in order to demonstrate their experience of the privatised state. Although this language may be arcane, ambivalent and psychologistic, it is nevertheless a genuine response to privatisation, despite the obvious ideological implications of any perspective which emphasises the individualistic roots of our contemporary social crisis.

An American Marxist puts it this way:

A collective consciousness of great diversity has been created. Experienced personally as individual and unique, it is simultaneously integral to and shaped by capitalist development. Non-marxist thinkers have always understood this development ideologically, abstracting either the pole of personal aloneness or the pole of social control. Their theories of the twentieth century portray either 'mass society', 'other directed man', 'men without qualities', 'organisation man', 'conformism', the 'rise of the masses', or, the polar opposite, 'existential man', 'irrational man', 'psychological man', 'post-industrial' or 'post-scarcity' man, man for whom hell is other people. In fact, capitalism has mass-produced specific forms of personal life, and of individuality, which simultaneously reinforce and threaten capitalist hegemony.[32]

In recognising the ideological connotation of those theories which 'abstract the pole of personal aloneness' we do not necessarily have to assent to the proposition that they are nothing but examples of middle-class ideology. If it is true that capitalism has produced a multiplicity of forms of personal life, then it is inappropriate to deny these forms some kind of theoretical expression. In other words, the ideological rooting of 'the privatised world' in middle-class perspectives does not, of itself, invalidate their reality or relevance.

It is precisely at this point that the case for a humanistic sociology stands or falls. My argument is that the experience of privatisation is dependent on the structural location of practitioners and participants in late capitalist societies in which the separation of the private and public spheres precipitates individualistic and mass society formulations. The fact that such formulations tend to be astructural and ahistorical does not detract from the believed-in reality of privatised experience. Hence, the privatised world is concretised for participants by their *experience* of the world. This means that a concrete humanism is concerned with *both the concrete situation, and the experience of that situation*. There is nothing earth-shattering in this – it replicates old arguments about the interplay between superstructure and infrastructure, but instead of simply relegating privatised experience to the realms of illusion and ideology, I am suggesting that forms of personal life dominate the consciousness of a large proportion of human beings in capitalist and industrial societies. If we are to talk of human liberation and emancipation, then it makes no sense to dismiss privatisation as being epiphenomenal or marginal to our understanding of the way in which participants experience the everyday world. This means that, to a certain extent, we cannot ignore the kind of evidence offered by practitioners whose focus of interest is centred on the problem of the fragmentation of consciousness in the contemporary world. Indeed, if we want to talk of false consciousness, then it is no use denying the reality of the fragmentation of consciousness as a phenomenon rooted in everyday life. The obviousness of this is often forgotten, when it is sometimes argued that the fragment-ation of experience and self is simply a peripheral consequence of the social division of labour. It is a major consequence.

While it could be maintained that, for *some* purposes, the biographical self remains the dominant emphasis in our view of the individual in western society, it is also true that the belief in fragmentation is pervasive among intellectuals as well as large sections of western populations who have been exposed to the supposed benefits of affluence and a higher education. These benefits, such as they are, have produced a high degree of introspective self consciousness which invariably leads to pessimism and defeatism. I say invariably, because it is difficult to discover in western literature and social thought, since the rise and defeat of Fascism, any real belief in the possibility of individual and social transformation. Put differently, while it may be difficult to demonstrate the empirical grounding of fragmentation in the everyday life of the majority of the population (in the sense that the biographical self is still their master stereotype), there can be no doubt that fragmentation is being 'sold' by the fragmented minority to increasing numbers of people. The actuality of fragmentation is reinforced by the propagandising of fragment-ation, or, to put it more strongly, more and more people are becoming privatised.

The question is 'why should so many participants accept the pessimistic imagery of this minority unless it somehow is resonant of their own actual experience?' If more and more people are trapped by the private sphere while simultaneously losing any real control over the work world, then perhaps it is not surprising that pessimism is the dominant mood of our time. Contemporary pessimism is not simply a form of academic and literary self indulgence (although, admittedly, this is often the case). Rather, pessimism is a concretisation of the subjective experience of millions of participants who somehow know that 'Something Happened' to their lives, but are not necessarily able to articulate that 'something'. The fact that Marxists claim that this pessimism is a form of defeatism, a form of ideological quietism, does not mean that we can simply afford to dismiss it out of hand.

At the end of the last chapter I asked two questions:

1 Even if we grant that identity and self processes can be accounted for in social and linguistic terms, does this have any theoretical import for sociology?

2 Granting the reality of the split between the private and public spheres, between personal troubles and public issues, in what ways does this split have any relevance for a sociology which defines itself as emancipatory?

My answers to both these questions have been indirect. I have continued to speak of the self and identity as though they concretise the lived experience of participants. But, by implication, I have suggested that the notion of the biographical self as a self contained entity which challenges the world as a universal hero, is a myth. The biographical self is under attack, not merely because it is epistemologically irrelevant, but also because the concrete experiences of human beings in industrial societies are fragmented.

Ideas of wholeness, autonomy, self determination and true identity are taken up with such ferocity precisely because they seem to provide a substitute for a lost world in which the biographical self was at 'home'. In the language of contemporary pessimism, the contemporary self is on a never-ending trip or journey to salvation, to certainty, to an inner reality which, in the end, turns out to be a carbon copy of the dream world projected by the media and the advertising industry. But, as Stan Cohen and Laurie Taylor put it:

> In everyday life, this sense of self seems doomed to remain a partial construction. It is never fully articulated in any one of our life worlds, for our sense of relativity ensures that we give less than full personal commitment to each one of them. Our sense of self flits about our everyday lives, it is a resource

> which we may summon when we are described as creatures of routine, when we are declared to be no more than what we do. It is an inner point of reference which helps us to defend ourselves against paramount reality, but when we come to look for it as a distinctive entity, a guarantee of our independence and individuality, it is peculiarly illusory. It is almost as if our true self has been stolen from us and we are left with only traces, echoes, memories. The intimations of self we have do not cohere; they hang about our lives but do not seem to constitute it.[33]

The notion of the true self that has been stolen from us, the sense of loss and separation informing the literature of alienation and anomie, the impotence in the face of political and social imperatives, all the benchmarks of privatisation can be discerned in the increasing tendency for social theory to retreat into partial perspectives in which the elusive self is elevated into a universal fraudulent performer, or it is made the focus of metaphysical pain. Yet it is, paradoxically, in the *particularised partial* views of those sociologies and philosophies which highlight the estranged self and the fragmentation of experience, that we may find the means to symbolise and articulate twentieth-century consciousness. This is not to say that we can employ these sociologies and philosophies to change the world, or even adequately to understand it, but it does mean our experience of this world can somehow be reconstituted in terms which ring true to a large number of people. However, there is a peculiar dilemma for those practitioners who talk about privatisation and the loss of identity from the vantage point of a secure middle-class existence. There is a very strong temptation to read one's own predicament into the world. One can write one's lectures and monographs in a study in an executive-designed house, in a middle-class estate, and convince oneself that privatisation is an inevitable and pervasive process. Moreover, one can begin to feel that this is the way the world is, and that consequently there is no way in which one can realistically place oneself on the chopping block of political commitment. Certainly, one can make the right sort of noises at the right sort of time. We can sign petitions, sometimes demonstrate – we can convince ourselves that, in the final analysis, we are somehow providing the means whereby our students can obtain a liberal education which allows them to make the right kind of informed rational choice; we can also convince ourselves that the books we write, the papers we give, the research we do, is ultimately grounded in some kind of valedictory praxis, or, that they somehow make a contribution to knowledge. It might well be some practitioners feel no guilt about their academic practice, or, if they do, manage successfully to repress it, but I must admit I have not found very many in the latter category, except perhaps those sociologists who believe that sociology is a profession.

In writing about such a topic as privatisation, then, one is very much aware that its relevance may be severely curtailed by the limiting boundaries of one's own experience. There is, in other words a strangely apolitical ambience to those viewpoints which are focused on the entrapment of the individual in the structures of his society. Entrapment implies passivity, acceptance of the *status quo* and the general belief in the immutability of social structures. A middle-class academic writing about the horrors of privatisation in the suburbs is, perhaps, responding autobiographically to his own entrapment and, in so doing, is merely reinforcing his own political impotence – or pandering to his own guilt about his academic status. Nevertheless, there *is* a privatised world in the suburbs, there *are* middle-class housing estates, there *are* high-rise developments in which men and women find themselves to be politically impotent and trapped. There are literally millions of people in western societies whose experiences are *partially* shaped by the ideological imperatives implicit in the mass-media, and so forth. In addition, the consequences of the social division of labour – that is, the increasing tendency for the private and work worlds to move away from each other, and the resultant pluralisation of life-worlds which this involves – all this is not a figment of the imagination. Nor, for that matter, is the accompanying fragmented consciousness which informs contemporary social existence. What *is* a figment of the imagination, what is blatantly defeatist, is the accompanying belief that all this is inevitable.

Defeatism and pessimism appear to be written into both academic sociology and aspects of western Marxism. It may well be that pessimism is the only realistic posture to adopt, given the complexity and apparent intractability of contemporary capitalism – it may well be that the experience of Fascism, the apparent defeat of the European working class, the permanent threat of thermonuclear extinction, the proliferation of personal troubles, our encapsulation in academic institutions which reinforce academic marginality – it may well be that all these factors enter in to the obsessive interest some of us exhibit in the privatised experience, but this interest may well be a reflection of our own experience of privatisation, our own introspective middle-class guilt, and our subsequent translation of this guilt into partial sociologies.

So, in the face of the black mood of despair that informs social theory, it is not surprising that defeatism is so prevalent. It is also

157

not surprising that so many practitioners (as well as participants) undertake the voyage in search of true identity. This is the ultimate admission that all the tools of analysis and empirical inquiry are incapable of handling the urgency of social, political and personal troubles.

Perry Anderson has written persuasively of the pessimism to be found in western Marxism. He suggests that this is demonstrated at three levels:

> *Firstly* [he argues that ever since the First World War] there was a marked predominance of epistemological work, focused essentially on problems of method. *Secondly*, the major substantive field in which method was actually applied became aesthetics – or cultural superstructures in a broader sense. *Finally*, the main theoretical departures outside this field, which developed new themes absent from classical Marxism mostly in a speculative manner – *revealed a consistent pessimism*. Method as impotence, art as consolation, pessimism as quiescence: it is not difficult to perceive elements of all these in the complexion of western Marxism. For the root determination of this tradition was its formation by defeat – the long decades of set-back and stagnation, many of them terrible ones in any historical perspective, undergone by the Western working class after 1920.[34]

Pessimism, then, informs both academic social science as well as western Marxism. In academic sociology we also have epistemological obsessions, an involvement in cultural processes and a deep-rooted pessimism about the relationship between self and society, and like western Marxism, western academic sociology smells defeat in the air. Yet, I suppose I have in this book defended, and argued for, a concrete humanism which tries to catch the here and now of experience. I have done so in the conviction that any theory of society which has emancipatory pretensions must pay attention to the experiential submerged world of individuals trying to make sense of their predicament, even though their own explanations of this predicament appear to be partial and lacking in epistemological sophistication or political relevance. In other words, although the privatised world offers practitioners opportunities for self-indulgence and pessimism, this does not entitle us to deny the fact of privatisation. Nor does it entitle us completely to ignore those partial sociologies which attempt to give forms of personal life theoretical expression. What may be unforgivable, however, would be to promote a sociology which is exclusively concerned with the primacy of personal troubles and states of consciousness.

158

7 Addendum: Private readings and the dictatorship of the script

Textual exegesis has developed into a fine art in the last few decades, not only among philosophers and literary critics, but among social theorists as well. Structuralism, Semiotics and Hermaneutics in their different ways have set off an explosion of 'readings' of Hegel, Marx, Weber, Freud and others. I have no intention of exploring the complexities of this development, except in the context of a general discussion of the status of interpretation in sociology. Perhaps it would be more accurate to say that I am concerned with the way in which sociologists 'read' society.

It might be supposed that a 'reading' involves a very complicated set of procedures, and this is, of course, true. In reading a text we are governed by certain conventions, relating to syntax, grammar and our expertise in semantic transformation. For the so-called general reader one would expect the 'reading' to reconstitute in his or her consciousness a sense of the 'reality' of the writer's world, not necessarily his intentions, but the fabric of meaning which the text generates for both reader and writer. But in the case of the critic reading the same work, there is the additional task of 'analysis'. What critical standards he employs will condition his evaluation of the text. These critical standards are both idiosyncratic and derivative. For example, it is unlikely that a critic who has been brought up on a diet of the 'classic unities' would warm to the delights of William Burroughs's *Naked Lunch*. This is not to say that he would not react in some unconventional manner by seeing Burroughs as an interesting example of modernist writing, but this does not seem to be on the cards. The point I am making is that, even in the rarified air of literary criticism, the text is not an isolated phenomenon, nor is the critic a solitary hero grappling with the intractability of an opaque text. The critic's vision is partly shaped by the tradition in which he has been raised,

159

and this is not to ignore the more obvious social influences at work. Hence, in reading a text, the critic is consciously (or unconsciously) utilising criteria derived from the readings of other texts. These other texts are the framework for the *present* reading – they provide the climate for interpretation, and the standard of comparison. (Of course, I am greatly simplifying the intricacies of this process.)

What about the sociologist? In theory, we are not supposed to be concerned with textual exegesis – we are supposed to examine and understand society, we are supposed to research the 'reality of social relationships'. In other words, we are supposed to address ourselves to the world outside books, and yet, most of us spend a great part of our lives reading each other's books. Moreover, we continue to 'read' the sociological classics because we are committed to the view that their versions of reality are the source of genuine understanding; that in fact they are the surest guide to the reality which they presuppose. In addition, today we are flooded by new readings, new interpretations and new interpretations of old interpretations. (To the cynical outsider this could appear to be an exercise in futility.) Now, while many of us spend a great part of our academic lives simply reading texts, it is also true that other sociologists and political scientists, economists and the like are doing, or accomplishing, research. They go out into the world, look at it, describe it, and, having used the appropriate techniques of data collection etc., write up their research reports in the hope that other like-minded researchers will find their work of interest and, more hopefully, become part of the empirical infrastructure of social science. But research itself is incorporated into the reading spiral. Papers are given, data and concepts evaluated, interpretations made and more texts are written. The text, the monograph and the 'paper' are the means whereby we confirm our academic reality.

If it is true that sociologists (and other academics) are caught up in 'reading' the world through texts, then does this mean that the text is the only way in which we can know that world? Or alternatively, does reading hide the world by distorting it beyond recognition? The optimistic view is that books and texts are instruments of insight giving us direct access to areas of experience which we would otherwise not encounter. Supposedly, this is the rationale behind the continued use of favourite texts in the teaching of sociology. Students are expected to read the 'classics', key research monographs, various contemporary works, and, if we are very daring, we might include samples of ethnomethodology and structuralism, etc. We tell students that these works are important because they reflect the central concerns of the sociological tradition and that, in addition, their interpretations of society, while not necessarily to be taken at face value, are rooted in the real experiences of practitioners who translated their observations into texts of lasting validity. In our lectures and tutorials we interpret, comment on and emphasise aspects of the writers' 'theory', description, and, in so doing, we add another dimension to the pyramid of interpretative procedures. We say to our students 'concentrate on primary texts, not secondary sources', and then we proceed to tell them that when they do read these 'secondary sources' some are better than others, and so on and so on.

The logic of this process is that we tend to find that the teaching of sociology is geared to the art of textual exegesis – the more successful the student is in learning the rules of this game, the more likely the chance of academic success. In a department where there is a broad consensus about the value of the classics, and especially when this consensus is apparent in the approach to the interpretation of texts, it is very difficult to gain support for 'other' texts or alternative readings of the entrenched works. This is not to say that there is intellectual censorship, rather it is to point to the dominance of a tradition which has nurtured the majority of practising sociologists. Obviously this must not be taken to mean we are prisoners of our texts – this would be to neglect crucial sociological factors which enter into the 'making' of a sociologist (especially, class, ideology and socialisation), but it does highlight the strange enclosed world of sociologists, and, indeed, most academics. How often has one been in the situation when one is 'discussing' a text with colleagues in which the words 'alienation', 'evidence', 'analysis', 'infrastructure' and 'superstructure' are employed in a taken-for-granted fashion. The object of the discussion is somehow to make sense of the conflicting readings of the interpreters. From the outside, such a discussion is a shambles, seeming to be resonant with sociological jargon; from the inside, the jargon has respectability, it is sanctioned by usage and tradition, and it is conceivable that there is some consensus on the 'meaning' of terms. As the discussion continues, it becomes evident that something peculiar is happening. Instead of clarification, ambiguity seems to be the end result of the long hours of debate. This happens not only in the context in which there are a number of diametrically opposed positions about a text, but also when one has reason to believe that the participants are broadly in agreement in respect to the text in question.

For example, if one has read the *Theses on Feuerbach* it is obvious that the 'reading' is not a simple dialogue between the text and reader. There are a great number of theoretical difficulties for anyone trying to understand the 'denseness' of Marx's thought and

161

language. However, after a great effort, you think that you have managed to 'see' what Marx is getting at – with the help or hindrance of a number of relevant commentaries. Then, in a discussion with one's friends and colleagues, the realisation comes that, although they have read the *Theses*, what they say seems to bear no resemblance to your reading. The obvious reasons for this may be that either you or they have misunderstood Marx, and, if this is the case, it is a simple matter to put right; but it is never as simple as this. What happens is that the more one gets involved in attempts to resolve the contradictory 'readings', the more uncertain the whole enterprise becomes. Those in the discussion who ostensibly agree with your interpretation might do so for varying reasons (some of which may have to do with the fact that they have the same political convictions, or they were exposed to the same 'course' at a particular university, or they read the texts and found no other possible interpretation), and yet their agreement is qualified by your own conviction that they too are confused. The question is, why all this ambiguity and confusion? Is it simply that it is a linguistic problem that can be cured by the appropriate linguistic therapy, or is there a far more deep-rooted reason? And what about our students who have to put up with all this, even though they might not suspect that there is a problem?

I am suggesting, in a convoluted manner, that the texts we revere *sometimes* become absolute frames of reference, from which it becomes increasingly difficult to escape, and that consequently, in spite of our best intentions, we 'read' society as a text. Instead of using the 'text' as a construction, we use it as a map – as a literal map. In other words, Durkheimians see the world as Durkheimians, Weberians as Weberians, Marxists as Marxists, ethnomethodologists as ethnomethodologists. Admittedly, I am overstating the case, but this overstatement is grounded in my own tenuous observation of 'everyday life' in sociology departments. The prior question of why one is a Marxist, a symbolic interactionist or a Parsonian, is of course the usual sociological approach to the theoretical and ideological commitments of this or that sociologist – the sociology of knowledge, or the sociology of sociology traditionally copes with the structural location of theoretical perspectives, but it does not handle textual exegesis. Generally texts are seen as good, bad or indifferent examples of the kind of sociology one finds convincing. (Our academic journals are full of reviews of books by hostile 'readers' who take great delight in exposing the stylistic and logical sins of their victims.) I have been constantly amazed at the way in which the entrenched sociological community tries to come to terms with ethnomethodology. Besides the usual tactics of 'incorporation', 'it's all been said before', 'trivialisation', 'it's so bloody obvious', there is also a desperate attempt to question academic credentials of its proponents. Moreover, this state of affairs can be replicated throughout the 'halls of academe'. The beautiful picture of the thrust and counter-thrust of Socratic debate is a myth. Alternative viewpoints, new departures, are the occasion for savage battles in which 'texts' are cited as the ultimate source of legitimation. Again, I must repeat, that this is an exaggerated picture – in practice most of us can, and do, distinguish between the 'world' of the text and the 'world'. The danger, as I see it, lies not so much in allowing the text to dominate one's perception of social reality, but rather in our tendency to legislate the meaning of other texts which we find to be not to our liking.

The legislation of meaning for opposing viewpoints and texts means that it becomes increasingly difficult to see or understand the reality of disparate worlds. This is especially true when the text in question is defined as belonging to a dubious ideological position. For example, in the university context, the compilation of book-lists for courses is an activity which encourages the selection of texts which we believe to be important, representative and relevant to our area of interest. Whether we like it or not, this process can be highly selective – it screens out, albeit unconsciously, those texts which we consider to be unsound or rubbish, and even when we are prepared to recommend 'theoretically' deviant work, this is done under the auspices of a benign condescension, as if to say 'you might want to look at this, it is an example of the sort of thing I have been criticising, it might amuse you, but don't take it too seriously'. Now, it could be argued that this selectivity is an unavoidable consequence of the education game – one can only recommend what you or I as a teacher have found significant – we are not acting as censors but exercising our independent judgment as to what constitutes the best available work in our field. Certainly, this is one unstated assumption behind all discussion of 'rationality' in education. One could have some sympathy for such a position if it were indeed the case, but I suspect that the commitment to rationality is similar to the Smith régime's commitment to democracy – it is nice to pay lip-service to provided it does not do too much damage to ongoing practice.

Like everybody else, I am just as guilty of this attempt to keep the discipline clear of contaminating influences by the technique of sponsoring 'desirable' texts and 'damning' the 'undesirable'. This is a state of affairs to be found in a lot of surprising places, especially in those disciplines which pride themselves on their ability to pursue rational inquiry in a disinterested and logical manner. For instance, the various schools of 'ordinary language

163

philosophers', while setting themselves a limited programme, are openly against 'metaphysics' and other kinds of speculative discourse. By implication, this rules out a fantastic amount of contemporary continental philosophy. Students educated at Oxford and Cambridge are thus not likely to have been encouraged to read Hegel, Heidegger, Sartre, Bachelard, except in a very perfunctory manner. In sociology the position is similar. As 'gate-keepers' we tend to construct our courses around great names and great texts, and we teach these courses in terms of a belief that the 'reading' of 'seminal' texts is a valuable first step in knowing something about reality. The fact that students often find them to be difficult and uninteresting is a monumental irrelevance. Today, other texts have found their niche in the academic game. Reading lists contain the names of Althusser, Habermas, Lévi-Strauss, Garfinkel, Goffman, Wittgenstein, Blum and McHugh, and a host of others. Yet the argument is still from texts – and it follows that if you were taught throughout your undergraduate days by devotees of a particular kind of sociology, it is more than likely that your reading of the world will correspond to theirs.

The world as text

What does it mean to say that we read the world as a text? Surely this cannot apply to all those people who do not read, at least do not read academic texts? Well then perhaps they 'read' the world as a novel, or a detective story or as science fiction? If we are saying that all that is involved is the interpretation of the world, then there is no problem. Everyone interprets the world – perception is not a neutral process – to a certain extent reality is constructed, but presumably we are not saying this. We are saying that, for a great many people exposed to the benefits of an education in sociology and other disciplines, the reading of texts produces a set of beliefs in the reality of the text which is then directly transferred to the world around them. What evidence does one have for such a peculiar claim? The evidence is derived from the language of sociology and the metaphors which have become a part of the normal discourse of the discipline. It is also derived from the associated belief that 'everyday life' exhibits to a very large degree the quality of dramatic structure which allows participants to textualise their experience in such a way that it becomes possible for an 'outsider' to read their scripts. To say that the language of sociology is metaphorical is not to say much, but the metaphors themselves are not simply exercises in poetic licence – they constitute cognitive maps of reality. If, for example, we take some of Durkheim's seminal texts, forgetting for the moment their theoretical significance for sociology, we are faced with a textual world which demands of us a suspension of belief in the actuality of some of the taken-for-granted aspects of 'everyday life'. Although I suppose most of us thought we knew what was meant by the word 'social', when we read Durkheim the 'social' takes on the burden of a very specific formulation. For a lot of people, this formulation replaces the common-sensical view to which they had previously adhered and, indeed, a strange metamorphosis takes place. They now literally 'see' the world through Durkheim's eyes. They become Durkheimians. Now I am not suggesting that a simple reading of *Suicide*, or *The Elementary Forms of Religious Life* immediately shapes cognition (for some people a first reading of Durkheim will have the opposite effect – they will run screaming back to their favourite novel), but I am suggesting that their reading takes place in the context of a system of pressures which subtly, and not so subtly, guide the reader (student) into an interpretative posture. The reader is told that, although there is an element of naïvety in the way in which Durkheim used statistics, or, perhaps, in his unsophisticated view of psychology, nevertheless he was engaged in a scientific enterprise which changed the future direction of sociology. In other words, the reading of texts is reinforced by teaching procedures which help the student to *see* the world.

This entire process is repeated for other theorists, so that the world is caught in a confusing maze of texts. Recently, the most striking instance of this process is the wide acceptance by so many practitioners of the dramaturgical model of social behaviour. After reading Goffman, it was difficult not to be drawn into his world – for some sociologists, including myself, his perception of the intricacies of 'face work' seemed to open up a fresh slant on reality. We found the test of the text to be in the world itself – so an entire vocabulary was imported into the 'everyday life' of a number of sociologists. Clearly one did not mistake the text for the reality, but, inevitably, reality conformed to the 'structure' of the text.

In a work of fiction the writer can impose a reality on the reader – the writer creates an encapsulated world of meaning which appears to obey an inner logic of its own, but it is a fictive reality, even when the writer concerned is a Balzac or Faulkner (whatever we might want to say about the question of realism in literature and art). We do not make the mistake of asserting the equivalence of text and reality. Yet there are occasions when the reading of a novel, or the examination of a work of art, forces us into a state of total acceptance. (Similarly, this happens with more dramatic consequences in the cinema.) Moreover, it could be argued that 'fictive' works have a way of dominating the consciousness of large

165

sections of the reading public, and this might be specially true of those who constitute a self conscious intelligentsia. For a very long time after the 'war' Kafka's 'visions' seemed to many to represent the reality of the human condition, and in another context I know one or two people who have discovered their own version of reality in the antics of Rhinehart's *Diceman*, but, be that as it may, a work of fiction is not a representation of society, although it enters into our perception of reality. But what about sociological texts? Are they fictions?

Elizabeth and Tom Burns write:

> The fictive worlds of the novel and drama are not mirrors of action. They are compositions which 'find out about the changing world on our behalf; they rearrange our complementaries'. . . . The resemblance that the fictive world has with the real world gives its authenticity; what gives it meaning, and us a sense of comprehending the real world better, is the acknowledgement by writer and reader, and playwright, actors and audience, of a universe of fictive worlds, with a grammar of conventions, rules of the game, and conceptual vocabulary of its own, which is again shared by writer and reader, playwright and audience etc.[1]

Now, we might want to suggest that sociological texts are also not 'mirrors of action', but do they 'rearrange our complementaries' as Frank Kermode[2] originally put it? Having read Marx, Weber, Durkheim, Goffman, Parsons, Garfinkel and all the others, can we claim that not only do we comprehend the 'real world' better, but that in addition, the texts themselves are not fictive renderings of that world? (A great many of sociology's critics would subscribe to the view that it is basically a farago of fictions – and inelegant ones at that.) Sociologists as a whole are convinced that the texts they read and write are not merely constructions and inventions. They are supposed to be tools of understanding and interpretations of the world, and as interpretations they encourage certain kinds of reading of evidence, and they discourage other readings. This means that the 'text' is a public attempt to make sense of social experience. When Durkheim wrote *Suicide*, he was offering an interpretation of relationships between suicide rates and structural determinants – he was not trying to sanctify a text. In following Durkheim, readers and interpreters modified, qualified and sometimes rejected his thesis, but while this process was conducted in terms of the evidence offered publicly in research papers etc., simultaneously the text was codified and institutionalised in university courses. So we are in a situation today in which we interpret an interpretation of an

166

interpretation. In practice this means that the interpretative process is a dialogue with books, and not a dialogue with the 'reality', which the books presuppose (granted the possibility that 'reality' is constituted by language, symbols, speech-acts, etc.).

It is one thing to say that texts coerce our reading of reality; it is altogether different to claim that everyday life is textualised. The problem of scripting has received considerable attention in the last few years. Very simply, the idea is that social actors write their own scripts, thereby textualising their behaviour. Scripting involves a continuous process of interpretation, both on the part of the actors themselves, and the outside 'reader' who tries to make sense of the script.

It is the situation which allows the actor to develop his interpretation of the script. Situations vary, and so do interpretations, but the important thing to keep in mind is that the appropriate script resembles other scripts, so that the outside observer believes that he can understand the meaning of the action. If there were no such resemblance, then the task of interpretation would be hazardous. The theatrical mode has been well documented in the sociological literature – its limitations and strengths do not concern me here. What I am concerned with is the actuality of scripting in everyday life. Are there really scripts which human beings translate into performances? If we are concerned with everyday routines then scripts are non-problematic – after all, what is so theatrical about putting on one's shoes in the morning, or drinking a cup of coffee? Nevertheless, it could be argued that it is not the action that is important, but the accompanying 'talk'. People talk to themselves when putting on shoes, or they talk to others; similarly with coffee-drinking. Talk constitutes the 'action' – it is the essential ingredient of a script. Although talk in such routine activities is often predictable – for instance, 'is your coffee strong enough?' or 'pass the sugar', there are occasions when coffee talk is far more dramatic. Again this depends not on the act of drinking coffee, but on the intrusion of other 'realities'. The talk appropriate to the breakfast table is sabotaged when one of the participants has recently been declared redundant or told that he has an incurable disease. There is no script which definitively handles this sort of situation; rather the script writes itself. Instead of 'pass the sugar', the scene becomes saturated with declarations of despair 'What are we going to do?' or perhaps it dispenses with talk altogether.

If we maintain that the script writes itself, then some of the assumptions about the way in which the outside observer or interpreter 'reads' these scripts are questionable. Usually, outsiders (sociologists, anthropologists and the like) have a repertoire of

167

scripts which they try to apply to the scene – in addition, they also carry around with them scripts they have absorbed from the reading of novels, or exposure to the cinema, theatre and television. In observing the scene at the breakfast table, in listening to the talk of participants, it is very easy to fall into the trap of believing that you have heard it all before – it might fit in very nicely with descriptions of family tensions found in standard sociological text-books, or it might remind one of typical episodes from kitchen-sink drama. The typicality of the script appears to be self evident to the observer in spite of variations of a stylistic character. Certainly, there are typical 'resources' to be found in the script. Having a cup of coffee at breakfast, in the example given above, is reminiscent of other scenes from other *contexts*. There is a general expectation that the script will be recognisable as an example of the generality of tragedy in everyday life. Hence, the reading of the concrete grounding of the talk is circumscribed by other readings deriving from other contexts. Can it be claimed that such a reading or interpretation does full justice to the script in question? Can it be caught in the interpretative posture of the reader?

In talking about scripts and texts in everyday life, we unavoidably use criteria from literary discourse. Whether a script is a radio announcement, a television commercial, a play or an academic text, there are certain conventions which shape its structure – these are dependent on the nature of the text, its form, its genre, and the limitations governing any kind of written discourse. Essentially, written texts are not speech acts – though it is often claimed that certain dramatists, novelists and poets approximate in their work to the reality of the speech or talk world. Do sociologists ever approximate to this world? For most of us I would guess not. The texts we read and write are constructed in terms of cognitive categories which are singularly divorced from the accounting and scripting procedures of talk. They presuppose a minimal proficiency in the art of textual construction – put differently, they have a structure which is not necessarily the structure of the speech world. Accordingly, do the scripts of everyday life remain inviolable and beyond interpretation, except to the participants? This is not necessarily true. For one thing, it assumes that the reader, the interpreter, the observer, is incapable of penetrating the mysteries of talk and performance. We assume that participants know what they mean when they engage in talk; they can read the script, so to speak. The observer can also read the script, and imaginatively participate in the action, because talk is not outside his or her experience. Thus, in the texts that sociologists write about everyday life, or in anthropological monographs, the fact that the structure of talk is not mirrored accurately may be a consequence of the formal constraints of written language.

However, this ignores other problems, especially those relating to what ethnomethodologists call 'accomplishing talk'. How do participants go about the business of accomplishing or creating a meaningful script, and how does the sociologist accomplish his own talk about participants' talk? How do we translate participants' talk into sociological talk? Translation is a central dimension in the process of trying to come to grips with the two worlds of participant and reader – it is here more than anywhere else that we are likely to get lost in a maze of opposing insights. In translating a foreign language text the problem is to reconstruct in one's own language the symbolic universe which the writer takes for granted; it involves more than an accurate rendering of the text itself – it also involves a reconstruction of the ambience of the writer's situation.

For example, there is no way in which the English reader can hope to understand Hegel unless he is acquainted with some of the contextual features of Hegel's work. He has to make sense of the cultural code in which Hegel expresses himself, and not merely the purely textual. In other words, translation is not easy. On the other hand, we might want to argue that once the code is broken, then there is no problem – it is simply a matter of putting the pieces of the jigsaw together, and, by extension, the translation of everyday life scripts into the language of sociology is also a question of being able to fit pieces of a jigsaw together. This is altogether too optimistic and mechanistic. It assumes that translation is the process of deciphering discrete units of everyday scripts which are then incorporated into the 'master scripts' of sociology. But, as George Steiner has argued, translation is such a basic part of all communicative and social action that it cannot be subsumed under the rubric of an abstract notion of the perfectibility of the translation process:

> In one sense, each act of translation is an endeavour to abolish multiplicity and to bring different world-pictures back into perfect congruence. In another sense, it is an attempt to re-invent the shape of meaning, to find and justify an alternate statement. The craft of the translator is, . . . deeply ambivalent: it is exercised in a radical tension between impulses to facsimile and impulses to appropriate recreation. In a very specific way the translator 're-experiences' the evolution of language itself, the ambivalence of the relations between language and world, between languages and 'worlds'. In every translation the creative, possibly fictive nature of these relations is tested. Thus, translation is no specialised, secondary

activity at the 'interface' between languages. It is the constant, necessary exemplification of the dialectical, at once welding and divisive nature of speech.[3]

The 'impulse to facsimile', as Steiner puts it, is a perennial occupation of sociologists who want to catch the full flavour of participants' language and conduct. Before the advent of the tape-recorder and other sophisticated electronic equipment, the accuracy of the sociologist's account of his data was presumed to be highly volatile and suspect. The tape-recorder makes all the difference, we are told, because it faithfully records speech as it occurs. Hence, translation into sociological language may be possible, but this assumes that translation is merely an attempt 'to bring different world-pictures back into perfect congruence'. In translating a novel from the French, the translator is not merely a servant of accuracy, he also appears to 're-invent the shape of meaning'. The reading of *The Charter House of Parma* in the original is not equivalent to its reading in English – the translator is not a passive instrument, and his translation will be strongly influenced by interpretative commitments deriving from the English literary scene, as well as his own experience. How different is the sociologist's attempt to translate everyday scripts into the language of sociology? Does the possession of the tape-recorder and suchlike enable him directly to apprehend his data?

The translation of everyday scripts into sociological language should, in principle, be a relatively uncomplicated procedure. After all, it is not as though sociologists are exploring a strange cultural climate – the scripts are supposedly readable because they are readily available on one's cultural doorstep, so to speak. There are countless opportunities to translate scripts into sociological language, but it is precisely here that difficulties abound. Nobody is really interested in 'perfect facsimile', yet the criticisms levelled against 'theorists' are mainly concerned with their departure from everyday life – in their over-abstraction from scripts, and in their 'reinvention' of reality. Granted that translation more often than not *gets away* from the data, are we then expected to let the scripts speak for themselves, without the benefit of an interpretative gloss?

This is plausible only if the data themselves really *do speak for themselves*. For example, if I ask 'How do you read the situation in South Africa?', the possible answers will depend on factors which are not simply matters of straightforward extrapolation from the facts or data. If the question is directed to an expert on South African affairs, then the answer would probably be in terms of history, social structure, economic development and political alignment – also perhaps statistics would be quoted to demonstrate the status of the answer. The same question directed to a black freedom fighter would have a different response. Even though he may or may not have access to the same analytical tools as the 'expert', he will certainly believe that the facts speak for themselves; but this does not have any point of intersection with the methodological insistence that argues for the suspension of interpretation. For participants, everyday life is full of significant scripts which are immediately understood, and are acted out in various situations. When a Black encounters difficulties with the 'pass laws' in South Africa, the scripts are not necessarily predetermined, but they certainly are not open to too much improvisation. How you negotiate with policemen who demand to see your pass is part and parcel of the state of being black in South Africa. It is in this sense that the facts speak for themselves so that it becomes possible for an 'outsider to read the scripts'.

This still leaves us with the problem of trying to relate the scripts to some broader frame of reference – a frame of reference usually sanctioned by allegiance to this or that theoretical scheme, and supported by key texts. How do we get from script to theory? Or, to put it another way, do the social sciences have adequate methods of translation which allow them to respect the integrity of the original data, as well as allowing them to exercise an element of inventiveness? Inventiveness might be a fundamental imperative in the translation of works of literature, but is it so necessary in social science? Surely, it could be argued that inventiveness leads to distortion and even to downright error. Now admittedly armchair speculation about the nature of society often has unfortunate results in that analogies are reified and text-books are written which bring the analogies to life (e.g. the organic and machine metaphors), but this could be said about any academic discipline which endeavours to translate empirical data into a conceptual scheme. The translation of script into theory requires more than a poetic imagination; it also requires a sense of the reciprocal tension between data and theory. It is no use picturing South Africa in terms of a peculiar combination of functionalism and conflict theory unless one is prepared to locate such a combination in the actual scripts of participants. If one does make an excursion into the 'reality' of everyday life by sampling scripts, as in the case of the Black being asked to produce his pass, then whatever theoretical baggage you bring with you is useless unless it points to the tensions within the situation itself. In other words, a sociologist who just happens to be around when the policeman makes his arrest will suffer from conceptual stasis if he does not suspend his inclination to theorise from an entrenched position which has already legislated the meaning of the script.

171

Tension is generated by the attempt to ride two horses simultaneously – that of strict script integrity and the monitoring of theoretical temptations. Hopefully this tension precipitates the 'inventiveness' which Steiner speaks about when works of literature are translated. In the specific context of South African social structure, a policeman arresting a pass offender is obviously not doing anything out of the ordinary. However, if, by some chance, a sociologist is present at this incident, tension is not simply a property of the translation process, it is present in the script itself, in the confrontation of the participants who know all the moves of the game and yet are still prepared for the unexpected – the policeman might accept the validity of the Black's reasons for non-possession of an up-to-date pass, or he may be scared of the threatening posture of onlookers, or he may be following the policy dictates of a new 'humane' approach to pass offenders. The sociologist, provided he has had some previous experience of this kind of situation, should be able to 'read' the script – that is, he should be able to tease out the complicating influences at work. When he does manage to do this, the probability is that it will be treated as an instance of a theoretical perspective – it will be absorbed into a vocabulary which already contains provision for so-called deviant cases. A functionalist-conflict theory mixture certainly does impose limits on what can be read into a situation or script, but our sociologist would not necessarily find this an obstacle, especially if he is convinced that the 'mixture' best explains or accounts for the peculiarities of the script. If this happens, the tension between script and theory is completely absent, for the simple reason that our sociologist has fallen into the trap of the 'perfect facsimile'. He has found what he expected to find: the script conforms to this theoretical commitments.

We seem to have arrived at a 'Catch 22' situation. On the one hand it is argued that the script is inviolate, it stands by itself and therefore translation is a question of 'perfect congruence', and on the other hand the argument is that the script never stands by itself – it needs interpretation, it needs to be subsumed in larger theoretical concerns; but – and it is a big 'but' – the question remains, how do we know that the theoretical concern does, indeed, subsume the script without completely violating its freshness and immediacy? Should we accept the thesis that we are really talking about two different languages which intersect only when the sociologist raids the empirical world in the guise of social researcher or participant observer? In a successful raid the sociologist comes back to his base and says 'look at what I have found' and then proceeds to place his finding in his 'collection'. Then other sociologists come along with their findings and trophies and add them to their collections, collections are compared and findings are queried, and the sociologist goes back again to the empirical quarry and adds further trophies to his collection. While this is going on, other practitioners 'look' at the collections. They start reclassifying the findings, they point to logical inconsistencies, they argue that some of the trophies should not appear where they do but in other collections, and in general, they engage in interpretation, they write books and comment on each other's books.

The idealised image that is projected in all this intellectual activity is of some beautiful dialectical process in which scripts and interpretations mutually interpenetrate, giving rise to theoretical creativity. In actuality, the opposite tends to be the case, because research and interpretation are conducted in isolation from each other. The divorce between theory and research is particularly evident in the social sciences, where both kinds of activity proceed as if they were independent of each other. However, this could be an illusion because even though research and theory are accomplished by two sets of practitioners, in the final analysis they write for each other. Sociologists write for sociologists, economists for economists, political scientists for scientists. Granted that there are some social scientists whose work is believed to have policy implications for this or that organisation or government, this does not detract from the fact that their audience is constituted of other social scientists. It may be that this is true of most academic discourse in that it is too technical for dissemination among a wider community, but in the case of the social sciences it could be argued that their very purpose and rationale is to break out of the narrow confines of academic discourse in order to reach as vast an audience as possible. But we know that this has not happened. Of course, the great names have been popularised – everybody has heard of Freud, Marx, Keynes, Sartre, perhaps Chomski and Lévi-Strauss, but so what!! In general, practitioners in the social sciences write books which other social scientists read, criticise and demolish – and this goes on in the insulated context of 'protected' institutions of higher learning.

In a very real sense we could say that sociologists, who in theory are interpreters and analysts of the social world, live out their own lives away from the concerns of the public sphere. They tend to be spectators and commentators, but not participants. The fact that many sociologists are Marxists and so forth does not mean that they can transcend the privatised state they find themselves in, no matter the extent of their political activity outside the university. There is an additional irony. When practitioners 'raid the empirical world' and endeavour to translate everyday language into their own theoretical jargon, participants find it almost impossible to recognise themselves or their language in this jargon. Who reads Garfinkel, Blum and McHugh, Althusser, Parsons, Durkheim, Weber, etc., etc.? Certainly not participants. And who, except practitioners, can understand them?

The real 'Catch 22' situation for sociologists is not only that they are politically ineffective, and consequently feel powerless to influence events, but also, even when they believe that their research is relevant and accessible, they find it difficult to convince others that this is so. The net result of all this is to generate an enclosed world in which texts, monographs and research reports are circulated from practitioner to practitioner in what Lefebvre claims is a 'permanent substitute for experience'.

Although we can exaggerate the influence of texts, there is little doubt that a great many of us are prisoners of the texts we read and write. For many of us, this state of affairs is very enjoyable – after all, there is nothing pleasanter than spending one's life among books. If we were simply to accept this there would be no problem, provided the community at large was prepared to go on financing our enjoyment. But I suspect that very few practitioners would admit that this is the sole rationale for their commitment to sociology. Enjoyment or not, it would seem to me that sociology and the other social sciences are becoming increasingly unable to bridge the gap between their academic encapsulation and the everyday concerns of participants, and this – if you like – is an extreme form of privatisation. Indeed, the fragmentation of knowledge, the hardening of boundaries between disciplines, the growth of specialised jargon, makes it more and more difficult for participants to believe that the social sciences can say anything significant to them.

References

1 Introduction: Negation of the self

1 John Rex, *Sociology and the Demystification of the Modern World*, Routledge & Kegan Paul, London, 1974, p. 10.
2 J. R. Barrington-Moore, *Reflections on the Causes of Human Misery*, Allen Lane, London, 1972.
3 Gibson Winter, *Elements for a Social Ethic*, Macmillan, New York, 1968, p. 25.
4 Maurice Natanson, *The Social Dynamics of George H. Mead*, Martinus Nijhoff, The Hague, 1973.
5 G. H. Mead, *Mind, Self and Society*, University of Chicago Press, 1967.
6 Michel Foucault, *The Order of Things*, Tavistock Press, London, 1970.
7 Louis Althusser, *For Marx*, Penguin Books, Harmondsworth, 1969, pp. 234–5.
8 Claude Lévi-Strauss, *The Savage Mind*, Weidenfeld & Nicolson, London, 1966.
9 Michel Foucault, *op. cit.*, p. 348.
10 Hugh Mehan and Huston Wood, *The Reality of Ethnomethodology*, John Wiley, New York, 1975, p. 137.
11 Maurice Roche, *Phenomenology, Language and the Social Sciences*, Routledge & Kegan Paul, London and Boston, 1973.

Part one

2 Everyday life and reality

1 Peter Berger, Brigitte Berger and Hansfried Kellner, *The Homeless Mind*, Random House, New York, 1973, pp. 112–13.
2 Henri Lefebvre, *Everyday Life in the Modern World*, Allen Lane, The Penguin Press, London, 1971, p. 55.

3 Geoffrey Pearson, *The Deviant Imagination*, Macmillan, London, 1975, p. 107.
4 *Ibid.*, p. 109.
5 Robert L. Heilbroner, *An Inquiry into the Human Prospect*, Calder & Boyars, London, 1975, p. 21.
6 Henri Lefebvre, *op. cit.*, p. 56.
7 Hugh Mehan and Huston Wood, *The Reality of Ethnomethodology*, John Wiley, New York, 1975.
8 Andrew Tudor, 'Misunderstanding Everyday Life', *Sociological Review*, August 1976.
9 Victor W. Turner, *The Forest of Symbols*, Cornell University Press, Ithaca, 1967.
10 Albrecht Wellmer, *Critical Theory of Society*, Herder & Herder, New York, 1971, pp. 26–7.
11 Harvey Sacks, 'An initial investigation of the usability of conversational for doing sociology', in D. Sudnow (ed.), *Studies in Interaction*, Free Press, New York, 1969.
12 Joseph Heller, *Something Happened*, Jonathan Cape, 1975.
13 John Rex, *Sociology and the Demystification of the Modern World*, Routledge & Kegan Paul, London, 1974, p. 218.

3 Privatisation and fragmentation

1 Peter Berger, Brigitte Berger and Hansfried Kellner, *The Homeless Mind*, Random House, New York, 1973.
2 *Ibid.*, p. 92.
3 Eduard Bernstein, *Evolutionary Socialism*, Schocken, New York, 1963.
4 Roy Willis, *Man and Beast*, Paladin Books, St Albans, 1975, p. 81.
5 Peter Berger, *et al., op. cit.*, p. 196.
6 Georg Simmel, *The Sociology of Georg Simmel* (ed.), K. H. Wolff, Free Press, New York, 1964, pp. 333–4.
7 *Ibid.*, p. 337.
8 Robert A. Nisbet, *The Sociological Tradition*, Heinemann, London, 1967, p. 48.
9 W. Kornhauser, *The Politics of Mass Society*, Routledge & Kegan Paul, London, 1959, p. 32.
10 Norman Birnbaum, *Toward a Critical Sociology*, Oxford University Press, New York, 1971, p. 87.
11 Karl Marx, *A Contribution to the Critique of Political Economy*, Lawrence & Wishart, London, 1971.
12 C. B. MacPherson, *Democratic Theory*, Oxford University Press, London, 1973, pp. 182–3.
13 T. B. Bottomore, *Sociology as Social Criticism*, George Allen & Unwin, London, pp. 114–31.
14 *Ibid.*, pp. 124–5.
15 John H. Goldthorpe, David Lockwood, Frank Bechhofer and Jennifer Platt, *The Affluent Worker in the Class Structure*, Cambridge University Press, 1969.

16 Pierre L. van den Berghe, *Man in Society*, Elsevier, New York, p. 129.
17 Eli Zaretsky, *Capitalism, the Family, and Personal Life,* Pluto Press, London, 1976, p. 34.
18 Shulamith Firestone, *The Dialectic of Sex*, Paladin, London, 1972.
19 Ann Oakley, *The Sociology of Housework*, Martin Robertson, pp. 17–18.
20 Henri Lefebvre, *Everyday Life in the Modern World*, Allen Lane, London, 1971, p. 92.
21 Bertell Ollman, *Alienation*, Cambridge University Press, London, 1971, p. 245.

Part two

4 The biographical self

1 Peter Berger, Brigitte Berger and Hansfried Kellner, *The Homeless Mind*, Random House, 1973, p. 186.
2 *Ibid.*, p. 187.
3 Peter K. Manning and Horacio Fabrega, 'The Experience of Self and Body: Health and Illness in the Chiapis Highlands', in *Phenomenological Sociology* (ed.), George Psathas, Wiley, New York, 1973, p. 254.
4 Jean Piaget, *Six Psychological Studies*, Random House, New York, 1967.
5 Luke Rhinehart, *The Diceman*, Panther Books, London, 1972.
6 R. Harré & P. E. Secord, *The Explanation of Social Behaviour*, Basil Blackwell, Oxford, 1972, p. 142.
7 William James, *Psychology: The Briefer Course*, New York, Holt, 1910.
8 Susanne K. Langer, *Mind: An Essay on Human Feeling*, vol. 2, Johns Hopkins University Press, Baltimore, 1972, p. 344.
9 Gordon Allport, *Becoming*, Yale University Press, New Haven, 1955.
10 Steven Lukes, *Individualism*, Basil Blackwell, Oxford, 1973, pp. 71–2.
11 Leon Festinger, *A Theory of Cognitive Dissonance*, Tavistock Publications, 1962, pp. 1–31.
12 Liam Hudson, *Human Beings*, Jonathan Cape, 1975, pp. 53–7.
13 R. Harré and P. E. Secord, *op. cit.*
14 Steven Lukes, *op. cit.*, pp. 71–8.
15 Jean-Paul Sartre, *Search for a Method*, Vintage Books, New York, 1968, p. 152.
16 Louis Althusser, *For Marx*, Penguin Books, Harmondsworth, 1969, pp. 229–30.
17 *Ibid.*, p. 233.

5 Identity and illusion

1 Jeff Coulter, *Approaches to Insanity*, Martin Robertson, London, 1973, p. 34.

2 Anthony F. C. Wallace, *Culture and Personality*, Random House, New York, 1961, pp. 84–117.
3 John E. Horrocks and Dorothy W. Jackson, *Self and Role*, Houghton Mifflin, Boston, 1972, p. 60.
4 Carl Rogers, *On Becoming a Person*, Houghton Mifflin, Boston, 1961.
5 Richard R. Robbins, 'Identity, Culture and Behaviour', in *Handbook of Social and Cultural Anthropology*, Rand McNally, 1973.
6 Erik H. Erikson, *Identity: Youth and Crisis*, Faber & Faber, London, 1968.
7 R. D. Laing, *The Divided Self*, Penguin Books, Harmondsworth, 1968.
8 Ludwig Binswanger, *Being in the World*, Basic Books & Souvenir Press, London, 1975.
9 Ralph Ruddock, *Roles and Relationships*, Routledge & Kegan Paul, London, 1969, pp. 109–10.
10 Jean-Paul Sartre, *Being and Nothingness*, Methuen, London, 1968.
11 Wilhelm Reich, *The Sexual Revolution*, Vision Press, London, 1968.
12 Erik Erikson, *op. cit.*
13 Maurice Natanson, *The Journeying Self*, Addison-Wesley, Reading, Massachussets, 1970, p. 14.
14 Don Locke, *Myself and Others*, Oxford University Press, 1968, London, pp. 72–9.
15. Arthur Brittan, *Meanings and Situations*, Routledge & Kegan Paul, 1973, London, pp. 121–6.
16 Alan Dawe, 'The Underworld of Erving Goffman', *British Journal of Sociology*, vol. 24, no. 2, 1973, pp. 246–53.
17 Erving Goffman, *Frame Analysis*, Penguin Books, Harmondsworth, 1975, pp. 1–8.
18 *Ibid.*, pp. 298–9.
19 Kenneth Plummer, *Sexual Stigma*, Routledge & Kegan Paul, London, 1974, p. 135.
20 Maurice Natanson, *The Social Dynamics of George H. Mead*, Martinus Nijhoff, The Hague, 1973.
21 Jack D. Douglas, *Understanding Everyday Life*, Routledge & Kegan Paul, London, 1971, pp. 3–44.
22 Zygmunt Bauman, *Towards a Critical Sociology*, Routledge & Kegan Paul, London, 1976, p. 67.
23 Erving Goffman, *Stigma*, Penguin Books, Harmondsworth, 1970.
24 Anton C. Zijderveld, *The Abstract Society*, Penguin Books, Harmondsworth, 1974, p. 11.
25 Peter Berger, Brigitte Berger and Hansfried Kellner, *The Homeless Mind*, Random House, New York, 1973.
26 Daniel Bell, *The Cultural Contradictions of Capitalism*, Heinemann, London, 1976, pp. 89–90.
27 Stan Cohen and Laurie Taylor, *Escape Attempts*, Allen Lane, London, 1976.
28 Claude Lévi-Strauss, *The Raw and the Cooked*, Jonathan Cape, London, 1976, pp. 340–1.
29 Mark Poster, *Existential Marxism in Post-War France*, Princeton

University Press, New Jersey, 1975, pp. 320–1.

30 Irving M. Zeitlin, *Re-thinking Sociology*, Appleton-Century-Crofts, New York, 1973, p. 217.

31 Salvador Giner, *Mass Society*, Martin Robertson, London, 1976.

32 Anton C. Zijderveld, *op. cit.*, p. 71.

6 A concrete humanism?

1 Erving Goffman, *Frame Analysis*, Penguin Books, Harmondsworth, 1975, pp. 13–14.

2 Karl Marx, 'Theses on Feuerbach', in *The German Ideology*, Lawrence & Wishart, London, 1970, pp. 121–3.

3 *Ibid.*

4 Sigmund Freud, *Civilization and its Discontents*, Hogarth Press, London, 1957.

5 Karl Marx, *op. cit.*

6 Joachim Israel, *Stipulations and Construction in the Social Sciences in The Context of Social Psychology*, Academic Press, 1972, pp. 137–8.

7 Karl Marx and Frederick Engels, *The German Ideology*, Lawrence & Wishart, London, 1970, pp. 51–2.

8 Hendrik M. Ruitenbeek, *The Individual and the Crowd: A Study of Identity in America*, Mentor Books, New York, 1964, p. 98.

9 Jack Douglas, *The Social Meaning of Suicide*, Princeton University Press, 1967.

10 Milton Yinger, *Toward a Field Theory of Behaviour*, McGraw Hill, New York, 1965, p. 189.

11 Lucien Seve, *Marxism and the Theory of Human Personality*, Lawrence & Wishart, London, 1975, pp. 27–8.

12 *Ibid.*, p. 31.

13 *Ibid.*, p. 26.

14 *Ibid.*

15 Margaret Coulson, 'Role: A Redundant Concept in Sociology', in *Role* (ed.) J. A. Jackson, Cambridge University Press, London, 1972.

16 Max Horkheimer and Theodor W. Adorno, *Aspects of Sociology*, Beacon Press, Boston, 1972, p. 46.

17 *Ibid.*

18 Herbert Marcuse, *One-Dimensional Man*, Routledge & Kegan Paul, London, 1964.

19 Henri Lefebvre, *Everyday Life in the Modern World*, Allen Lane, London, 1971.

20 Perry Anderson, *Considerations on Western Marxism*, New Left Books, London, 1976, pp. 75–96.

21 Lucien Seve, *op. cit.*, p. 26.

22 Roger Poole, *Towards Deep Subjectivity*, Allen Lane, London, 1972, p. 27.

23 Charles A. Valentine, *Culture and Poverty*, University of Chicago Press, 1968.

24 Herbert Marcuse, *op. cit.*, p. 174.

25 Matthew Speier, *How to Observe Face to Face Interaction: A*

Sociological Introduction, Goodyear Publishing, Pacific Pallisade, 1973, p. 59.

26 Anthony Wootton, *Dilemmas of Discourse*, George Allen & Unwin, London, 1975, p. 59.
27 Herbert Marcuse, *op. cit.*, p. 174.
28 Barrington Moore, jr., *Reflections on the Causes of Human Misery*, Allen Lane, London, 1972, pp. 1–2.
29 Hans Enzenberger, *The Consciousness Industry*, Seabury Press, New York, 1976, p. 101.
30 Max Horkheimer, *Critical Theory*, Seabury Press, New York, 1972, pp. 289–90.
31 C. Wright-Mills, *The Sociological Imagination*, Oxford University Press, New York, 1959.
32 Eli Zaretsky, *Capitalism, The Family, and Personal Life*, Pluto Press, London, 1976, p. 73.
33 Stan Cohen and Laurie Taylor, *Escape Attempts*, Allen Lane, London, 1976, p. 206.
34 Perry Anderson, *op. cit.*, p. 93.

7 Addendum: Private readings and the dictatorship of the script

1 Elizabeth and Tom Burns (eds), *Sociology of Literature and Drama*, Penguin Books, Harmondsworth, 1973, p. 22.
2 Frank Kermode, *The Sense of an Ending*, Oxford University Press, London, 1967.
3 George Steiner, *After Babel*, Oxford University Press, London, 1975, p. 235.

Index

Routledge Social Science Series

Routledge & Kegan Paul   London, Henley and Boston

39 Store Street, London WC1E 7DD
Broadway House, Newtown Road, Henley-on-Thames,
Oxon RG9 1EN
9 Park Street, Boston, Mass. 02108

Contents

*Authors wishing to submit manuscripts for any series in
this catalogue should send them to the Social Science Editor,
Routledge & Kegan Paul Ltd, 39 Store Street,
London WC1E 7DD*

● *Books so marked are available in paperback*
All books are in Metric Demy 8vo format (216 × 138mm approx.)

International Library of Sociology

General Editor John Rex

GENERAL SOCIOLOGY

Barnsley, J. H. The Social Reality of Ethics. *464 pp.*
Belshaw, Cyril. The Conditions of Social Performance. *An Exploratory Theory. 144 pp.*
Brown, Robert. Explanation in Social Science. *208 pp.*
● Rules and Laws in Sociology. *192 pp.*
Bruford, W. H. Chekhov and His Russia. *A Sociological Study. 244 pp.*
Cain, Maureen E. Society and the Policeman's Role. *326 pp.*
●**Fletcher, Colin.** Beneath the Surface. *An Account of Three Styles of Sociological Research. 221 pp.*
Gibson, Quentin. The Logic of Social Enquiry. *240 pp.*
Glucksmann, M. Structuralist Analysis in Contemporary Social Thought. *212 pp.*
Gurvitch, Georges. Sociology of Law. *Preface by Roscoe Pound. 264 pp.*
Hodge, H. A. Wilhelm Dilthey. *An Introduction. 184 pp.*
Homans, George C. Sentiments and Activities. *336 pp.*
Johnson, Harry M. Sociology: *a Systematic Introduction. Foreword by · Robert K. Merton. 710 pp.*
●**Keat, Russell,** and **Urry, John.** Social Theory as Science. *278 pp.*
Mannheim, Karl. Essays on Sociology and Social Psychology. *Edited by Paul Keckskemeti. With Editorial Note by Adolph Lowe. 344 pp.*
Systematic Sociology: *An Introduction to the Study of Society. Edited by J. S. Erös and Professor W. A. C. Stewart. 220 pp.*
Martindale, Don. The Nature and Types of Sociological Theory. *292 pp.*
●**Maus, Heinz.** A Short History of Sociology. *234 pp.*
Mey, Harald. Field-Theory. *A Study of its Application in the Social Sciences. 352 pp.*
Myrdal, Gunnar. Value in Social Theory: *A Collection of Essays on Methodology. Edited by Paul Streeten. 332 pp.*
Ogburn, William F., and **Nimkoff, Meyer F.** A Handbook of Sociology. *Preface by Karl Mannheim. 656 pp. 46 figures. 35 tables.*
Parsons, Talcott, and **Smelser, Neil J.** Economy and Society: *A Study in the Integration of Economic and Social Theory. 362 pp.*
Podgórecki, Adam. Practical Social Sciences. *About 200 pp.*
●**Rex, John.** Key Problems of Sociological Theory. *220 pp.*
Sociology and the Demystification of the Modern World. *282 pp.*
●**Rex, John** (Ed.) Approaches to Sociology. *Contributions by Peter Abell, Frank Bechhofer, Basil Bernstein, Ronald Fletcher, David Frisby, Miriam Glucksmann, Peter Lassman, Herminio Martins, John Rex, Roland Robertson, John Westergaard and Jock Young. 302 pp.*
Rigby, A. Alternative Realities. *352 pp.*
Roche, M. Phenomenology, Language and the Social Sciences. *374 pp.*

Sahay, A. Sociological Analysis. *220 pp.*
Simirenko, Alex (Ed.) Soviet Sociology. *Historical Antecedents and Current Appraisals. Introduction by Alex Simirenko. 376 pp.*
Strasser, Hermann. The Normative Structure of Sociology. *Conservative and Emancipatory Themes in Social Thought. About 340 pp.*
Urry, John. Reference Groups and the Theory of Revolution. *244 pp.*
Weinberg, E. Development of Sociology in the Soviet Union. *173 pp.*

FOREIGN CLASSICS OF SOCIOLOGY

●**Durkheim, Emile.** Suicide. *A Study in Sociology. Edited and with an Introduction by George Simpson. 404 pp.*
●**Gerth, H. H.,** and **Mills, C. Wright.** From Max Weber: *Essays in Sociology. 502 pp.*
●**Tönnies, Ferdinand.** Community and Association. (*Gemeinschaft und Gesellschaft.*) *Translated and Supplemented by Charles P. Loomis. Foreword by Pitirim A. Sorokin. 334 pp.*

SOCIAL STRUCTURE

Andreski, Stanislav. Military Organization and Society. *Foreword by Professor A. R. Radcliffe-Brown. 226 pp. 1 folder.*
Carlton, Eric. Ideology and Social Order. *Preface by Professor Philip Abrahams. About 320 pp.*
Coontz, Sydney H. Population Theories and the Economic Interpretation. *202 pp.*
Coser, Lewis. The Functions of Social Conflict. *204 pp.*
Dickie-Clark, H. F. Marginal Situation: *A Sociological Study of a Coloured Group. 240 pp. 11 tables.*
Glaser, Barney, and **Strauss, Anselm L.** Status Passage. *A Formal Theory. 208 pp.*
Glass, D. V. (Ed.) Social Mobility in Britain. *Contributions by J. Berent, T. Bottomore, R. C. Chambers, J. Floud, D. V. Glass, J. R. Hall, H. T. Himmelweit, R. K. Kelsall, F. M. Martin, C. A. Moser, R. Mukherjee, and W. Ziegel. 420 pp.*
Johnstone, Frederick A. Class, Race and Gold. *A Study of Class Relations and Racial Discrimination in South Africa. 312 pp.*
Jones, Garth N. Planned Organizational Change: *An Exploratory Study Using an Empirical Approach. 268 pp.*
Kelsall, R. K. Higher Civil Servants in Britain: *From 1870 to the Present Day. 268 pp. 31 tables.*
König, René. The Community. *232 pp. Illustrated.*
●**Lawton, Denis.** Social Class, Language and Education. *192 pp.*
McLeish, John. The Theory of Social Change: *Four Views Considered. 128 pp.*
Marsh, David C. The Changing Social Structure of England and Wales, 1871-1961. *288 pp.*
Menzies, Ken. Talcott Parsons and the Social Image of Man. *About 208 pp.*

● **Mouzelis, Nicos.** Organization and Bureaucracy. *An Analysis of Modern Theories. 240 pp.*

Mulkay, M. J. Functionalism, Exchange and Theoretical Strategy. *272 pp.*

Ossowski, Stanislaw. Class Structure in the Social Consciousness. *210 pp.*

● **Podgórecki, Adam.** Law and Society. *302 pp.*

Renner, Karl. Institutions of Private Law and Their Social Functions. *Edited, with an Introduction and Notes, by O. Kahn-Freud. Translated by Agnes Schwarzschild. 316 pp.*

SOCIOLOGY AND POLITICS

Acton, T. A. Gypsy Politics and Social Change. *316 pp.*

Clegg, Stuart. Power, Rule and Domination. *A Critical and Empirical Understanding of Power in Sociological Theory and Organisational Life. About 300 pp.*

Hechter, Michael. Internal Colonialism. *The Celtic Fringe in British National Development, 1536–1966. 361 pp.*

Hertz, Frederick. Nationality in History and Politics: *A Psychology and Sociology of National Sentiment and Nationalism. 432 pp.*

Kornhauser, William. The Politics of Mass Society. *272 pp. 20 tables.*

● **Kroes, R.** Soldiers and Students. *A Study of Right- and Left-wing Students. 174 pp.*

Laidler, Harry W. History of Socialism. *Social-Economic Movements: An Historical and Comparative Survey of Socialism, Communism, Co-operation, Utopianism; and other Systems of Reform and Reconstruction. 992 pp.*

Lasswell, H. D. Analysis of Political Behaviour. *324 pp.*

Martin, David A. Pacifism: *an Historical and Sociological Study. 262 pp.*

Martin, Roderick. Sociology of Power. *About 272 pp.*

Myrdal, Gunnar. The Political Element in the Development of Economic Theory. *Translated from the German by Paul Streeten. 282 pp.*

Wilson, H. T. The American Ideology. *Science, Technology and Organization of Modes of Rationality. About 280 pp.*

Wootton, Graham. Workers, Unions and the State. *188 pp.*

CRIMINOLOGY

Ancel, Marc. Social Defence: *A Modern Approach to Criminal Problems. Foreword by Leon Radzinowicz. 240 pp.*

Cain, Maureen E. Society and the Policeman's Role. *326 pp.*

Cloward, Richard A., and **Ohlin, Lloyd E.** Delinquency and Opportunity: *A Theory of Delinquent Gangs. 248 pp.*

Downes, David M. The Delinquent Solution. *A Study in Subcultural Theory. 296 pp.*

Dunlop, A. B., and **McCabe, S.** Young Men in Detention Centres. *192 pp.*

Friedlander, Kate. The Psycho-Analytical Approach to Juvenile Delinquency: *Theory, Case Studies, Treatment. 320 pp.*

Glueck, Sheldon, and **Eleanor.** Family Environment and Delinquency. *With the statistical assistance of Rose W. Kneznek. 340 pp.*

Lopez-Rey, Manuel. Crime. *An Analytical Appraisal. 288 pp.*
Mannheim, Hermann. Comparative Criminology: *a Text Book. Two volumes. 442 pp. and 380 pp.*

Morris, Terence. The Criminal Area: *A Study in Social Ecology. Foreword by Hermann Mannheim. 232 pp. 25 tables. 4 maps.*
Rock, Paul. Making People Pay. *338 pp.*
●**Taylor, Ian, Walton, Paul,** and **Young, Jock.** The New Criminology. *For a Social Theory of Deviance. 325 pp.*
●**Taylor, Ian, Walton, Paul,** and **Young, Jock** (Eds). Critical Criminology. *268 pp.*

SOCIAL PSYCHOLOGY

Bagley, Christopher. The Social Psychology of the Epileptic Child. *320 pp.*
Barbu, Zevedei. Problems of Historical Psychology. *248 pp.*
Blackburn, Julian. Psychology and the Social Pattern. *184 pp.*
●**Brittan, Arthur.** Meanings and Situations. *224 pp.*
Carroll, J. Break-Out from the Crystal Palace. *200 pp.*
●**Fleming, C. M.** Adolescence: Its Social Psychology. *With an Introduction to recent findings from the fields of Anthropology, Physiology, Medicine, Psychometrics and Sociometry. 288 pp.*
● The Social Psychology of Education: *An Introduction and Guide to Its Study. 136 pp.*
●**Homans, George C.** The Human Group. *Foreword by Bernard DeVoto. Introduction by Robert K. Merton. 526 pp.*
● Social Behaviour: *its Elementary Forms. 416 pp.*
●**Klein, Josephine.** The Study of Groups. *226 pp. 31 figures. 5 tables.*
Linton, Ralph. The Cultural Background of Personality. *132 pp.*
●**Mayo, Elton.** The Social Problems of an Industrial Civilization. *With an appendix on the Political Problem. 180 pp.*
Ottaway, A. K. C. Learning Through Group Experience. *176 pp.*
Plummer, Ken. Sexual Stigma. *An Interactionist Account. 254 pp.*
●**Rose, Arnold M.** (Ed.) Human Behaviour and Social Processes: *an Interactionist Approach. Contributions by Arnold M. Rose, Ralph H. Turner, Anselm Strauss, Everett C. Hughes, E. Franklin Frazier, Howard S. Becker, et al. 696 pp.*
Smelser, Neil J. Theory of Collective Behaviour. *448 pp.*
Stephenson, Geoffrey M. The Development of Conscience. *128 pp.*
Young, Kimball. Handbook of Social Psychology. *658 pp. 16 figures. 10 tables.*

SOCIOLOGY OF THE FAMILY

Banks, J. A. Prosperity and Parenthood: *A Study of Family Planning among The Victorian Middle Classes. 262 pp.*
Bell, Colin R. Middle ʻClass Families: *Social and Geographical Mobility. 224 pp.*

Burton, Lindy. Vulnerable Children. *272 pp.*

Gavron, Hannah. The Captive Wife: *Conflicts of Household Mothers. 190 pp.*

George, Victor, and **Wilding, Paul.** Motherless Families. *248 pp.*

Klein, Josephine. Samples from English Cultures.
1. Three Preliminary Studies and Aspects of Adult Life in England. *447 pp.*
2. Child-Rearing Practices and Index. *247 pp.*

Klein, Viola. The Feminine Character. *History of an Ideology. 244 pp.*

McWhinnie, Alexina M. Adopted Children. *How They Grow Up. 304 pp.*

● **Morgan, D. H. J.** Social Theory and the Family. *About 320 pp.*

● **Myrdal, Alva,** and **Klein, Viola.** Women's Two Roles: *Home and Work. 238 pp. 27 tables.*

Parsons, Talcott, and **Bales, Robert F.** Family: Socialization and Inter-action Process. *In collaboration with James Olds, Morris Zelditch and Philip E. Slater. 456 pp. 50 figures and tables.*

SOCIAL SERVICES

Bastide, Roger. The Sociology of Mental Disorder. *Translated from the French by Jean McNeil. 260 pp.*

Carlebach, Julius. Caring For Children in Trouble. *266 pp.*

George, Victor. Foster Care. *Theory and Practice. 234 pp.*
Social Security: *Beveridge and After. 258 pp.*

George, V., and **Wilding, P.** Motherless Families. *248 pp.*

● **Goetschius, George W.** Working with Community Groups. *256 pp.*

Goetschius, George W., and **Tash, Joan.** Working with Unattached Youth. *416 pp.*

Hall, M. P., and **Howes, I. V.** The Church in Social Work. *A Study of Moral Welfare Work undertaken by the Church of England. 320 pp.*

Heywood, Jean S. Children in Care: *the Development of the Service for the Deprived Child. 264 pp.*

Hoenig, J., and **Hamilton, Marian W.** The De-Segregation of the Mentally Ill. *284 pp.*

Jones, Kathleen. Mental Health and Social Policy, 1845-1959. *264 pp.*

King, Roy D., Raynes, Norma V., and **Tizard, Jack.** Patterns of Residential Care. *356 pp.*

Leigh, John. Young People and Leisure. *256 pp.*

● **Mays, John.** (Ed.) Penelope Hall's Social Services of England and Wales. *About 324 pp.*

Morris, Mary. Voluntary Work and the Welfare State. *300 pp.*

Nokes, P. L. The Professional Task in Welfare Practice. *152 pp.*

Timms, Noel. Psychiatric Social Work in Great Britain (1939-1962). *280 pp.*

● Social Casework: *Principles and Practice. 256 pp.*

Young, A. F. Social Services in British Industry. *272 pp.*

SOCIOLOGY OF EDUCATION

Banks, Olive. Parity and Prestige in English Secondary Education: a Study in Educational Sociology. *272 pp.*

Bentwich, Joseph. Education in Israel. *224 pp. 8 pp. plates.*

●**Blyth, W. A. L.** English Primary Education. *A Sociological Description.*
1. Schools. *232 pp.*
2. Background. *168 pp.*

Collier, K. G. The Social Purposes of Education: *Personal and Social Values in Education. 268 pp.*

Dale, R. R., and **Griffith, S.** Down Stream: *Failure in the Grammar School. 108 pp.*

Evans, K. M. Sociometry and Education. *158 pp.*

●**Ford, Julienne.** Social Class and the Comprehensive School. *192 pp.*

Foster, P. J. Education and Social Change in Ghana. *336 pp. 3 maps.*

Fraser, W. R. Education and Society in Modern France. *150 pp.*

Grace, Gerald R. Role Conflict and the Teacher. *150 pp.*

Hans, Nicholas. New Trends in Education in the Eighteenth Century. *278 pp. 19 tables.*

● Comparative Education: *A Study of Educational Factors and Traditions. 360 pp.*

●**Hargreaves, David.** Interpersonal Relations and Education. *432 pp.*

● Social Relations in a Secondary School. *240 pp.*

Holmes, Brian. Problems in Education. *A Comparative Approach. 336 pp.*

King, Ronald. Values and Involvement in a Grammar School. *164 pp.*
School Organization and Pupil Involvement. *A Study of Secondary Schools.*

●**Mannheim, Karl,** and **Stewart, W. A. C.** An Introduction to the Sociology of Education. *206 pp.*

Morris, Raymond N. The Sixth Form and College Entrance. *231 pp.*

●**Musgrove, F.** Youth and the Social Order. *176 pp.*

●**Ottaway, A. K. C.** Education and Society: An Introduction to the Sociology of Education. *With an Introduction by W. O. Lester Smith. 212 pp.*

Peers, Robert. Adult Education: *A Comparative Study. 398 pp.*

Pritchard, D. G. Education and the Handicapped: *1760 to 1960. 258 pp.*

Stratta, Erica. The Education of Borstal Boys. *A Study of their Educational Experiences prior to, and during, Borstal Training. 256 pp.*

Taylor, P. H., Reid, W. A., and **Holley, B. J.** The English Sixth Form. *A Case Study in Curriculum Research. 200 pp.*

SOCIOLOGY OF CULTURE

Eppel, E. M., and **M.** Adolescents and Morality: *A Study of some Moral Values and Dilemmas of Working Adolescents in the Context of a changing Climate of Opinion. Foreword by W. J. H. Sprott. 268 pp. 39 tables.*

●**Fromm, Erich.** The Fear of Freedom. *286 pp.*

● The Sane Society. *400 pp.*

Mannheim, Karl. Essays on the Sociology of Culture. *Edited by Ernst Mannheim in co-operation with Paul Kecskemeti. Editorial Note by Adolph Lowe. 280 pp.*

Weber, Alfred. Farewell to European History: *or The Conquest of Nihilism. Translated from the German by R. F. C. Hull. 224 pp.*

SOCIOLOGY OF RELIGION

Argyle, Michael and **Beit-Hallahmi, Benjamin.** The Social Psychology of Religion. *About 256 pp.*

Glasner, Peter E. The Sociology of Secularisation. *A Critique of a Concept. About 180 pp.*

Nelson, G. K. Spiritualism and Society. *313 pp.*

Stark, Werner. The Sociology of Religion. *A Study of Christendom.*
  Volume I. *Established Religion. 248 pp.*
  Volume II. *Sectarian Religion. 368 pp.*
  Volume III. *The Universal Church. 464 pp.*
  Volume IV. *Types of Religious Man. 352 pp.*
  Volume V. *Types of Religious Culture. 464 pp.*

Turner, B. S. Weber and Islam. *216 pp.*

Watt, W. Montgomery. Islam and the Integration of Society. *320 pp.*

SOCIOLOGY OF ART AND LITERATURE

Jarvie, Ian C. Towards a Sociology of the Cinema. *A Comparative Essay on the Structure and Functioning of a Major Entertainment Industry. 405 pp.*

Rust, Frances S. Dance in Society. *An Analysis of the Relationships between the Social Dance and Society in England from the Middle Ages to the Present Day. 256 pp. 8 pp. of plates.*

Schücking, L. L. The Sociology of Literary Taste. *112 pp.*

Wolff, Janet. Hermeneutic Philosophy and the Sociology of Art. *150 pp.*

SOCIOLOGY OF KNOWLEDGE

Diesing, P. Patterns of Discovery in the Social Sciences. *262 pp.*

● **Douglas, J. D.** (Ed.) Understanding Everyday Life. *370 pp.*

● **Hamilton, P.** Knowledge and Social Structure. *174 pp.*

Jarvie, I. C. Concepts and Society. *232 pp.*

Mannheim, Karl. Essays on the Sociology of Knowledge. *Edited by Paul Kecskemeti. Editorial Note by Adolph Lowe. 353 pp.*

Remmling, Gunter W. The Sociology cf Karl Mannheim. *With a Bibliographical Guide to the Sociology of Knowledge, Ideological Analysis, and Social Planning. 255 pp.*

Remmling, Gunter W. (Ed.) Towards the Sociology of Knowledge. *Origin and Development of a Sociological Thought Style. 463 pp.*

Stark, Werner. The Sociology of Knowledge: *An Essay in Aid of a Deeper Understanding of the History of Ideas. 384 pp.*

URBAN SOCIOLOGY

Ashworth, William. The Genesis of Modern British Town Planning: *A Study in Economic and Social History of the Nineteenth and Twentieth Centuries. 288 pp.*

Cullingworth, J. B. Housing Needs and Planning Policy: *A Restatement of the Problems of Housing Need and 'Overspill' in England and Wales. 232 pp. 44 tables. 8 maps.*

Dickinson, Robert E. City and Region: *A Geographical Interpretation 608 pp. 125 figures.*

The West European City: *A Geographical Interpretation. 600 pp. 129 maps. 29 plates.*

● The City Region in Western Europe. *320 pp. Maps.*

Humphreys, Alexander J. New Dubliners: *Urbanization and the Irish Family. Foreword by George C. Homans. 304 pp.*

Jackson, Brian. Working Class Community: *Some General Notions raised by a Series of Studies in Northern England. 192 pp.*

Jennings, Hilda. Societies in the Making: *a Study of Development and Re-development within a County Borough. Foreword by D. A. Clark. 286 pp.*

●**Mann, P. H.** An Approach to Urban Sociology. *240 pp.*

Morris, R. N., and **Mogey, J.** The Sociology of Housing. *Studies at Berinsfield. 232 pp. 4 pp. plates.*

Rosser, C., and **Harris, C.** The Family and Social Change. *A Study of Family and Kinship in a South Wales Town. 352 pp. 8 maps.*

●**Stacey, Margaret, Batsone, Eric, Bell, Colin,** and **Thurcott, Anne.** Power, Persistence and Change. *A Second Study of Banbury. 196 pp.*

RURAL SOCIOLOGY

Haswell, M. R. The Economics of Development in Village India. *120 pp.*

Littlejohn, James. Westrigg: *the Sociology of a Cheviot Parish. 172 pp. 5 figures.*

Mayer, Adrian C. Peasants in the Pacific. *A Study of Fiji Indian Rural Society. 248 pp. 20 plates.*

Williams, W. M. The Sociology of an English Village: *Gosforth. 272 pp. 12 figures. 13 tables.*

SOCIOLOGY OF INDUSTRY AND DISTRIBUTION

Anderson, Nels. Work and Leisure. *280 pp.*

●**Blau, Peter M.,** and **Scott, W. Richard.** Formal Organizations: *a Comparative approach. Introduction and Additional Bibliography by J. H. Smith. 326 pp.*

Dunkerley, David. The Foreman. *Aspects of Task and Structure. 192 pp.*

Eldridge, J. E. T. Industrial Disputes. *Essays in the Sociology of Industrial Relations. 288 pp.*

Hetzler, Stanley. Applied Measures for Promoting Technological Growth. *352 pp.*

Technological Growth and Social Change. *Achieving Modernization. 269 pp.*

Hollowell, Peter G. The Lorry Driver. *272 pp.*

●**Oxaal, I., Barnett, T.,** and **Booth, D.** (Eds). Beyond the Sociology of Development. *Economy and Society in Latin America and Africa. 295 pp.*

Smelser, Neil J. Social Change in the Industrial Revolution: *An Application of Theory to the Lancashire Cotton Industry, 1770–1840. 468 pp. 12 figures. 14 tables.*

ANTHROPOLOGY

Ammar, Hamed. Growing up in an Egyptian Village: *Silwa, Province of Aswan. 336 pp.*

Brandel-Syrier, Mia. Reeftown Elite. *A Study of Social Mobility in a Modern African Community on the Reef. 376 pp.*

Dickie-Clark, H. F. The Marginal Situation. *A Sociological Study of a Coloured Group. 236 pp.*

Dube, S. C. Indian Village. *Foreword by Morris Edward Opler. 276 pp. 4 plates.*

India's Changing Villages: *Human Factors in Community Development. 260 pp. 8 plates. 1 map.*

Firth, Raymond. Malay Fishermen. *Their Peasant Economy. 420 pp. 17 pp. plates.*

Gulliver, P. H. Social Control in an African Society: a Study of the Arusha, Agricultural Masai of Northern Tanganyika. *320 pp. 8 plates. 10 figures.*

Family Herds. *288 pp.*

Ishwaran, K. Tradition and Economy in Village India: *An Interactionist Approach.*
Foreword by Conrad Arensburg. 176 pp.

Jarvie, Ian C. The Revolution in Anthropology. *268 pp.*

Little, Kenneth L. Mende of Sierra Leone. *308 pp. and folder.*

Negroes in Britain. *With a New Introduction and Contemporary Study by Leonard Bloom. 320 pp.*

Lowie, Robert H. Social Organization. *494 pp.*

Mayer, A. C. Peasants in the Pacific. *A Study of Fiji Indian Rural Society. 248 pp.*

Meer, Fatima. Race and Suicide in South Africa. *325 pp.*

Smith, Raymond T. The Negro Family in British Guiana: *Family Structure and Social Status in the Villages. With a Foreword by Meyer Fortes. 314 pp. 8 plates. 1 figure. 4 maps.*

Smooha, Sammy. Israel: Pluralism and Conflict. *About 320 pp.*

SOCIOLOGY AND PHILOSOPHY

Barnsley, John H. The Social Reality of Ethics. *A Comparative Analysis of Moral Codes. 448 pp.*

Diesing, Paul. Patterns of Discovery in the Social Sciences. *362 pp.*

●**Douglas, Jack D.** (Ed.) Understanding Everyday Life. *Toward the Reconstruction of Sociological Knowledge. Contributions by Alan F. Blum. Aaron W. Cicourel, Norman K. Denzin, Jack D. Douglas, John Heeren, Peter McHugh, Peter K. Manning, Melvin Power, Matthew Speier, Roy Turner, D. Lawrence Wieder, Thomas P. Wilson and Don H. Zimmerman. 370 pp.*

Gorman, Robert A. The Dual Vision. *Alfred Schutz and the Myth of Phenomenological Social Science. About 300 pp.*

Jarvie, Ian C. Concepts and Society. *216 pp.*

●**Pelz, Werner.** The Scope of Understanding in Sociology. *Towards a more radical reorientation in the social humanistic sciences. 283 pp.*

Roche, Maurice. Phenomenology, Language and the Social Sciences. *371 pp.*

Sahay, Arun. Sociological Analysis. *212 pp.*

Sklair, Leslie. The Sociology of Progress. *320 pp.*

Slater, P. Origin and Significance of the Frankfurt School. *A Marxist Perspective. About 192 pp.*

Smart, Barry. Sociology, Phenomenology and Marxian Analysis. *A Critical Discussion of the Theory and Practice of a Science of Society. 220 pp.*

International Library of Anthropology

General Editor Adam Kuper

Ahmed, A. S. Millenium and Charisma Among Pathans. *A Critical Essay in Social Anthropology. 192 pp.*

Brown, Paula. The Chimbu. *A Study of Change in the New Guinea Highlands. 151 pp.*

Gudeman, Stephen. Relationships, Residence and the Individual. *A Rural Panamanian Community. 288 pp. 11 Plates, 5 Figures, 2 Maps, 10 Tables.*

Hamnett, Ian. Chieftainship and Legitimacy. *An Anthropological Study of Executive Law in Lesotho. 163 pp.*

Hanson, F. Allan. Meaning in Culture. *127 pp.*

Lloyd, P. C. Power and Independence. *Urban Africans' Perception of Social Inequality. 264 pp.*

Pettigrew, Joyce. Robber Noblemen. *A Study of the Political System of the Sikh Jats. 284 pp.*

Street, Brian V. The Savage in Literature. *Representations of 'Primitive' Society in English Fiction, 1858–1920. 207 pp.*

Van Den Berghe, Pierre L. Power and Privilege at an African University. *278 pp.*

International Library of Social Policy

General Editor   Kathleen Jones

Bayley, M. Mental Handicap and Community Care. *426 pp.*

Bottoms, A. E., and **McClean, J. D.** Defendants in the Criminal Process. *284 pp.*

Butler, J. R. Family Doctors and Public Policy. *208 pp.*

Davies, Martin. Prisoners of Society. *Attitudes and Aftercare. 204 pp.*

Gittus, Elizabeth. Flats, Families and the Under-Fives. *285 pp.*

Holman, Robert. Trading in Children. *A Study of Private Fostering. 355 pp.*

Jones, Howard, and **Cornes, Paul.** Open Prisons. *About 248 pp.*

Jones, Kathleen. History of the Mental Health Service. *428 pp.*

Jones, Kathleen, with **Brown, John, Cunningham, W. J., Roberts, Julian,** and **Williams, Peter.** Opening the Door. *A Study of New Policies for the Mentally Handicapped. 278 pp.*

Karn, Valerie. Retiring to the Seaside. *About 280 pp. 2 maps. Numerous tables.*

Thomas, J. E. The English Prison Officer since 1850: *A Study in Conflict. 258 pp.*

Walton, R. G. Women in Social Work. *303 pp.*

Woodward, J. To Do the Sick No Harm. *A Study of the British Voluntary Hospital System to 1875. 221 pp.*

International Library of Welfare and Philosophy

General Editors   Noel Timms and David Watson

● **Plant, Raymond.** Community and Ideology. *104 pp.*

● **McDermott, F. E.** (Ed.) Self-Determination in Social Work. *A Collection of Essays on Self-determination and Related Concepts by Philosophers and Social Work Theorists. Contributors: F. P. Biestek, S. Bernstein, A. Keith-Lucas, D. Sayer, H. H. Perelman, C. Whittington, R. F. Stalley, F. E. McDermott, I. Berlin, H. J. McCloskey, H. L. A. Hart, J. Wilson, A. I. Melden, S. I. Benn. 254 pp.*

Ragg, Nicholas M. People Not Cases. *A Philosophical Approach to Social Work. About 250 pp.*

● **Timms, Noel,** and **Watson, David** (Eds). Talking About Welfare. *Readings in Philosophy and Social Policy. Contributors: T. H. Marshall, R. B. Brandt, G. H. von Wright, K. Nielsen, M. Cranston, R. M. Titmuss, R. S. Downie, E. Telfer, D. Donnison, J. Benson, P. Leonard, A. Keith-Lucas, D. Walsh, I. T. Ramsey. 320 pp.*

Primary Socialization, Language and Education

General Editor Basil Bernstein

Adlam, Diana S., *with the assistance of Geoffrey Turner and Lesley Lineker.* Code in Context. *About 272 pp.*

Bernstein, Basil. Class, Codes and Control. *3 volumes.*
 1. *Theoretical Studies Towards a Sociology of Language. 254 pp.*
 2. *Applied Studies Towards a Sociology of Language. 377 pp.*
● 3. *Towards a Theory of Educatiomal Transmission. 167 pp.*

Brandis, W., and **Bernstein, B.** Selection and Control. *176 pp.*

Brandis, Walter, and **Henderson, Dorothy.** Social Class, Language and Communication. *288 pp.*

Cook-Gumperz, Jenny. Social Control and Socialization. *A Study of Class Differences in the Language of Maternal Control. 290 pp.*

●**Gahagan, D. M.,** and **G. A.** Talk Reform. *Exploration in Language for Infant School Children. 160 pp.*

Hawkins, P. R. Social Class, the Nominal Group and Verbal Strategies. *About 220 pp.*

Robinson, W. P., and **Rackstraw, Susan D. A.** A Question of Answers. *2 volumes. 192 pp. and 180 pp.*

Turner, Geoffrey J., and **Mohan, Bernard A.** A Linguistic Description and Computer Programme for Children's Speech. *208 pp.*

Reports of the Institute of Community Studies

●**Cartwright, Ann.** Parents and Family Planning Services. *306 pp.*
 Patients and their Doctors. *A Study of General Practice. 304 pp.*

Dench, Geoff. Maltese in London. *A Case-study in the Erosion of Ethnic Consciousness. 302 pp.*

●**Jackson, Brian.** Streaming: *an Education System in Miniature. 168 pp.*

Jackson, Brian, and **Marsden, Dennis.** Education and the Working Class: *Some General Themes raised by a Study of 88 Working-class Children in a Northern Industrial City. 268 pp. 2 folders.*

Marris, Peter. The Experience of Higher Education. *232 pp. 27 tables.*
 Loss and Change. *192 pp.*

Marris, Peter, and **Rein, Martin.** Dilemmas of Social Reform. *Poverty and Community Action in the United States. 256 pp.*

Marris, Peter, and Somerset, Anthony. African Businessmen. *A Study of Entrepreneurship and Development in Kenya. 256 pp.*
Mills, Richard. Young Outsiders: *a Study in Alternative Communities. 216 pp.*
Runciman, W. G. Relative Deprivation and Social Justice. *A Study of Attitudes to Social Inequality in Twentieth-Century England. 352 pp.*
Willmott, Peter. Adolescent Boys in East London. *230 pp.*
Willmott, Peter, and Young, Michael. Family and Class in a London Suburb. *202 pp. 47 tables.*
Young, Michael. Innovation and Research in Education. *192 pp.*
●Young, Michael, and McGeeney, Patrick. Learning Begins at Home. *A Study of a Junior School and its Parents. 128 pp.*
Young, Michael, and Willmott, Peter. Family and Kinship in East London. *Foreword by Richard M. Titmuss. 252 pp. 39 tables.*
The Symmetrical Family. *410 pp.*

Reports of the Institute for Social Studies in Medical Care

Cartwright, Ann, Hockey, Lisbeth, and Anderson, John L. Life Before Death. *310 pp.*
Dunnell, Karen, and Cartwright, Ann. Medicine Takers, Prescribers and Hoarders. *190 pp.*

Medicine, Illness and Society

General Editor W. M. Williams

Robinson, David. The Process of Becoming Ill. *142 pp.*
Stacey, Margaret, *et al.* Hospitals, Children and Their Families. *The Report of a Pilot Study. 202 pp.*
Stimson, G. V., and Webb, B. Going to See the Doctor. *The Consultation Process in General Practice. 155 pp.*

Monographs in Social Theory

General Editor Arthur Brittan

●Barnes, B. Scientific Knowledge and Sociological Theory. *192 pp.*
Bauman, Zygmunt. Culture as Praxis. *204 pp.*
●Dixon, Keith. Sociological Theory. *Pretence and Possibility. 142 pp.*
Meltzer, B. N., Petras, J. W., and Reynolds, L. T. Symbolic Interactionism. *Genesis, Varieties and Criticisms. 144 pp.*
●Smith, Anthony D. The Concept of Social Change. *A Critique of the Functionalist Theory of Social Change. 208 pp.*

Routledge Social Science Journals

The British Journal of Sociology. *Editor – Angus Stewart; Associate Editor – Leslie Sklair. Vol. 1, No. 1 – March 1950 and Quarterly. Roy. 8vo. All back issues available. An international journal publishing original papers in the field of sociology and related areas.*
Community Work. *Edited by David Jones and Marjorie Mayo. 1973. Published annually.*
Economy and Society. *Vol. 1, No. 1. February 1972 and Quarterly. Metric Roy. 8vo. A journal for all social scientists covering sociology, philosophy, anthropology, economics and history. All back numbers available.*
Religion. Journal of Religion and Religions. *Chairman of Editorial Board, Ninian Smart. Vol. 1, No. 1; Spring 1971. A journal with an interdisciplinary approach to the study of the phenomena of religion. All back numbers available.*
Year Book of Social Policy in Britain, The. *Edited by Kathleen Jones. 1971. Published annually.*

Social and Psychological Aspects of Medical Practice

Editor   Trevor Silverstone

Lader, Malcolm. Psychophysiology of Mental Illness. *280 pp.*
● **Silverstone, Trevor,** and **Turner, Paul.** Drug Treatment in Psychiatry. *232 pp.*

Printed in Great Britain by
Lowe & Brydone Printers Limited, Thetford, Norfolk